# SPORT, TIME, AND SOCIETY

# SPORT, TIME, AND SOCIETY

## The British at Play

## DENNIS BRAILSFORD

London and New York

First published 1991
by Routledge
11 New Fetter Lane, London EC4P 4EE
29 West 35th Street, New York, NY 10001

© 1991 Dennis Brailsford

Typeset in 10/12 pt Palatino by
J&L Composition Ltd, Filey, North Yorkshire
Printed in Great Britain by
T J Press (Padstow) Ltd, Padstow, Cornwall

*British Library Cataloguing in Publication Data*
Brailsford, Dennis
Sport, Time, and Society: the British at play.
1. Great Britain. Leisure activities. Social aspects
I. Title
306'48'0941

*Library of Congress Cataloging in Publication Data*
Also available

ISBN 0–415–00766–6

For Nicholas, Jennifer, and Nigel

# Contents

# List of plates

# Preface

We live, like it or not, in a sporting world. Sport is everywhere. It is no longer confined to what were once its own compartments, the sports pages in the press, or its own television programmes. Now sport is news, and general news at that. To ignore the plethora of organized play has become so difficult that it even entails averting the eyes from the cereal packet to avoid the face of the soccer striker, the baseball pitcher, or the latest sprint champion.

It is the collapse of the barriers of time that has made the present sporting world a possibility. Sport has conquered the calendar that confined it in the past, and can now invade every hour of every day of the year. The expanding opportunities for play have been decisive in changing its role in human affairs. The occasions on which sport could take place and the time span allowed for it have been fundamental to the nature of sporting activity, yet their part in its growth has been surprisingly little considered. Much more attention has been given to what sports were played, how they were played, the motives that prompted them, and their functions, than *when* they took place, or other elements in their timing. The frequency of sports, their duration, their pace, and their rhythm do, none the less, lie at the centre of their history.

Sport, as discussed here, needs some preliminary definition. Changing concepts through the ages of what constitutes 'sport', developments in its forms, and restatements of its roles, all call for a catholic approach, and here the word will be held on a relatively loose rein. Its boundaries with organized entertainment are drawn to exclude drama, the theatre, the music hall, and the circus, and with domestic amusements to exclude parlour and card games, while little attention is given to purely childhood play, which often operates within its own time scales. Positively, the two elements seen to characterize sport are competition and scale. There is usually contest, and there is usually size – either large body movement or the involvement of large numbers, or both. Moreover, since sport is not being considered primarily in terms of physical or health education, but as a social phenomenon, no hard and fast distinctions are made between its various participants, whether players, promoters, arbiters, or spectators. Nor is there any sharp division made between 'leisure' and 'free time', emphasized by Sebastian de Grazia in his challenging call to the cultured life, *Of Time, Work, and Leisure*.[1] Such differentiation is only made where it is directly relevant to the sporting scene.

More pertinent is de Grazia's discovery that the analysis of leisure led him into 'a review of a whole way of life, the extent of its traditions, education, technology, creativeness, and liberty'. While the reach of this work is less ambitious, the kaleidoscopic interactions between sport and time still call for wide reference – to religion and economics, to commerce and manufacture, and to political and social theory and practice. Some of the by-ways are too seductive to be completely shunned, in what is essentially an exploration.

The time dimension is an unbroken thread, running through the whole history of sport. Its study may help to bring the whole historical experience of sport – primarily, but not exclusively, the British experience – to our current considerations. The fashionable concentration of most sport historians is with the post-industrial world, and this is understandable. The recent past is more apparently relevant to the sport of today, and is infinitely more accessible than the sporting record of more distant generations. The temptation to push back the remoter past has, though, to be treated with caution. All-embracing theories of modernization, with models to support them, are valid perhaps as shorthand expressions, but they always run the danger of ending rather than furthering historical speculation on the nature and growth of sport. Scepticism suggests a more tentative approach – the model is inclined to make it all too easy, its elements too neatly categorized, its air one of finality. This is especially so when it invites, at least by implication, a cut-off from much of our sporting past. Writing here beneath the Dorset Downs, in the shadow of an Iron Age hill fort, looking over to the foundations of a Roman temple on the one hand and a fourteenth-century parish church on the other, it is far from easy to accept notions of discontinuity in the human story.

Clio, alas, is the most fickle of the muses. All historical writing is transient. Historians, whether of sport or any other matter, have to write out of, and for, their own times, in terms that are meaningful to themselves and their contemporaries. New generations need new histories, and today's theories are tomorrow's heresies. This, it has to be granted, applies as much to the pragmatist, who makes no overt declaration of any overriding panoramic view, who picks up such generalizations as fall his or her way from time to time from the facts that slowly reveal themselves, as it does to the systematic theorist and model maker. 'No theory – no history', we are sometimes warned, but all historians do have their philosophies, even if they are only implied in their emphases, their selections and omissions. In the end it may be no more than a question of their own confidence in their consistency, but doubt was never a bar to good history.

There is comfort in the fact that even Descartes had to make do with a provisional morality which he never got round to analysing and confirming. The contemplation of the theme of sport and time leaves an abiding impression of the interplay between the permanent and the transient, between the unchanging human inclination to play and the always changing contexts, forms, and motives of its expression. If it should be that no other great truth emerges, no other theoretical banner gets hoisted more than half-way up the flag pole, then the young literature teacher in Malcolm Bradbury's *The History Man* comes nearest to providing the apologia:[2]

> 'Ah, yes,' says Howard, 'but how do you teach it?' 'Do you mean am I a structuralist or a Leavisite or a psycho-linguistician or a formalist or a Christian existentialist or a phenomenologist?' 'Yes,' says Howard. 'Ah,' says Miss Callendar, 'well, I'm none of them.' 'What do you do then?' asks Howard. 'I read books and talk to people about them.' 'Without a method?' asks Howard. 'That's right,' says Miss Callendar. 'It doesn't sound very convincing,' says Howard. 'No,' says Miss Callendar, 'I have a taste for remaining a little elusive.' 'You can't,' says Howard. 'With every word you utter, you state your world view.' 'I know,' says Miss Callendar, 'I'm trying to find a way round that.' 'There isn't one,' says Howard, 'you have to know what you are.' 'I'm a nineteenth century liberal,' says Miss Callendar. 'You can't be,' says Howard, 'this is the twentieth century, near the end of it. There are no resources.' 'I know,' says Miss Callendar, 'that's why I am one.'

The one snag is that Annie Callendar herself ended up in bed with Howard Kirk.

# Acknowledgements

Help has come from many quarters in the production of this book, and particularly from colleagues in the University of Birmingham. The University Library, both through its general services and its two specialist sports units, has been an indispensable resource. I am indebted to John Bromhead and the National Centre for Athletics Literature for help with pictorial material and for permission to reproduce prints taken from the centre's archives. Jim Davies of the library's Photographic Department also gave valuable technical assistance. Among colleagues in the School of Sport Sciences, Charles Jenkins has been unfailing in his encouragement and positive criticism, and without his observations the book's shortcomings would have been all the greater than they are. Those that remain are, of course, all my own.

Each chapter of the book is separately and, I trust, fully annotated, so that the notes themselves constitute an effective bibliography. For original source material I am indebted to the officers of the Lord's Day Observance Society for allowing generous access to the society's records, and, among those who supplied me with useful unpublished references, to R. J. Davies and Pamela McClintock.

Finally I am in constant debt to my wife for her assistance with research, her proofreading, and her down-to-earth comments – but above all for her good-humoured tolerance.

Dennis Brailsford
Preston, Weymouth, Dorset
October 1989

# 1

# Echoes from a lost world

Just before dawn, on a spring morning many centuries ago, little groups of country folk might be faintly visible in the chill mist as they made their way out into the open fields. They had to be there before the sky lightened, for it was the day on which the awakening sun would dance in the sky as it rose. It was the moment of the year to stand in awe of the goddess Eostre, and to dance joyfully with her at the revival of the cold earth after its winter sleep. It became, then, a time to celebrate the resurrection of a new god, on Easter Day, a god who had only dimly displaced the ageless deities of the past. Over the centuries, too, local expectations had brought their changes to the central magic of the dancing sun. In Germany it would leap three times, at sunset if it failed to do so at dawn. In Norfolk it would perform an agonizing dance through the morning haze, and Devonians saw it whirling round and round, jumping at will.[1]

Centuries later, on an April day in 1987, crowds gathered outside again. They flocked in their thousands to celebrate with sport this self-same festival. Few of them would dance in the streets on their way home, but they could still marvel or moan, as their forebears did, over won or lost hopes. Is it any more than a historical quirk that Easter Monday is one of the busiest weekdays in the English sporting calendar, rivalled only by Boxing Day? Is it an accidental continuity owing more to the innate conservatism of western man's social habits than to any deeper compulsions? After all, many ancient feasts once rivalling Yule and Eostre – Christmas and Easter – now survive only in the remoter reaches of the folklore sections of libraries, or in the small print of the *Book of Common Prayer*. Yet these two have persisted, and a third, Whitsuntide, was only superseded in Britain by a still anonymous 'Spring Bank Holiday' some twenty years ago. While their sporting significance may vary over the widespread western world, the endurance of celebration at about the times of the winter solstice and the vernal equinox suggests the satisfying of some long-standing human urges which have survived momentous upheavals. Among each new generation of today's Easter and Christmas-tide spectators, fewer and fewer of them might consciously acknowledge even the Christian associations with the holidays to which they hold so firmly. Yet they are anniversaries which have stubbornly remained, through massive shifts in thought, belief, and attitude, in social structure, and in the systems of labour and leisure. Their importance has varied from time to time and from place to place, their sporting emphases have shifted from day to day within their seasons, but they are still observed, in an unbroken succession from those dawn dancers in the mist and their winter fellows, the grotesquely masked revellers of yuletide.[2]

Twentieth-century sport is no phoenix, arisen fully fledged from the barren ashes of a dead past. There is no wiping clean what has gone. Always the canvas retains some faint impression of the old images under the bright new tints. Certainly much of our playing past is apparently lost. There are major elements in our sporting lives that are no older than the revolution in organized play of the last quarter of the nineteenth century, but this does not preclude the existence of some roots which reach down to the Middle Ages, or even to a far-away pre-Christian past.

The tenacious hold of Easter, for instance, on the British sporting calendar is readily apparent from a look at two successive April Mondays. The 27 April 1987 was a humdrum sporting day. The ardent racegoer had to trek to either Brighton or Wolverhampton for some unremarkable flat racing, or else be content with what the Nottinghamshire countryside could offer over the sticks at Southwell. With Monday the least popular weekday for play in the major winter team games it was hardly worth the search for a football match. There was just one Football League fixture, and no Rugby games at all in either code. The only mildly notable sporting events on this particular Monday were the eight cricket County Championship matches which, thanks to an earlier than usual start to the season, found themselves braving the spring breezes.

It had all been very different on the previous Monday. Every football club, soccer or rugby, had been in action, nearly all of them playing afternoon or even morning games, not the evening matches usual on weekdays. Wherever they lived, the punters had a race meeting within reach. Kempton Park, Newcastle, Nottingham, and Warwick all had attractive cards, and there were no fewer than eight National Hunt meetings, scattered from Carlisle in the north to Towcester in the West Midlands, and from Chepstow in Wales to Fakenham in East Anglia. The Irish had their own Grand National at Ferryhouse. The difference was that 20 April was Easter Monday.

The Easter and Christmas holidays bring the only full-scale departures from the weekend domination of the winter programmes of the major sports. Boxing Day, and increasingly New Year's Day, have the same full fixture lists as Easter Monday, often with matches between neighbouring teams, avoiding overnight travel and making for popular local rivalries. At least half the Christmas games are morning matches, with none at all in the evenings, the time for parties and merrymaking. There are a few variations. Rugby football, for instance, south of the border, has not yet shared the wholesale Scottish enthusiasm for New Year's Day play, though racing had four jump meetings on 1 January 1987, following an ambitious fare of eight on Boxing Day.[3] In the United States, the New Year sees the climax of the college football season, with day and night games on New Year's Eve, and the Pasadena Rose Bowl and other bowl contests on the following day.

For most of their history, the Christmas and Easter holidays, like most other festivals, had their own distinctive sporting characters. The climate restricted most Christmas recreation to indoors, or to vigorous open-air activities. It was the season for family feasting, some brief respite from the common drabness of the daily diet, for drinking, for such games as bobbing for apples, and making music. Many towns and villages had their customary ritual processions, noisy and festive, their wassailing, the ringing of bells, and mummers' plays.[4] The main competitive sport was football, in one or other of its forms. Communal contests, like that at Kirkham in Lancashire, often took place on Christmas Day itself. Christmas Day football was played over the whole of the British Isles. In Scotland, at Scone, the married men strove against the bachelors, while at Inveresk the wives tackled the spinsters. Hardy Scots fishwives took to golf on any holiday[5] – those at Musselburgh competed on New Year's Day for a creel presented by the local golf club.[6] There was Christmas Day football in Ireland at the Restoration, and in Cardiganshire in Wales. There was an hour-long lunch interval here to one Christmas game. Players and spectators alike resorted freely to the beer barrel, and the afternoon session descended, unsurprisingly, into a free-for-all – the footballers 'began to quarrel and swear and kick each other' and were soon 'fighting like bulldogs'.[7]

Easter sport usually had both more variety and greater sobriety. It could embrace virtually any competitive activity popular at the time, from quoits, bowls, bell-ringing, and cock-fighting in the early eighteenth century, to steeplechasing, football, cycling tours, and rowing in the late nineteenth.[8] Today, though, its sporting fare is little different from that of Christmas. In North America, where Easter is of less special sporting significance, the harshness of winter made outdoor sports surrender the early months of the year to ice hockey and basketball, which contributes to a continuing springtime distinction. By

3

Easter, football has long gone, and as often as not the promise of summer is in the brightening air with the first games of the new baseball season. In Britain, though, the differences between Christmas and Easter programmes are minor. Christmas can only offer National Hunt racing, while by Easter flat racing has started, rugby clubs are on tour, and there are numerous seaside hockey tournaments. These aside, it would be hard to identify an unmarked fixture list as belonging to Boxing Day or Easter Monday.

The capacity to accommodate whatever form of play happened to evolve has been one of the sustaining features of these enduring festivals. They have kept free of general taboos – such as those restricting Sunday behaviour – and whenever constraints have limited a particular part of the holiday it has always managed, amoeba-like, to change its shape to fit the new context. The capacity of playing styles to adapt to new conditions has been matched by the equal ability of the holidays to adapt their own forms.

This has been important for festivals which came to include, as their centrepieces, two of the most solemn Christian holy days. There have been shifts in attitudes towards play on Christmas Day and Good Friday, arising from a diffuse range of causes – from changing theological views on the holiness of saints' days and other annual feasts, from the weight given to religion itself, from altered labour practices, and from local, regional, and national predilections. The relatively recent avoidance of these two days by the British spectator sports has come about from reasons which are almost wholly secular, though operating in opposite directions. Christmas Day sport effectively stopped when the transport unions negotiated a free day, the petrol stations closed, and the country sank back into domestic jollification and the television. Good Friday, on the other hand, in spite of continuing to be a Common Law Holiday, has become a normal working weekday for most businesses, though many of them, apart from stores, do not reopen before the Wednesday of Easter week. Christmas Day soccer disappeared in the 1960s from the combined effects of making New Year's Day a public holiday in England and Wales (as it had been in Scotland) and the wider availability of floodlighting. Pressure on fixture lists was lessened, and the Christmas Day matches now had the new holiday as substitute.[9] Good Friday play was eroded more gradually, and there is still the occasional day game, especially if clubs have a backlog of fixtures to make up.[10] There are still, too, likely to be the usual handful of Friday evening games owing little to the holiday and arranged by struggling lower division clubs who seek desperately to add a few hundred more to the gate by avoiding Saturday afternoon clashes with more prosperous neighbours.

Similar pictures of Good Friday, less sharply etched, have emerged in the other major team games.[11] The changes over recent generations are symptomatic of the long resilience of the two festivals. They have been possible because of the traditional *extent* of these holidays, which has meant that their play elements have not been put at risk by being denied on one particular day. Each has, over the centuries, become a *season* of celebration, embracing individual feast days, but not confined to them. After the transmutation of the pagan midwinter festival into Christmas, for example, it gradually acquired many different local stresses spread over the whole term between Christmas Eve, 24 December, and the Monday after Twelfth Day, when parishes had their ploughs blessed to make the new farming year fruitful. Over much of Europe it could be attenuated even further, from the feast of St Nicholas on 6 December. In England it had official recognition as a season in such statutes as that of Henry VIII forbidding bowling to the lower orders, except at Christmastide.[12] In agricultural communities the depths of winter allowed more respite from normal labour than any other part of the year and the Christmas break could be granted its spread over two full weeks. It was the more intensive farming methods of the later eighteenth century that began to limit the customary freedom.[13] Even craft work was difficult in the short, dark days of December and January, and the first manufacturers were not averse to a generous Christmas shut-down, especially if they could find recompense elsewhere. Josiah Wedgwood promised his pottery workers 'a long Christmas' in 1776 if they would give up their summer habits of making off, willy-nilly, to parish wakes up and down the county.[14] On the other hand, the early textile mill-owners, whose purses ached when their frames were silent, could not always find enough charity in their hearts to grant even a free Christmas Day, until the 1833 Factory Act forced most of them to do so.[15]

The building trades in Britain now regularly take a two-week break covering Christmas and the New Year, and many other businesses find it unprofitable to reopen briefly between the two Bank Holidays. Few vestiges though, sporting or otherwise, remain of the other special days which once illuminated the Christmas season. The sporting emphasis on Boxing Day itself is modern. Although prize-fights and pedestrian matches begin to appear on Boxing Day in the industrial areas from the second quarter of the nineteenth century,[16] 26 December had no regular sporting importance until the effects of the 1871 Bank Holiday Act began to be felt. Other Christmas church festivals, Holy Innocents' Day on 28 December, and Epiphany on 6 January, were never occasions for competitive play. The latter, as Twelfth Day, was noted by James Boswell as a day 'on which a great deal of jollity goes on in England'[17] (as distinct from the Scotland which he had just left), though it was largely secular and domestic, and residually remembered still as the time by which Christmas decorations must be taken down and the

Christmas tree discarded. Plough Monday sport was quite another matter, and some of its activities linger on locally, perhaps as somewhat forced survivals. Not that the men of Haxey and Westwoodside would admit as much, nor that there is any mere antiquarianism about their struggle to carry the 'hood' to their local tavern. They play their traditional 'football' game for real. Where such contests took place, typically on Plough Monday or Shrove Tuesday, though on other feast days as well, they inherited ancient practices far bloodier than priestly blessings of the plough. They recall distant fertility rites, the ball the symbolic head of a sacrificial victim whose blood would enrich the fields of the winners. Primitive drives can still seem near the surface from the ferocity of today's struggles for the Haxey Hood, though the conflict has long been cauterized by a medieval tale of a lady losing her headgear and having it rescued, with due reward, by local peasants, who contested for the privilege of doing so.[18]

The equally faraway origins of Easter itself, and its indelible stamp on the lives of Christian converts, are evident in the church's assumption of even its pagan title, the Anglo-Saxon *Eastre* and the Old High German *Ostara*.[19] Improving weather, the longer daylight hours, the anticipation of fresh foods again, and the high hopes of the budding year had always made this a more open and outdoor celebration than yuletide. The sense of release which it embodied was strengthened by formalizing the inevitable food shortages of later winter into the self-denial of Lent, followed by the deliverance and jubilation of the Resurrection. The release could sometimes appear too complete to the austere. Bishops like Bartholomew of Exeter at the end of the twelfth century were troubled by the persistence of pagan practices at these festivals.[20] Friars, like the Dominican, John Bromyard, some 200 years later, found the good works of Lent giving way too liberally to the rejoicings of Eastertide, when thoughts turned 'to the open, the merry greensward, May-games and revelry, whither they will go with heads rose-garlanded for the feasts and shows'.[21] Over the centuries, though, the major complaints over Easter recreation have centred on Good Friday. Like Christmas Day it was imbued with a devotional solemnity often thought incompatible with public play. When the Duke of Newcastle had a fall, which broke his horse's neck, Archbishop Laud asked in his diary, 'Should not this day have other employment?'[22] Bielby Porteus, later as Bishop of Chester to be the moving spirit behind the 1780 Act banning Sunday sport, castigated his Lambeth parishioners for their neglect of Good Friday,[23] and in the 1920s the Bishop of Swansea and Brecon led a campaign to end Good Friday play. He urged the 'big clubs' and the Football League to follow what he saw as the example of most smaller clubs and not arrange matches on this day.[24] In the face of the long-standing religious criticisms it is paradoxical that Good Friday

6

and Christmas Day play finally withered for overwhelmingly secular reasons.

Some traditional Good Friday play did make tenuous claims to religious meaning, but this had usually been left far behind. The whipped top was Pontius Pilate, as was the tethered bird, or one perched high in a large earthenware pot, and pelted with sticks and stones.[25] This 'amusement' tended to spread over the other spring feasts, enough to prompt a campaign against it by the London constables on Shrove Tuesday, 1768.[26] Specific to Good Friday 'in the past', according to Pierce Egan in 1832, was the annual wrestling at one of the early homes of cricket, White Conduit Fields,[27] but the tendency was for Good Friday to take on a more subdued tone. There were the day's rail excursions to local beauty spots, popular with Victorian workers,[28] whose rough and ready predecessors, colliers 'in the first rank for savage ignorance and wickedness of every kind', listened to Wesley's preaching so attentively on Good Friday, 1743.[29] In the later years of the nineteenth century the middle-class sports clubs were also likely to show more deference to the singular observance of Good Friday than to the recurring demands of Sunday abstinence.[30]

Whatever doubts there might have been over the sporting suitability of Good Friday, there were few over the rest of Eastertide. As at Christmas, the holiday came to extend over several days. Government offices were closed for the first three days of the week in 1800, and 'Easter Tuesday' and 'Easter Wednesday' had their own titles. While much of the Easter play would spread over the whole holiday, some events became attached to particular days – Easter Tuesday, for instance, saw the annual football game between the fishermen and the colliers at Workington,[31] and a handball competition among the girls of Keswick.[32] Easter Tuesday prize-fights,[33] though, signified nothing out of the ordinary, as Tuesday had long become the main 'fighting day' throughout the season.

It was Easter Monday which was the great festive and sporting day of the holiday from the later Middle Ages onwards. This was natural enough. It was the day which came immediately after Easter Day itself, and Monday was the day when town workers were always likely to turn to amusement and recreation.[34] There were the traditional football games, and even cricket – as early as 1700 an Easter Monday match was being advertised for Clapham Common[35] – as well as all the contemporary fun of the fair. The rich flavour of the holiday at the end of the eighteenth century comes out vividly in accounts of such semi-serious events as the Epping Hunt. This attracted large Easter Monday crowds, to the unbounded pleasure of local innkeepers, whose subscriptions helped to keep the 'hunt' going, and who were 'not backward in their charges'. In 1795 a carted stag was released, chased by a motley collection of hounds, by horsemen and pedestrians, and taken alive in a pond after just over an hour. Refreshment booths were everywhere, and there was a gambling table with an alluring croupier, 'dressed in a riding habit', whose 'bewitching face and fascinating address, had the desired influence to induce the country Johns to sport their silver liberally'. Other contests followed the hunt. There were two or three boxing matches, nine-pins for a gold-laced hat, and a farmer's lad failed to run a mile in five minutes. There was a full-scale cock-fighting tournament, a singlestick match, and, in the evening, an assembly for the subscribers and others.[36] It was all a fascinating mix of the old and the new – the traditional pursuit of prey, at the customary time, but no kill to the hunt, thousands of spectators, and unashamed commercialism. And elsewhere in the London area, on the same day, there was a jackass race at Battlebridge, bull-baiting at Holloway, a cock-match at Tottenham, and a smock race for ladies at Hornsey.[37]

The Epping Hunt had descended further into farce by 1811, when the assorted hounds were as much frightened as the stag by the size of the crowd and the cries of the hunters. After twenty minutes, only five couple were still following the stag, many sportsmen had been unseated and their horses were grazing lazily on the sparse turf. Meanwhile, the stag had made itself comfortable in a thicket, from which it was taken alive to the Horse and Wells tavern at Woodford. There the gallant early retirers from the chase 'plucked him almost bald, to decorate their hats with trophies of his hair'.[38]

It was a noteworthy decline in the communal significance of a traditional Easter event. The old holiday had been at its most flourishing, in both its extent and the variety of its sporting opportunities, in the later years of the past century. Under sterner employment conditions, and with the spread of alternative free time (particularly on Saturday afternoons), its range began to be restricted, though Easter Monday working remained unusual. The Bank Holiday Act of 1871, formally extended to cover docks, customs houses, and the like in 1875, then helped to regularize the multiplicity of holiday practices. Passed originally, in the minds of Members of Parliament, to facilitate business by making bank closures predictable, and with no mandatory force beyond that, it soon set the standard to which all employees looked, as of right. The act confirmed the established holidays of Christmas Day, Boxing Day, Easter Monday, and Whit Monday, and added a new one in the first Monday in August.[39]

Much else was changing, apart from the formalizing of the holiday calendar. Recreational activities changed dramatically, for instance, under the influence of the railway. A train trip at Easter or Whitsuntide became one of the most popular ways of enjoying a day's freedom. The potential of the new steam travel was quickly appreciated and by 1839 the daily service between London and Gravesend was being trebled at the two spring holidays.[40] Existing spectator sports, particularly pedestrianism and horse-racing, began to exploit the two holiday Mondays more fully. Easter Monday horse-racing had a long history, reaching back to 1598 in Scotland, when a bell was presented for a race at Stirling.[41] By the 1880s there were Bank Holiday meetings serving four of the largest English cities – Kempton Park, at the edge of London, Manchester, Newcastle, and the ill-fated Four Oaks Park near Birmingham.[42] Football turned to the holiday and the new cycling clubs were soon arranging Easter and Whitsuntide tours.[43] A pattern was set which remained basically unchanged for over fifty years.

These enduring festivals of Christmas and Easter were never seriously threatened, even in the darkest days of popular recreation.[44] The many other celebrations owing their sanction to the church calendar of the Middle Ages and beyond had no such durability. From Shrove Tuesday to Michaelmas, they, and their former contribution to sporting life, have all withered away. They lapsed during the long process of change from a medieval calendar tuned to the rhythms of farming and religion, based on the seasons and the saints' days, to one punctuated by the unvarying logic of the week and the month. They suffered alike from the weakening of the intermittent holy days in the cause of Sunday observance and from the demands for regular labour in the cause of continuous production.

Sometimes the specific sports followed on a particular holiday contributed to its demise. This was so with Shrove Tuesday, whose spiritual role became wholly buried under an annual outburst of communal football, cock-fighting, and other animal sports,[45] all of them at risk as consciences grew more tender and property interests more powerful. May Day, the marker for the birth of summer, has been nominally revived in Britain as a statutory bank holiday on the first Monday in the month, but it has gained little credence and found no identity in the sporting calendar. Even though the county cricket season is, by then, into its stride, there is unlikely to be any play unless one of the one-day competition games happens to have been rained off on the previous Saturday! The new politically inspired May Day carries no inheritance in either timing or content from the old festival of music, dance, and play, and arrived too late to find the place in the hearts of organized labour which it often enjoys in Commonwealth countries and over much of Europe, both East and West. Little wonder that a government of another colour announced, in July 1987, that its status was 'under review', though one of the suggested alternatives, St George's Day, for all its patriotic overtones, is almost equally rootless.[46]

The lapse of sports associated with the summer solstice – varied, but predominantly based on foot-racing – was hastened by the switch from the Julian to the Gregorian calendar in 1752,[47] when the country 'lost' its eleven days, and folk became confused over *when* Midsummer's Day actually was. Observance of the 'old' Midsummer's Day on 4 or 5 July appears to have faded within a generation[48] and the 'new' day only gained some ritual acknowledgement with modern revivalism. Ascension Day (falling variably in early May according to the date of Easter) was broadly associated with racing and other athletic sports, possibly a growth out of the ancient custom of beating the parish bounds on that day.[49] From the relative acceptability of its sports, Ascension Day might have been expected to fare better than it did, but its closeness to the Whitsuntide holiday some ten days later was always a disadvantage. The writing was on the wall when the Mayor of Carlisle refused, in 1814, to donate the usual prize for the annual Ascension Day race, even though, on this occasion, the freemen of the town then supplied the prize themselves, elected their own mayor for the day, and enjoyed an excellent day's sport, 'with the greatest hilarity and good humour'.[50]

Two great British sporting holidays of the first half of the twentieth century have not yet figured in this survey – Whitsuntide itself, as ancient as any festival in the calendar,[51] and August Bank Holiday, only as old as the 1871 Act, but soon unrivalled as the great outdoor day of high summer. While the first Monday in August had previously had no official sanction, still less any medieval justification, many sporting events had taken place then, as they did on other summer Mondays.[52] The Bank Holiday gave some limited legitimacy to a long-established recreational habit, and was quickly seized upon by industrial Britain. Summer sports had their fling. The great cricket rivalries of Whitsuntide – Yorkshire against Lancashire, Nottinghamshire and Surrey – found a holiday time for their return matches, race meetings abounded, and packed trains steamed to the seaside resorts. The fact that the Bank Holiday *week* often tended to become the annual long break somewhat undermined the status of the individual day by taking would-be spectators away from home on vacation, but the statutory move of the Bank Holiday to the last Monday in August in 1971[53] has never found any echoes in people's hearts. It falls too early to fulfil the role of America's Labour Day, bringing the summer season to a close, and has remained an anonymous and unconvincing postscript to the holiday year. The logic in the change, made in a mood of high confidence in social engineering, did little more than prove that recreational habits are not governed by reason alone.

The transfer of the Whitsuntide holiday from Pentecost to the last Monday in May was prompted by similar motives, by such apparently sound reasons as predictability, a better spread of breaks, and (in defiance of all experience of the British climate) the hope of better

10

weather. In the past it could fall anywhere between 10 May and 13 June. A confusion, mildly reminiscent of the calendar change of the 1750s, has been the result. Half of the customary Bank Holiday cricket matches have moved to the new holiday weekend, and half have stayed with the old. The change came at a time when annual holidays were again being extended, the Spring Holiday – to give it its new name – became another full week's break for the schools, and people 'went away'. While Whit Monday's importance in the post-war recreational calendar had already been diluted by the wider availability of leisure generally, the sudden disappearance of what had been a major and highly durable play festival remains remarkable. This is all the more so as, in the past, Whitsuntide had modified its traditional pursuits to meet nineteenth-century expectations better than any of the other main festivals. The racing, cock-fighting, dancing, and general buffoonery which had grown out of the original elements of pagan ritual,[54] politely gave way to sedate processions and the new controlled spectator sports.[55] The visiting country cousins made it 'Gaping Sunday' in the northern towns, it became the time for new clothes, and local Whit Week celebrations often fell into the decorous guiding hands of churches, temperance reformers, and friendly societies, whose sober sports and parades replaced the riotous fêtes of the past.[56]

Was it the lapse in Christian belief which allowed Whitsuntide to die so quietly? For centuries, though, Christian celebrants must have found the descent of the Holy Ghost much harder to comprehend than the birth and death of Christ, without this proving any deterrent to their annual revels. At least part of the answer must lie in Whitsuntide's comparative lack of any decorative symbolism or widely observed rituals. Its role as the time for baptisms (*White* Sunday, from the christening gowns) was long forgotten, and buying a new suit or dress is no longer an annual event to be celebrated. By contrast, Christmas is heavy with visual symbols and ritualistic practices – greetings cards, fir trees, and reindeer, Father Christmas, plum pudding, and presents – and Easter has its eggs, chicks, hot cross buns, and Easter bonnets. Superficial or not, such images powerfully underpin the two holidays, both emotionally and commercially. Since few are more than a century old they may, of themselves, do little to strengthen claims for a meaningful medieval ancestry to the two continuing festivals. What they do demonstrate is that people have responded to these new accretions, that Christmas and Easter have continued the age-long responsiveness to the mutations of belief and fashion. They suggest that there are indeed still long and vital race memories prompting celebration and play at these moments of the turning year around the winter solstice and the spring equinox.

Such a notion would seem less far-fetched if it were not for the current habit of thinking of the medieval world as far away and irretrievable so far as its sports are concerned. The survival of elements of medieval play in today's sport does, though, become less surprising when we remember the recurring revivalism which has kept alive various visions of the Middle Ages over the centuries. In the arts, medievalism has made its repeated appeals – to Edmund Spenser, Keats, and Burne-Jones, for instance. The notion of a Merry England, vaguely associated with some dimly recalled past, was alive enough in the 1950s to be laughed drunkenly out of court by Kingsley Amis's Lucky Jim.[57] It has been an influential concept, if often a flawed one. In sporting terms the medieval and the classical often had a tendency to become intermingled, as most notably in John Dover's Cotswold Games, consciously revived on the hill above Chipping Campden about 1612, and where a blind Homeric harpist presided over such bucolic English contests as shin-kicking.[58]

History is often what people want it to be. Dover's was just one of many attempts to find a simple sporting happiness from a younger world. Such projects became common in the early nineteenth century, when they eventually found their text in Lord John Manners's *Plea for Holy Days*. Manners, one of Disraeli's 'Young England' coterie, lamented the souring of the national character from the loss of the old 'manly' sports. His remedy was to revive the former holy days, combining 'feast and festival', under the benign influence of the church.[59] It was one of several responses to what had come to be perceived as the 'problem' of popular recreation under the restrictive conditions of the Industrial Revolution. Among the new ventures, all of them harking to a greater or lesser degree back to the past, were the St Ives Games in Cornwall, Colonel Mason's Necton Sports (from 1817), the Uffington Olympics, Robert Paxton's Till-side Border Games ('innocent amusement, healthy relaxation and pleasant pastime', according to *Bell's Life*), the Much Wenlock Olympics and – looking forward to modern athletics as well as backwards – Baron de Beranger's Stadium Olympic Week in the grounds of Cremorne House, Chelsea.[60] Worthy as such attempts at renewal were, their weakness lay in their failure to come to terms with the alien conditions of life and labour around them. Only the Highland Games, tapping the released fervours of Scottish nationalism, and later nurtured by professional athletics, managed to put down any deep roots or endure as more than curios.[61]

Their interest lies in the persistence of the medieval theme. It was the lost dream of an integrated life, one in which labour and leisure, play and praise, were all one. It was often only a dimly perceived vision and, of course, it left the medieval reality far behind – a reality of brief lives, limited diet, hunger, cold, damp, and scant relaxation. However, just as the rhythms of the old holiday still continue to beat beneath the smooth metallic surface of today's sporting calendar, some other elements from medieval play still remain remarkably close.

There may be little of consequence surviving from the structure of much of medieval sport. Because some of the primitive play forms – hitting a missile with a stick, or kicking a ball – happen to be identifiable with modern games does not necessarily imbue them with any particular contemporary relevance. 'Football' contests, for instance, were amorphous, in that the size and strength of teams was a matter of chance, the playing area was unlimited and the rules undefined. Only in the behaviour of a minority of today's football spectators is there a reminder of the violent rivalries of the old football struggles, which traditionally took advantage of the relaxation of normal constraints at festival times.[62] Football has always had its outbursts of riotous behaviour – an important new dimension to the occasional violence is the public attention given to it. Eyebrows were doubtless raised at the terse press reports of 50 injured spectators and 38 police treated at the infirmary after the replayed Scottish Cup Final in 1909, and at the one hundred or so wounded laid out on the pitch at half-time in a Belfast Celtic match some years earlier.[63] But there was no furore. Football existed on the edges of 'normal' life. Now it is back in the centre, and we have a new shared experience with the Middle Ages. Our sport, like theirs, is all-pervading, and has been woven back into the central fabric of living. We are experiencing the rapid reversal of that process of marginalizing sport which began as early as the fourteenth and fifteenth centuries, when play, even at the popular level, began to gain in variety and specialization – with, for instance, the appearance of bowling greens and alleys[64] – and the opportunities for its enjoyment became more frequent and less wholly reliant on church festivals. The repeated criticisms of the friars provide oblique evidence of this growth.[65]

And medieval sport does afford occasional glimpses of play elements which have become identified as 'modern'.[66] Recent research[67] has confirmed the long-standing impression that the tournament had reached high sophistication well before the Tudors (who sought to keep it alive) came to the English throne. This knightly contest, the combatants charging at each other on their ponderous mounts, lances poised, over the forty paces of the lists, was highly organized and subject to a complex body of national rules.[68] The tourney took place on a defined area – the tilting ground at Kenilworth Castle, Warwickshire, is an admirable surviving example – and the spectators were firmly separated from the players, both spatially and functionally. Foul play, such as striking an opponent when his back was turned, or he was disarmed, was penalized, the scoring system was precise, and written records were kept of matches and results.[69]

What the tourney did embody, of relevance to the sports of our own century, were the twin concepts of the *challenge* and the *champion*. The challenge subsequently became the means by which formal competition was set in train in a whole range of sports. Where it remains, in more than nominal form, it has become increasingly anachronistic, but the idea of the champion, in its medieval aspect of *surrogacy*, has by contrast been going from strength to strength in recent times. The challenge began in defence of honour in the combat sports, spread to other forms of competition, and was cemented in by centuries of playing for stake money. As sports gained a degree of organization in the later eighteenth century, its real significance began to diminish. Ornate and defiant threats by pugilists to would-be opponents gave way to business-like messages, in which the hand of the backer was easily discernible.[70] In horse-racing the two-horse challenge match continued to dominate at Newmarket (where it remained important right through the nineteenth century) but generally the sweepstake and the prize race were taking over.[71] Cricket remained devoted to the challenge match and its stakes until about the 1820s, when gambling began to lose favour. Mid-century issues of *Bell's Life*, though, still carried numerous challenges from the pugs and the peds, and the concept was originally, as its title affirms, incorporated into the competition for the Football Association Challenge Cup. At first it *was* a challenge trophy. The preliminary ties were designed to find a challenger to the holder in the final – a short-lived mode of operation as it denied the holder both high-level opposition and lucrative fixtures, and it was abandoned by the time the Football League was formed in 1888.[72] The system lasted much longer in tennis, where the exemption of the holder until the challenge round in the Wimbledon men's competitions and the women's singles was not dropped until 1922.[73] As competitors in all sports became more numerous, and more nearly equal in standard, the challenge became harder and harder both to justify and to manage. Only in closed competitions, such as the Oxford and Cambridge boat race, where the arrangements are made through private correspondence between the two secretaries, does the old notion of the challenge still have some relevance. Where it persists elsewhere, notably in yachting's America's Cup, it gives rise to constant problems over what is or what is not allowable, and to disputes which, by 1989, had landed the competitors in the law courts.

If the endurance of the challenge demonstrates the slow dying of some medieval sporting concepts, the present relevance of the idea of the champion shows their continuing capacity for expansion. There is nothing out of date about the notion of the champion. The simple interpretation of the term, as the best performer, is being applied to increasing numbers of sports on the international scale. Where once only boxing, of the major sports, could boast its 'World Champions', and baseball's 'World Series' always smacked of hyperbole, now there

14

are World Cups in soccer, field hockey, and cricket, to name but a few, and there are numerous world championship competitions, from winter sports to judo. The growing significance of the idea of the champion, though, lies primarily in its original medieval connotation. The champion was the substitute, the representative of the leader, national or local, in church or state, there to defend and uphold his sponsor's cause. The champion had, accordingly, to be seen as the best. It is this surrogate function which has re-emerged so strongly in the twentieth century. As sport has grown in global importance, a nation's whole reputation can hang, in no small way, on its performances on the international playing-fields. Its champions have again become the standard-bearers of a cause that is beyond themselves.

For the moment, it serves as a reminder that aspects of our present sporting lives do have their distant origins. It is not merely some of our sporting occasions that are inherited from a far-off past. The recreational life of the Middle Ages, remote as it may be from our own, does not belong entirely to a dead and alien gothic world of darkness. There are continuities, and it should not be surprising if some of these become more apparent now than in the recent sporting past. Sport has returned to the centre of the human stage, to perform again an intrinsic role, as it once did in medieval life. It is again an all-pervading activity, an inevitable part of late-twentieth-century living. By its very ubiquity, our ultra-modern sport is more likely than its immediately preceding forms to take on features from a more distant sporting experience. It may remain the child of the Industrial Revolution, but it also has to acknowledge now its other more remote ancestry. Different gods may now preside over sporting triumphs and disasters, but they remain gods, and recognizable to all. The new centrality of sport is always likely to allow significant elements from its old centrality to shine through. Even through the traumas of our second Industrial Revolution, the ancient pulses can still beat, drawing men and women to their seasonal recreations, prompting features in their play which, among all the strangeness that they would find here, would still have meaning for our dawn dancers from the misty April morning. Despite all the maze of technology, they would recognize again in our sports an activity which is part and parcel of our social, economic, and political lives, and which embodies, too, many of our attitudes and beliefs. And *that* they would not find strange at all.

# 2

# Making much of time

The Members of Parliament who turned up at Westminster on 25 December 1656 looked around in disgust. There were too many empty benches in the House. To make matters worse, they had found many of the shops closed as they made their way through the city. They expressed their displeasure at such lapses into old, erroneous ways. They had not beheaded a king and reshaped both church and state to preserve such popish festivals as Christmas Day.[1] All snares set in the pathway to salvation had to be ruthlessly removed, even if it meant sending the military into private houses to search kitchens, pantries, and ovens to make sure that no misguided housewife had special meats or cakes prepared for the forbidden feasts. They would welcome the Lord Protector's forthcoming appointment of his major-generals to enforce obedience to the new order.

Not since the phallic maypoles, symbols of lewd and heathenish celebration, had been dragged down from the village greens over a decade ago had there been such vigorous signs of determination to control the citizens' behaviour in all its aspects. The closed bear-pits and theatres, the intruding soldiers, and Pepys's vain search for a tavern on Sunday night ('not finding any open, we durst not knock'[2]) were the visible signs of deep division in attitudes towards life and belief, work and play. They were much more than mere tinkerings with customs and calendars and they pointed to modes of recreation which owed nothing to the inherited holidays of the medieval church and even questioned the whole function of play itself.

Many of the outer garments of Puritanism are now no more than tattered rags. Even in its homeland, the English Sunday, one of the creed's most enduring bequests, has lost most of its effectiveness as a barrier against sports. Apart from keeping the betting shops closed, and so making racing impracticable, the law has become so transparent that Sunday has, with the barest side-stepping, become one of the country's most popular sporting days. But even if the direct and discernible effects of the Puritan message have now largely slipped into the past, the influence of that message on the development of sport, its nature and its opportunities, has been strong and sustained. The Puritans first of all made sport a matter for serious and critical debate. Their immediate effects on its status and evolution were certainly negative in the main. Yet the ethos of modern sport, its manners and its social acceptability, all owe much to that Puritan frame of mind that began in religion and ended in a social and economic system powerful enough to bring much of the world, bruised perhaps, but surviving, through the Industrial Revolution into the twentieth century. Lacking in benevolence towards play, the Puritans brought new ideas on time to its consideration. They began not only the long process of redefining its proper occasions, but also, and indirectly and unwittingly, that of shaping it into more regular and precise forms. Their criticisms of sport aimed at its abolition. What they achieved, though it took three centuries to do so, was its ultimate reformation and rehabilitation.

In its own heyday, Puritanism made its impact on sport and recreation both through the reshaping of the leisure calendar and through persistent attacks on play itself, for its misuse of time and its evil associations. Its radicalism was largely accidental. The original intention of the English Reformation was for the Anglican church to remain a national version of the universal Catholic church, the king at its head instead of the pope, and with an English Bible and an English Prayer Book. Protestants who wanted to go further than this were denied high office, but otherwise suffered only spasmodic harassment. The reformers in Europe found themselves either holding the reins of political power or being persecuted. In neither case could sport and leisure figure very highly in their priorities. Their English counterparts, by contrast, were left free to deliberate, to preach, and to convert. It was from these deliberations that many of the values ultimately associated with modern sport derive. These first Puritans sought the true light with the English Bible as their main, indeed often their sole, guide. With it, they diligently explored every implication of Protestantism's basic tenet of individual responsibility to God. As they pushed on, everything inherited from the old religion became suspect, and had to be rigorously examined. Play itself was soon put to the question. Not only was it closely associated with the feast days embedded in Catholicism, but it also raised serious questions about the proper use of God-given time.

The employment of time became particularly significant as the consequences of the Calvinistic doctrine of predestination became clear. If salvation was reserved for a predetermined band of the elect, how did an individual know whether he or she was one of the chosen? It would show, came the answer, in his life here, in his piety and religious observance, and in his public and private acts. Moreover, since the chance to demonstrate conspicuous worthiness on a grand scale came only to the few, these signs of grace had to be available in situations open to all – in the prayer and praise of family life, in diligent and honest labour, and in a sober and godly bearing on all occasions.

So the attitude to time itself changed dramatically. The medieval world, at root, had seen all life as but a patient – and usually short – wait for eternity. The brevity and pains of the life below were endurable in the light of the life to come, which was assured so long as the formal calls of the church were obeyed. Now urgency, the need for positive action, replaced the passive stoicism of the past. Time became the essential element in life's central purpose – that of demonstrating election to future glory. There was no single minute to spare from this overwhelming earthly purpose.

At some stages of history, sport and play might have laid admissible claims to a share of this precious commodity, time. In late Victorian and Edwardian England, the playing field could present itself as the forcing ground for fair play, justice, and manliness. There was little, though, in the sport and play which the Puritans saw around them that appeared to ease the way to eternal life. It had been hard enough for the Renaissance educators, well disposed though they were, to find justifications for sport. From Vergerius in fifteenth-century Italy to Sir Thomas Elyot in sixteenth-century England they were always having to hedge in their already modest proposals for play.[3] The Puritan, for his part, found only sin and error in the people's customary play. He was not looking for signs of communal well-being, for the simple satisfactions of the game, for the happiness of the participants or the relief of the strains of their working lives. What he found was only 'the abominable idol of fleshly pleasure', play that was marked by 'idleness, pride, drunkenness, quarrelling and brawling',[4] 'wicked in curses and swearing', and 'wasteful in gaming and spending'.[5] To be sure these iniquities were all there, on the green, in the open fields, and even in the churchyard, and they were even more marked on the traditional feast days, with their casting off of usual restraints. February was, for centuries, the sad month for the annual plague of infanticides, tragic endings to May Day's carnal pleasures. Few amusements of any sort could now claim innocence. Stage plays became 'plain devourers of maidenly virginity and chastity',[6] with their examples of vicious conduct, and even mixed dancing was claimed to have been always 'utterly unlawful, sinful, shameful, carnal, sensual, and devilish as hateful to God, as hurtful to men'.[7]

Such sport and recreation could make no justifiable calls on the time of the virtuous. Even the late and comparatively moderate voice of Richard Baxter, whose *Christian Directory* belongs to the Restoration years and

1 One of the oldest bowling greens in the country, in Christchurch Priory grounds, Dorset, survives as an example of the church's former role in popular play (Author's collection)

the political defeat of the Puritan cause, remains dubious over the need for play at all. His cautionary subheading, 'Directions about Sports and Recreations and against excess and sin therein',[8] speaks for itself, and in the end he concludes that 'honest bodily labour' which 'joineth pleasure and profit together' is a 'fitter kind of exercise' than any games played 'only to delight a carnal fantasy'.[9] When the most generous Puritan advice was that the only justifiable sport was that which tended to the glory of God that 'the scope and end of all recreations is that God may be honoured in and by them', little in contemporary play was going to pass the test.[10]

It was a question of suitable *occasions* for play, as well as of play itself. One of the most enduring practical legacies of Puritanism was a fundamental reshaping of the leisure calendar. The feast days which lay at the heart of medieval popular recreation were bitterly attacked. The one single holy day for which the reformers could find any biblical sanction was Sunday, though they held that title to be heathenish and preferred the Jewish 'Sabbath'. All other so-called holy days had to be mere inventions of the old church, probably introduced at the instigation of the devil, through his agent the pope. They were deliberately designed to replace honest work with hours of sloth and sin, 'whereby half of the year and more was overpassed ... in loitering and vain pastimes, etc. in restraining men from their handy labours and occupations'.[11]

There was a two-fold recreational thrust in this changed emphasis. It would, on the one hand, remove many of the inherited opportunities for play and, on the other, bar sports from the one regular rest day which remained. The abolition of holy days would be dramatic in its effects. There had been at least 150 major religious feasts in the medieval calendar, running from Circumcision on 1 January to St Silvester's Day on 31 December, and alphabetically from St Adrian's (9 January) to St Wulstan's ten days later.[12] The scope these gave for leisure has certainly sometimes been exaggerated.[13] It was not until the fourteenth century that work after church on Sunday began to diminish, and it remained usual at harvest and other busy farming seasons. None the less, amid all the variety that existed, the church feasts did allow many to enjoy frequent if spasmodic breaks for play.

Some medieval craftsmen's work patterns were formalized. At the top of the employment tree, the king's masons, in the fifteenth century, had thirty-seven holy days and all Sundays free from work, with early finishes on Saturdays and before most of the holy days.[14] If workers in less prestigious crafts fared less well, they still enjoyed considerable freedom. The London wiremongers, for instance, had thirteen free holy days on what were ranked as 'double' feasts, early finishes on Saturdays, and free Sundays.[15] The greater part of the population, those working on the land, were harder pressed, especially as they often depended for food on what they could raise on their own plots, in such times as they could find.

The stress on Sunday had begun to show in the hundred years between the masons' work schedule and that of the wiremongers in 1481. Sunday had been elevated to a 'double' feast – a major holiday – while many minor holy days had been lost. If the Puritans promoted Sunday at the expense of all other religious occasions, they were not the first to discover its holiness. The potential threat to the country's recreational life had been hinted at even before the Reformation, with the friar, John Bromyard, for instance, regretting that greater Sunday freedom from work also brought more bear-baitings.[16] The assurance of some degree of release every seven days gave a measure of predictability and continuity to people's play, and it is no accident that sports did gain in variety in the fifteenth century, as demonstrated by the growing lists of games in proclamations and edicts. On the other hand, the same motives which fostered the weekly holy day also sought to reserve it more completely for devotion and good works – not at first easy with a population which had always associated all its holy days with both prayer *and* play.

Sabbatarianism gained in strength through the middle years of the sixteenth century. True to its moderate intentions, the official Anglican stance on Sunday observance remained conservative. The 1551 Act of Uniformity allowed Sunday labour not only at harvest, but also 'at any other times of the year when necessity shall require to labour, ride, fish or work any kind of work'. The law might continue to require church attendance, and then give a comfortable allowance for either work or play afterwards, but the mood was changing. Even the church's own injunctions began to take on an acerbic tone, claiming that 'in our time, God is more offended than pleased, more dishonoured than honoured upon the holy day; because of idleness, pride, drunkenness, quarrelling and brawling'.[17] As the stricter minds turned critical eyes on the pursuit of play itself, they found it all the more objectionable for its persistent Sabbath-breaking. Finally, the wave of anti-Catholic feeling in the 1570s, with Queen Elizabeth's life endangered by papist plots and the Spanish a constant threat, gave Sabbatarianism its opportunity to flower. By 1595, when Nicholas Bound gave it a theology in his long-forgotten but highly influential *Doctrine of the Sabbath*, the functional benefits of Sunday observance had already dawned even on many of the ungodly, in terms of public order, social control, and economic advantage. Bound claimed that to keep Sunday holy was nothing less than a divine and immutable law, deriving from Genesis and the Creation, predating even man himself. It was merely reinforced by the Mosaic code and the fourth commandment, and not dependent upon either. It was a persuasive theory which fell upon ready ears, and remained relatively unscathed until disputed by Hessey and other theologians in the nineteenth century.[18] For all that time it effectively kicked Sunday play out of the doctrinal ball-park.

If Sabbatarianism presented one serious threat to popular play, its complementary arm, seeking the abolition of other holy days, was equally limiting. Soon Puritan craftsmen were actually striving for the liberty to work on all days other than the Sabbath, and throughout the seventeenth century there was continual conflict between the Established Church, seeking to maintain traditional observances, and that part of the population which held Sunday to be the only holy day with true biblical sanction. There were numerous prosecutions for failure to observe saints' days under Archbishop Laud, and the complaints continued after the Restoration.[19] In the rich and righteous Vale of Evesham it was said of the farmers, in 1674, that 'on the Sabbath days they forbear but on the holy days in seed time and harvest they follow their bodily and ordinary labour and permit their servants to do so'.[20] The word 'permit' is as telling as the timing of the complaint. The return of the monarchy had brought relief from some of the tightest constraints on the people's sport, but it had brought no long-term security.

On the face of things, the Puritans had become a defeated force in Britain. Even the name fell into disuse. Those of them who had founded the New England colonies were soon to be outnumbered by immigrants with less firm religious tenets. The social message of Puritanism, however, had come to have considerable appeal to many who were at best lukewarm towards its theological enthusiasms. The deep honesty of the Puritan work ethic was apparently as profitable to the pocket as it was satisfying to the soul. The search for more regular work patterns to suit the infant capitalist system found a response in the regular weekly holiday and the disappearance of the unpredictable and wayward feasts of the past. And given the disturbing lawlessness and licence of much popular play, any system which held it in closer bounds and limited its occasions had an irresistible attraction to administrators and guardians of law and order.

Thus the Puritan legacy was assured of a continuing influence on the future of sport and recreation, and it is an influence which is still not wholly played out. There have been periods, as in much of the eighteenth century, when it remained relatively muted. Its latent potential for reappearance was always there, though, not only in the discipline of the sterner sects,[21] but also in the minds of moderate dissenters such as Job Orton, who had a deep aversion to 'methodists and other disorderly people'.[22] It was not just Sunday sport but popular recreation itself that was frowned upon. In their own turn, the

22

Methodists themselves sought the 'reform' of popular recreation, but in a manner which was almost wholly negative until the last quarter of the nineteenth century.[23] The same Puritan strains in Methodism did much to persuade the working-class movements earlier in the century to keep sport and physical recreation at arm's length,[24] and contributed to their low priority in most Mechanics' Institutes.[25] Even after sport had become tolerable, if not totally respectable, in the minds of the majority, questioning moral voices continued to echo the old Puritan doubts, particularly directed against its 'contamination' by professionalism and against the growing crowds who watched rather than played, those 'thousands of boys and young men' described by Lord Baden-Powell in his *Scouting for Boys* in 1908 as 'pale, narrow-chested, hunched-up, miserable specimens, smoking endless cigarettes, numbers of them betting, all of them learning to be hysterical as they groan or cheer in panic unison with their neighbours'.[26] The Puritan distaste for popular sport had bitten hard and deep.

Wholesale disavowals of competitive sport are now comparatively rare. *Aspects* of sport do, of course, come in for endless criticism and discussion. This is part of its life blood, a symptom of its universal significance. Its opponents generally resign themselves to forlorn complaints over its monopoly of the television channels. Outright condemnation is left to the few, such as Bernard Levin, who sees sport as dream world, enthusiasm for it as escape from reality, and the national euphoria at international sporting success 'inexplicable'.[27] For the majority, sport is just as much a part of 'reality' as making cars, selling stocks and shares, or cooking hamburgers. The Puritan doubts about sport and recreation may well seem to have been washed away. The spread of free-thinking and self-indulgence that marked the decades after the Second World War rid many human appetites, including that for play, of much of their inherited guilt. When 'Gorgeous' Gussie Moran appeared at a post-war Wimbledon in frilly silk knickers she was opening the door to a new sporting world.[28]

What its new message will be is too early to say. The original conflicts and questions prompted by the Puritan movement, and, indeed, even the debates of Victorian Evangelicals, may appear to have little bearing on contemporary sporting themes. At a time, though, when Thatcherism is reawakening Puritan memories of free-market capitalism allied with moral paternalism, it is appropriate to recall that modern sport was moulded in the Puritan and Evangelical traditions, diluted as their influence may now have become. Modern sport grew within the constraints and conditions which the Puritan inheritance had planted in the hearts and minds of those who were to be its most influential promoters, who were to secure its reformation to meet the terms of the post-industrial world.

The long dominance of attitudes rooted in the original tenets of Elizabethan Puritanism ensured that sport could only emerge into the full sunlight of approval if it conformed to some demanding expectations. It had to shed its reputation for excess and disorder, throw off its associations with drink and foul language, and divorce itself from what often seemed its intrinsic element – gaming. It had also, and this above all in the minds of many, to find its *time*, to find legitimate occasions which offended neither God nor Mammon. The sporting revolution of the late nineteenth century succeeded because it found absolution from sport's original sins. Only in the present century, with its status assured and certain, has sport been able to afford conspicuous new lapses from purity.

The pathway to grace was slow and uneven. The early spectator sports saw little need to win public approval. The aristocratic patronage, on which they considerably depended, was powerful enough to ignore the still muted moral voices. Even so, gestures towards decency were made. Pugilism might be an illegal sport in itself, but it avoided the added offence of mounting fights on the Sabbath. With the rarest of exceptions,[29] horse-racing and cricket followed suit. As Victorian morality took over, cricket brought itself gradually within the pale, having already banned gambling from Lords (if not always effectively) in the 1820s, and taken action against players alleged to have 'sold' games.[30] The turf's moral problem was that gambling and horse-racing have always been inextricably intertwined. Its only hope was to make the gambling as honest as possible, and there still remains a generation alive for whom the racecourse has an air of sin about it, the clouds of suspicion only briefly lifting on Derby and Grand National days. As to prize-fighting, the bare-knuckle sport never stood any hope of survival, given the physical cruelty which it added to sport's other sins. The new sports which grew up in the nineteenth century had a much easier time of it. They did not have to adapt their old ways to new demands, but knew from the start the expectations which they had to fulfil. Amateur athletics and rowing had their initial struggles with inherited practices, but activities such as croquet, tennis, golf, and swimming were launched with growing confidence in their capacity to surmount the traditional moral objections.

The first British signs of an easing of the ethical demands on sport appeared in the 1930s, with the introduction of new and seemingly less disreputable forms of gambling. The stigma attached to betting on the results of contests began to lose its force, first with the racecourse Totalisator – the 'Tote', which returned most of the stake money to winning punters – and then with football pools, which were an instant and phenomenal financial success.[31] The pools met surprisingly subdued opposition. The courts decided that forecasting results was a skill and that the Gaming Acts did not apply, and then there was the widespread impression that the pools would reduce the small gambler's dependence on that other new lure, greyhound-racing. 'Going to the dogs' had quickly become a snap description of the road to ruin. By 1960, not only had gambling become more broadly accepted, it had also become legal. The ban on off-course betting was lifted and licensed betting shops[32] replaced the bookie's runner, down at heel, flat-capped, cigarette drooping from the corner of the mouth, and known down every working-class street. It could hardly be otherwise after the state had put its own seal on gambling by introducing Premium Bonds, allegedly 'savings', but with their monthly prize draws.

That the football pools should appear somewhat less iniquitous than betting on horses and dogs was another of the surprising off-shoots of nonconformist morality. It had always firmly placed domestic duties and the virtues of the hearth above participation in dubious communal pursuits, and whereas to bet legally on racing the punter had to be at the racecourse, or the track, the football coupon did not of necessity draw him away from the fireside. Family life may now have weakened with the spread of divorce, but other changes – particularly those stressing the equality of the sexes, and the general and more equally shared growth of leisure – have extended the notion of what the family should do as a unit. Sport and recreation have become again what they were in the pre-industrial days – much more family activities, much more likely to involve both wives and husbands.[33] The consequences for sport are telling.

Sport, to be successful, must no longer be a competitor with home life, a threat to the moral comforts of domesticity, but must be accessible to the whole family. This has been easier to achieve with some sports, and in some places, than with others. Cricket, with its opportunities for easy socializing during the leisurely course of play, and the relative comfort in which it was usually watched, attracted women spectators from Edwardian days and earlier, though at first, and for economic as well as social reasons, it tended to be middle-class women who predominated. Football and baseball, as examples from male-dominated sports, faced greater difficulties. Baseball succeeded by having special family games, give-aways to youngsters at some, a more dramatic presentation, and keeping prices down to a level which a family could afford. British football, by contrast, and with a few notable exceptions,[34] remains essentially a male preserve at the highest levels – a major reason behind its repeated crowd problems.

The foul language, obscene chanting, overt racism, and physical violence found in some such crowds is exactly the mass behaviour which the whole Puritan tradition rejected. Yet the actual play itself, like all modern sport, is deeply if distantly indebted to that same tradition

25

for many of its positive qualities. The play ethic became the ultimate mirror image of the Protestant work ethic – the contractual honesty of business, so firmly subscribed to by the Puritans and their successors, became fused with the self-regarding concept of *honour*, from another, older, and elitist inheritance, to produce the idea of fairness in play. It is an idealistic notion in both the common and the philosophical senses. It embodies a perfectionist code of play behaviour and a recognition that the moral force behind that code lies beyond the confines of the game itself. 'Fair play', taken in its full meaning, implies something more than accepting an appointed arbiter's decision. The cricketer who walks away from his wicket when he knows that he has edged the ball into the wicket-keeper's gloves, or the fieldsman who acknowledges that the ball was grounded when he appeared to catch it, both relieve the umpire of a decision which might well be the wrong one. Such actions epitomize the spirit of fair play, taken to its extreme by that early select amateur soccer club, the Corinthians, who resolved to dispense with their goalkeeper if one of the newly introduced penalty kicks for foul play should ever be awarded against them.

As sporting success came to involve both national prestige and high finance, such standards became all the harder to sustain. The Argentinian footballing genius, Diego Maradonna, not wholly cynically perhaps, could claim that it was not his hand, but the hand of God, which 'headed' the ball into the English net in a World Cup match. But it was not the God of the Puritans.[35] 'Nice guys finish last' may now seem a more powerful slogan than 'Play up! Play up! And Play the Game!' The ideal, though, of honest dealing was a main buttress of sport's rise to world importance, the very importance which has made finishing first or last matter so much that it challenges the means by which the result can be achieved.

There are other peculiarly British consequences of the impact on sport of Puritan ideas, notably the notion that it should not become too purely pleasurable,[36] but there remains one further significant element in their contribution to the universal theme of sporting time.

Time and motion were dominating themes in seventeenth-century thinking. Advances in the measurement of both[37] fed the preoccupations of scientists and philosophers, poets and preachers. By the beginning of the century it had become possible to measure seconds, as well as hours and minutes. Time was not the sole preserve of the spiritual reformer, and neither Marvell's 'To His Coy Mistress' nor Herrick's 'To the Virgins, to make much of time' was directed at objects which would win the approval of the pious. For those, though, who elevated time's proper employment into a prime religious principle, its apportioning, its rationing between one activity and another became compelling duties. If, as experience showed, sports and games could not be swept away, they could at least be confined. Even for Jeremy Taylor, Anglican bishop and no Puritan, sport was to be carefully measured and used in moderation, 'taken as physic, or as wine at most'.[38] And if man's own predilections for play would not submit readily to time limits, then the sports themselves had to be contained.

There were other contributory reasons for the gradual hedging in of play's time spans – the eighteenth century's search for order, for instance, and the nineteenth's insistence on tightly controlled labour – but the roots of the growth lay in the seventeenth century's new awareness of time itself, and in the restraining stresses which Puritanism had given to that awareness, so far as recreation was concerned.

One feature of medieval play's widespread lack of formal structure was its frequent open-endedness – it had its day or half-day, and often darkness was its only final whistle. The contrast with modern sports is wholesale, with virtually all today's contests controlled and limited by the clock.[39] Attempts by cricket to escape from its confines by having 'time-less' test matches (in order to secure positive results on the plumb wickets of the 1930s) effectively ended when the final game of a series between South Africa and England dragged itself out over ten playing days, and nearly 2,000 runs, and still had to be left as an unfinished draw when the visitors had to catch their boat back to Britain! So cricket returned to its bounds, and those bounds have been further and further refined, varied according to the style of game being played, and with the discipline of the clock reinforced by requiring a set number of overs to be bowled.[40] Lawn tennis, likewise, introduced the sudden-death play-off to put an end to the marathon sets where points relentlessly went with the server and could run to forty games or more. Many football competitions, too, now resort to penalty shoot-outs to avoid replaying drawn matches.

In some sports, particularly those popular in North America, the control by the clock has become even more precise, with only actual *playing* time taken account of – as distinct, say, from soccer, where the ball may be in play for as little as half of the allotted ninety minutes. This has refined still further the game skills called for in the management of time. Retaining possession, and keeping the ball in the opponent's half of the field to hang on to a lead towards the end of a game, in any of the British football codes, are simple exercises compared with the stopping of the clock in American football or basketball. There the last ten seconds of the match can be critical – and they are *known* to be the last ten seconds. The excitement of the game's final move, as its last breaths tick away, is a novelty confined to the twentieth century.

The growing capacity to measure time more finely has profoundly altered the nature of many competitive sports. Electronics can now make distinctions in fractions of a second that lie well beyond the capacity of the human eye. A dead heat in a modern championship swimming bath is now almost unknown. Racing contests of all sorts have responded to the increasing facility. In the eighteenth century, when running for wagers was more often against the clock than against an opponent, events of much shorter than a mile were practically unmeasurable in terms of time. Such claimed times as were recorded are often suspect.[41] Only in the early nineteenth century did times for performances begin to be quoted regularly in minutes *and* seconds,[42] and the door was opened to shorter races. The best-known records of the past had been for endurance events such as the famous Barclay Match of 1,000 miles in 1,000 hours,[43] but now times could be confidently established for sprints and speed began to count as much as stamina.[44] It is no accident either, although there were other forces at work as well, that the appearance of stop-watches in the hands of trainers on Newmarket Heath coincided with the growth of short-distance races for younger horses.[45] The progress to ever more tightly timed sporting competition was well on its way.

So, even though the Puritans and the many heirs to their tradition may not have been able to abolish public sports, as many in their hearts would have liked to do, they did achieve much. And what they did promote was, paradoxically, often to sport's eventual benefit. They reduced its crudity, improved its honesty, and set it within firm limits of time. We owe more that is positive to them than we are in the habit of granting. The old sports that the original Puritans saw around them on their village greens, with their drunkenness, their licence, and their irregularity of timing, could never have survived into an industrialized and urbanized world. They and their successors inculcated standards into British life which at length proved strong enough to displace the amorality of both a fading aristocracy and a rising working class. They were standards and expectations which came in the end to dominate all aspects of Victorian behaviour – including, and inevitably if it was to prosper, its sport. The 'gentling' of the masses was never a Puritan aim, but it was a process which their influence made all the more feasible.

It was an influence, too, which spread, with varying effects, over the whole English-speaking world – the inspiration, for example, in all the British Dominions of Sunday observance laws which were more severe (by being more deliberately formulated and precise) than those of the home country. It lay behind not only the strictures against play in colonial New England, but also the 'Blue Laws' which kept sport in a Sabbath stranglehold in many parts of the United States until well into the present century. The Puritan power, though, was far from unlimited. It always had its unappealing aspects – intolerance, bleakness, and an inbuilt tendency to hypocrisy – and has had its constant struggle with the Dionysian strain in man. The carousing players on the green or in the skittle alley could be dispersed, but seldom much further than the alehouse. And when they held the reins of power themselves, it was a Puritan government which first demonstrated the limits to political action when it goes against the desires and prejudices of the people, when it tries to deprive them of their accustomed pleasure, their amusements, and their play.

# 3

# The governing of play

> Clearly more needs to be done to control football hooliganism since the steps taken so far have been shown to be inadequate. Further measures have been proposed which the Government will be looking at and will discuss, where appropriate, with the football authorities.[1]

This ministerial statement to the House of Commons in June 1988 would still have had an almost routine air about it, even if it had been stripped of its clichés and its dampening jargon. Certainly feelings ran high against the groups of youths who had, with the help of local provocation, made great nuisances of themselves in Germany during the recent European Cup football tournament, but the government response was predictable. Had there been a simple road to soccer peace, the authorities would have already found it. What the administration was about to produce was, in fact, the Football Spectators Bill, with its speculative and highly controversial system of identity cards for admission to Football League games.

The modernity of the Commons announcement lay not in its content but in its origins. Violence in and around sport is as old as sport itself, but now it was being pronounced upon by an actual Minister for Sport. Until a generation ago, rioting spectators in England, if they happened to catch the Commons' attention, would have been the responsibility of the Home Secretary, and rampaging Britons abroad a problem for the Foreign Secretary. When the body-line controversy flared up between England and Australia in 1935–6 it landed in the Welsh lap of ex-railwayman J. H. Thomas, as Colonial Secretary. The existence of a Minister for Sport reflects sport's new centrality in the national life. Even a government theoretically devoted to *laissez-faire* economics and state minimalism has seen fit to continue the office, though the minister's brief may well extend no further than finding alternatives to the scant public funding already given to recreation and keeping the football fans quiet.

Governments have habitually found more problems than opportunities in their citizens' sporting proclivities. Sporting crowds have always seemed a potential threat to public order either directly,[2] or, more occasionally, as covert gatherings for seditious action.[3] Concern for public order must always rank high in any government's priorities, but apart from that a government devoted to the play of free-market forces finds itself in a dilemma over its approach to sport. It would, in its bones, like to 'keep politics out of sport', yet it knows, in its head, that this is impossible. If politics is the art of living together, then the community's play, no less than its form of government, its laws, and its work practices are part of the political process. However strong the contemporary disposition to non-interference with sport might be, it proves hard to live up to. English governments in the eighteenth century, for instance, saw their domestic role as limited to the maintenance of the satisfactory political arrangements which the country already enjoyed. Any view that sport was part of government's responsibilities would have been firmly rejected. Yet governments did interfere – in the control of gaming and horse-racing,[4] in the suppression of the prize-fighting emporia and the outlawing of the prize-ring,[5] and the effective banning of Sunday spectator sports.[6]

The continuing fact of a Ministry for Sport is tacit acknowledgement that non-involvement is no longer an option. Sport presents government with a complex international operation and gives rise, both at home and abroad, to issues which lie beyond itself. Morally, government has to oppose the strident racialism of some sporting crowds. Internationally, and with less apparent conviction, it has to support the Commonwealth Gleneagles Agreement against sending national teams to South Africa. Sport, in fact, is not only *in* politics, even for governments which might prefer it not to be, but it is often near the centre of the political stage. In sport itself, in its international dimension, the major issues are as likely to be political as athletic, even if they sometimes come in disguise.[7] Lord Killanin has stated that 95 per cent of the problems he had to deal with as President of the International Olympic Committee were political, and that no one 'needs less convincing that politics are "in" sport and always have been'.[8]

This is not the first time in our history that sport has posed awkward political questions. The nature and timing of play gave rise to vital constitutional controversy for much of the early Stuart period. If, in the sixteenth century, sport became a topic for religious debate, in the seventeenth it became a regular theme of political dispute. They were not our times, and they were not our sports – there was little organization, limited financial investment, and virtually no international competition. The debate, though, could still have its significance, if only for the long-enduring nature of its scars. The Sunday Observance Act of 1625, with its limitations on Sunday play, did, after all remain on the statute-book until 1969.[9]

The political disputes over sport in the seventeenth century had several characteristic features. The motives that lay behind the sporting debate were diverse – religious, social, economic, and constitutional. Contention over sport was often an alibi for more dangerous conflicts, and the consequences for sport of political action were not always intentional. They became as telling for future generations as for their own times, since they set up much of the administrative framework within which sport had to operate for the next two centuries, particularly in so far as the occasions for play and their frequency were concerned.

Parallels with our own experience are not hard to find. As sport has moved nearer and nearer to centre-stage, so more and more facets of human experience have been brought to bear upon it. This is reflected, for instance, in its academic expansion. Until the mid-twentieth century, the study of sport was largely confined to physical training, anatomy and physiology, and eulogizing histories of individual games and players. Today it embraces not only a broad swathe of the medical sciences, but has its recognizable sub-disciplines – psychology, socio-logy, economics, philosophy, comparative studies, sport literature, sport geography, and so on – as well as a growing body of critical historical research, bringing sport more firmly into the ambit of social history where it properly belongs.

We have, moreover, again found sport a useful alibi, a replacement for more damaging contests. As war becomes an ever more frightening, expensive, and destructive business, a threat indeed to the planet as a whole, some substitute for the expression of national rivalries has to be found, and sport has increasingly filled this role.[10] And there are many examples from the present century of political decisions which have had unintended or incidental effects on sport. Among them are changes in statutory holidays, the launch of Premium Bonds (for their implications for gambling), immigration and employment laws (for their effects on the signing of foreign players), and laws on restraint of trade which have loosened the hold of clubs on their professionals.

Holidays, gambling, and the effects of recreation on trade were all live issues for our seventeenth-century forebears and they were all drawn into what became the central political conflict of period. The Crown saw itself as inheriting traditional powers, which it sought to maintain, while a body of opposition in Parliament and country saw itself equally as defending traditional rights. The major lever available to Parliament was its substantial control of the national purse by voting taxes, while its precedents for independent action in other fields were patchy and uncertain. One subject on which it had regularly legislated, even if it was at the behest of the Crown, was sport. There were numerous medieval and Tudor statutes defining the opportunities for recreation and their proper use.[11] The frequency of enactments directing energies to archery practice[12] is indicative that any effects they had were short-term, but they were part of a body of legislation which had established this as a matter within the ambit of Parliament, at least in its own eyes.

Where members had acted in the interests of military training in the past, they now felt free to consider sport in other contexts. Even under the well-respected Elizabeth I, one of the topics on which parliamentary muscles had been flexed towards the end of the reign was that of Sunday sport. Bills for 'the better and more reverent observing of the Sabbath' were passed in both 1585 and 1601, to restrain Sunday play and Sunday trade. Although they were both vetoed by the queen, they had put down a marker of parliamentary interest in the people's recreation. The new monarch from Scotland, James I, with his elevated views on the nature of kingship, was unlikely to acknowledge it.

Given a widespread parliamentary concern for a more orderly recreational life, and two kings, in James and his son, Charles I, who combined a chronic shortage of money with ambitious views on their right to direct their subjects' behaviour, conflict was inevitable, if only on the narrow sporting question. The underlying struggle during the forty years before the Civil War was constitutional, stoked too by changing religious and economic interests. Where was the line to be drawn between the authority of the Crown and that of Parliament?

It scarcely seemed to be a conflict in which questions of sport would rank highly. Yet whenever the first two Stuarts called Parliament together – and they did so only when the coffers were empty – the members always set about, as their very first business, discussing popular sport and recreation.[13] One reason is that this was a subject on which there was likely to be a broad measure of agreement on the benches. Puritan MPs were always in a minority, and their real aim of wholesale religious reform stood no chance of success. They had to look to causes which could command the backing of the moderate majority, whose suspicions of the Crown were more political and economic than spiritual. A stricter Sunday, particularly one which set limits on Sunday play, had its strong appeal to commercial interests and to the many members who had local responsibilities for law and order. It was as though the deeper issues at stake were too inflammable to approach directly, and Sunday sport provided a convenient alternative battleground, only giving way to the prime causes of dissent when, in 1628, yet another of the many Bills for the 'Reformation of Sunday abuses committed on the Lord's Day' was dropped to make room for the 'great business' of the Petition of Right, which put the Commons' claims at last squarely before the Crown. The battle had moved from the practice ground to the main stadium.

An examination of the respective standpoints of the two sides during this long intermittent sparring match is revealing. The differences between them seem so minor to twentieth-century minds as to confirm that the real conflicts were less over the law itself than over the right to determine that law. It was by no means the last occasion when politicians have not been talking about what they claimed to be.

Once the Parliamentarians took over government in the 1640s and 1650s they could give full rein to a radically Puritan sporting policy. The close similarity of supposedly opposing viewpoints in the earlier Stuart years, though, comes out clearly in a comparison between James I's proclamation, the Declaration of Sports, which was essentially the statement of the Crown's position, and the one successful parliamentary intervention, the Sunday Observance Act of 1625. The declaration, better known later as the Book of Sports, did little more than explicate the existing law, but that was enough to infuriate those who sought its amendment. It was promulgated in response to complaints from Lancashire that local justices were putting down the recreations that the people customarily enjoyed once Sunday worship was over.[14] This, said James, was encouraging drunkenness, idleness, and unrest, and preventing men from taking the exercise they needed to keep them fit for military service, should the need arise. He also noted the obvious but seldom stated fact that if play was barred from Sundays and holy days, there would be no occasions left for people 'to have leave to exercise', as they had to work at all other times.[15] The declaration demanded church attendance as the price of play. Afterwards, all 'lawful' sports were to be allowed, including leaping and vaulting, dancing and May games. Only those barred by statute were forbidden. The sole innovation in the proclamation was to confine Sunday recreations to the home parish,[16] so preventing large crowds from gathering – a provision which, coming from other sources, might have won much support.

The 1625 Sunday Observance Act was forced upon a reluctant Charles I some seven years after his father's declaration. Expensive foreign adventuring and an empty purse compelled him to accept this fifth attempt by Stuart Parliaments to put a law on Sunday behaviour on the statute-book. In spite, though, of the long persistence of members and the equally sustained obduracy of the Crown, it was a far from revolutionary measure, in the circumstances of the day. It only differed, in fact, from the declaration by firming up the ban on travel out of the parish for Sunday play, adding 'common plays' to the prohibited Sunday amusements and setting out penalties for transgressors.[17]

The real question in dispute was over who should pronounce on sports and Sunday behaviour – the king by proclamation, or Parliament

34

by statute. Such issues concerning the source of authority in sports are again live ones in our own day. Indeed, given its ever greater immersion in the complexities of the contemporary world, and its growing internationalism, problems over the nature of control constantly become more intricate. Where shall the ultimate decisions on a sport's disciplinary questions lie, with its controlling body or with the courts? And where should the division of responsibilities lie between national and international bodies? Neither the ordinary courts nor the ruling bodies of sports are ideally suited for this new task, if for quite different reasons. The courts often fail to appreciate the complications and niceties of individual sports and would prefer to leave disputes in the hands of the governing bodies.[18] They, for their part, can be slipshod both in the ways their rules are drafted and in the manner in which they are applied. The outstanding example of their tendency to flout even the rules of natural justice was the long-standing Football Association rule requiring clubs or individuals accused of offences to prove their innocence![19] As sport becomes more sophisticated it seeps into new legal areas – drug-taking to enhance athletic performance, for instance, overlaps with criminality but does not coincide with it, and each country has its own interpretation of what should be the concern of sports administrators and what the concern of the courts. The intricacies of controlling international sport are well illustrated by the ban on European participation by English football clubs. Where does – or where should? – sovereignty lie in such issues? Should the question of lifting the ban be determined in Britain by the Minister for Sport, or in Europe, and if the latter, by what body, and where should any appeal lie? Is there any role, as the players themselves suggest, for the European Court of Human Rights? It may well be that the future will show that answers to such questions on the sources of authority in sports will prove much more influential than any specific judgements that happen to be pronounced, just as, in 1625, the passing of an Act was, of itself, much more important than what the Act happened to say.

Controversy over the allocation of time to sport did not end with the defeat of the Puritan and Parliamentary cause. The Restoration of the monarchy, after the Interregnum, provided a footnote that was on the face of things unexpected. The 1677 Sunday Observance Act has been accounted for as a check on the Catholic tendencies feared from Charles II's heir, his brother, who became James II. This, though, was only partly so. The Commons had brought up no fewer than five separate Bills on the subject, starting in the early years of the restored monarchy, when there was every expectation that the royal loins would prove as fruitful in the marriage bed as they were outside it. The only sporting consequence of the 1677 Act, which was directed at Sunday trading, was that it could prevent professional sportsmen from following their 'ordinary calling' on the Sabbath, but both the Act and the many contemporary parliamentary debates give clear evidence of a continuing wish for a more sober Sunday, including keeping play at arm's length.[20] The relative quiet of the Commonwealth Sunday had kept its appeal, even to many who had been Puritanism's most obdurate enemies, and the 'Caroline Laws' were securely placed on the statute-book, to be the pillars of Sabbatarianism and a constant hindrance to Sunday sport for the next two and a half centuries. An irresistible combination of piety and vested interests, whether of brewers or trade unionists, was to keep them in at least nominal force until 1969, and by then their relevant prohibitions were also protected by other legislation, such as the 1780 Sunday Observance Act and the 1930 Shops Act. If the so-called Cavalier Parliament of Charles II demonstrated that the radicalism of one age can become the orthodoxy of the next, the history of the laws on Sunday play can equally illustrate the endurance of political action on sport to well beyond its time, and for motives undreamed of by its originators.

This long-lived legislation, however, is by no means all that the seventeenth century has to show by way of government intervention in recreation. During the Commonwealth there was a drastic attempt to wholly reshape the country's play and leisure life. It may have been a relatively brief experiment, but its thorough-going nature has never been rivalled in Britain, and seldom anywhere in the world.[21] It was no less than an attempt to rewrite the whole sporting calendar. More repressive Sunday edicts were only to be expected once the Parliamentarians took over government, and they came in abundance. Each new measure found some fresh sporting target. In 1644 it was wrestling, archery, bell-ringing, feasting, dancing, and the catch-all of 'Games, Sports or Pastime whatsoever'.[22] In the next year the proscribed Sunday activities were extended to specify dicing, card-playing, football, stool-ball, hawking, hunting, fishing, and fowling.[23] By 1657 there was little that the imagination could add – 'leaping' was thrown in, presumably to make it clear that children's sports were also included,[24] and finally 'all persons vainly or profanely walking on that day' were to be prosecuted.[25] The ambition of government to control its citizens' bodily movements could hardly be pushed further.

The sporting revolution was not, though, to stop there. The papist festivals, those traditional occasions for popular play, all had to go. Christmas, Easter, Whitsuntide, and the whole gamut of holy days were struck from the calendar at a stroke by the Ordinance Abolishing Festivals in June 1647. For once, even the promoters of the edict recognized that the repression of play had to have its limits, and they instituted a new holiday for 'scholars, apprentices, and other servants' on the second Thursday of every month. At first, the holiday was at the discretion of employers, but clearly this was not effective and it was

36

made compulsory within a few weeks, but with the caution that any riotous behaviour by the young on their free day would bring its punishment, and they were to be turned out of the taverns by 8.00 p.m.[26]

The crunch came when government took decisive steps to make its policies, recreational and otherwise, thoroughly operative.

Until the establishment of professional police forces early in Victoria's reign, central government always had problems in making its writ run consistently over the whole country. Laws on sport, so long as no powerful local interest was offended, were particularly hard to apply, as the repeated attempts to compel archery practice through the Middle Ages readily show. The appointment of a network of Justices of the Peace by Henry VII went some way to improve the application of the law, but social legislation was still often weakened by the gradual decline of the country-wide church courts which had once taken responsibility for much of this field. Nor did the fact that many of the unpaid local constables were also innkeepers do much to strengthen recreational law, as they were themselves the most likely offenders against many of its provisons. The repetition of statutes on Sunday sport indicates that this remained an obstacle to government policy, and when that policy involved a wholesale reversal of recreational habits it was likely to be all the harder to put into practice.

Local examples confirm the continuing avoidance of the laws on leisure activities during most of the Commonwealth period. Not only did Sunday offences abound , but the old celebrations refused to fade away.[27] There were still the Christmas festivities, which grated on diligent members of the House of Commons, and drunken revellers were always likely to disturb the late December peace.[28] Reports from local representatives speak of many sporting irregularities. The Dorset Standing Committee was warning of football and cudgel matches, which could bring disaffected crowds together,[29] and when Cromwell sent out his major-generals to bring the nation to heel they found many causes for concern. 'I am much troubled with these market towns,' wrote one of them, 'vices abounding and magistrates fast asleep.'[30] Insurrection was a growing fear, and the major-generals' brief on leisure activities underlines this. They were, of course, to apply the laws on Sunday Observance to the hilt, but they were also to have a keen eye to prevent horse-race meetings, cock-fights (which had been forbidden by an ordinance of their own in 1654),[31] and bear-baitings, not primarily for either religious or moral reasons but because treason 'is usually hatched and contrived against the State on such occasions'.[32] The major-generals discharged their duties with the same ruthless efficiency with which they had once disposed of the Cavalier armies – and they, and with them the Commonwealth government, were hated for it. Cromwell died and within months, in May 1660, Charles II 'came into his own again'.

Sport had not been eradicated under the Commonwealth, particularly for the upper classes,[33] but popular recreation had been constrained, and forced into unfamiliar moulds. With the Restoration, all notions of banning the old feasts and holy days were soon discarded. The Commonwealth attempt to revolutionize the leisure calendar slipped into oblivion, from which, incidentally, for all its inherent interest, not even sports historians have ever rescued it.[34] Its most obvious permanent lesson is that laws on recreation are the easier to apply the more closely they coincide with overall inclinations of the people, which could well constitute a warning over the Football Spectators legislation, opposed as it is by virtually all those to whom it is intended to apply. Unpopular laws demand highly efficient and forceful policing to succeed, and the methods needed for their implementation may prove more unacceptable than the laws themselves.

Sporting habits tend to be deep-seated. Traditional play, on traditional occasions, is always more likely to evolve, at greater or lesser speed, than to be susceptible to sudden wholesale change by decree. The limited acceptance by sportsmen of the new statutory holiday calendar of late-twentieth-century Britain is, even in an age accustomed to rapid change, a telling example. Other times provide many instances of failed government intervention. The perennial resistance to archery practice was so endemic that many towns failed to build their butts, or keep them repaired, and even if the archers were mustered, they preferred competitive shooting at fine targets to practising long-range military skills.[35] The laws against bowling were even more flagrantly disregarded, so much so that the Middlesex magistrates in 1614 actually appointed sub-constables to supervise individual bowling alleys.[36] A unique event, in the same style, was the use of the local militia to keep order at the prize-fight – illegal, as such occasions were – between Josh Hudson and Tom Cannon at Warwick racecourse in 1824.[37] The ring's whole existence depended upon the weakness or complaisance of local authorities, but it seldom had such positive co-operation.

On the other hand, there have been cases where government action on sporting matters has been remarkably effective. It could be almost incidental, like the insertion of a clause into the Regulation of Railways Act of 1868 banning the provision of special excursion trains for prize-fights, which effectively killed off, as a public spectacle, an already dying sport. Legislation, such as that banning animal sports, worked when it went with the majority public taste, and it has usually been respected too when it has been in response to national emergencies. In both world wars in the twentieth century there has been severe restriction of spectator sport, with grounds requisitioned, players called up, and the sporting calendar severely curtailed. In 1916 the Whitsuntide Bank Holiday was cancelled and in the early 1940s travel for holidays was almost impossible. It had not always been so easy for governments, even in wartime, to flout custom. Military drill for part-time volunteer soldiers was a common eighteenth-century Sunday practice,[38] but an attempt to authorize this formally in the 1757 Militia Bill was defeated. Only under the threat from Napoleon was Sunday training legalized.[39]

While governments' attitudes toward sport and recreation have frequently been cautious and negative, they have also had good cause to find time for exercise. Ever since the Spartans exposed naked infants on mountainsides, rulers have sought to ensure the military fitness of the male population. Other motives for exercise and recreation did not figure largely in British government policy before the nineteenth century. Although the early public health measures then were half-hearted and slow to take effect, the 'Condition of England' did become a regular topic of debate in the 1820s and 1830s, and it began to be acknowledged that the physical well-being of the people was part of government's responsibilities. Time for recreation, and space for it to take place in, henceforth became recognizable priorities for government. In the present century, from the 'Keep Fit' movement of the 1930s to the 'Sport for All' campaign of the 1980s, the state has lent its support to efforts to improve health through play. Only in the 1980s in Britain did the government's role in promoting health through recreation begin to be questioned, at least so far as financial responsibility was concerned. Public money, it was argued, was not necessary for the promotion of sport at any level, or for any motive.

Although other British governments of the recent past have shown a more positive interest in sport as an adjunct to health education, they have seldom felt moved to promote athletic achievement at the highest levels, in the cause of international prestige. There might be widespread national depression at the poor performance of teams and players from time to time – as in the immediate post-war years when the English footballers lost to the Swiss and the Scots to Belgium, the Test team could not win a single match in a series against New Zealand, the boxers lost their world titles, and the only British winner at the Helsinki Olympics was a horse. Through all this gloom, governments stood stoically by, embodiments, whatever their political colour, of the amateur tradition, with its suspicion of coaching, training, or any undue preparation for sporting competition. Finding opportunities for sport was one thing – building it up into an internationally competitive industry was quite another. The appointment of a Sports Minister in the Wilson Government of the 1960s was some belated and partial recognition of interest in the welfare of British competitors, but sport has never been given the priority or resources which have fostered its growth in many socialist and Third World countries. For them, success on the international sports fields has been a comparatively cheap means of

2–3 While governments have usually been ambivalent towards sport, they have always been prepared to associate it with their policies if it has suited their purpose (*opposite*: National Centre for Athletics Literature)

winning world-wide recognition. There is no novelty in such use of play in the cause of nationalism. Gymnastics was a powerful force in the fostering of national awareness in Sweden and Germany in the later nineteenth century, Highland Games made their own mild contribution in Scotland, and an even more pointed independence movement was set up in Ireland, in the Gaelic Athletic Association, determined 'to resist by every means in their power the extension of English pastimes in this country'.[40]

Government's first interest in sport, though, still revolves around issues of public order, as it does with any activity which brings large crowds together in an exciting context. This alone would ensure the interaction of sport with politics, without the other national and inter-national factors which now draw the two irresistibly together. Avery Brundage, that misguiding hand of the International Olympic Com-mittee, wrote in 1967 that 'we must not become involved in political issues nor permit the Olympic Games to be used as a tool or a weapon for an extraneous cause'.[41] A correspondent to the *Sporting Magazine* nearly 200 years ago was nearer the mark when he urged politicians to recognize their sporting responsibilites. 'It is', he wrote, 'a prudential policy in a government to regulate the pleasures of the people, and have for them public sports and games, such as may allure their minds to virtue, or inure their bodies to strength and activity.'[42] Such is still the wish of governments everywhere, even if its unfashionable idealism means that the wish remains unuttered.

In discussions of the role of government in sport, 'government' usually remains faceless. Individuals seldom emerge. It is unorthodox enough today, even in political history, to ascribe decisive influences to the lone individual. The great man or woman tends to become the instrument or catalyst for underlying forces which were seeking a channel through which to operate. In social history this must seem even more strongly the case, and that branch of social history which examines the evolution of sport has certainly had to distance itself from its original unacademic enthusiasms and hero-worship. Personalized myths, whether of William Webb Ellis's creation of rugby football or Abner Doubleday's invention of baseball, had rightly to be discarded. It is a tendency, though, that can be carried too far. In the political conflict of the seventeenth century, the sporting theories and ambitions of James I and the play interests of Charles II can never be dismissed as irrelevant. Similarly, other royalty at other times have exerted identifiable influence on sports and games. Their participation has added to their status and supported their claims on time.

To stay with James I. Along with his elevated notions on the divine nature of kingship, James also brought from Scotland some ideas on physical education, a passion for hunting and animal sports, and two games new to his southern kingdom. In his book, *Basilicon Doron*, on the education of princes, he set out a list of acceptable physical recreations.[43] In his search for good hunting territory he found a remote Cambridgeshire heath and built a wooden hunting lodge at an obscure hamlet known as Newmarket, where the huntsmen soon became more excited by racing their horses than hunting with them. He shared the new passion, and acquired the first Arab horse to be imported. James had, too, a catholic interest in animal sports, which took in not only the baiting of bulls and bears, and cock-fighting – the wages of the Master of the Cockpit were said to equal those of the two secretaries of state together[44] – but also extended to such peculiar novelties as matching the wild animals kept in the Tower menagerie.[45]

His Scottish courtiers actually introduced two new games. One, a cross between croquet and golf, left no permanent mark other than its name, Pall Mall, given to the long, broad avenue where it was played. The other, golf, was to lie largely dormant, as a game for Scottish exiles, until its expansion in the later nineteenth century. If, similarly, the practical impact of James's sporting innovations was negligible in his own day, their long-term consequences were sometimes considerable. He had, in particular, both established the location of the future headquarters of British racing and determined its potential leadership as courtly and aristocratic. They were legacies that remain alive today. What was more immediately telling was James's general sporting disposition, so clearly anti-Puritan, and in the light of the circumstances of the day bound to aggravate disputes over play rather than work towards their solution.

Charles II had few theories beyond self-preservation. Himself a keen sportsman, he was content, in an easier climate, to keep any anti-sport lobby at a distance, without any resort to theory. Dancing, tennis, quoits, bowls, and horse-racing were all restored to favour at court,[46] and Charles himself became almost as much a part of sporting myth as of sporting history. The eighteenth century regularly looked back to his reign, and often to the king in person, for the origin of its popular sports. The rules of cock-fighting, printed annually in the *Racing Calendar*, claimed to 'have been in practice ever since the reign of Charles II', and some bowls clubs used to display cards with 'rules settled by his Most Excellent Majesty Charles II'.[47] There is more secure evidence for his influence on the rules of racing, the earliest of which were drawn up for the Newmarket Town Plate, founded by him in 1665.[48]

Ever since, horse-racing has been the sport to benefit most consistently from royal patronage, from Queen Anne's founding of Ascot to the current enthusiastic involvement of the queen and queen mother in the breeding and racing of their own horses and their frequent attendance at meetings. Without such powerful social backing horse-racing would hardly have survived as unscathed as it did from its own corruption and attacks on gambling in the early Victorian age. Was it more than mere coincidence that this low-water mark in British sport coincided with the presence at the queen's side of a consort who, even when he went riding, had a carriage following behind in case it rained? It certainly meant something to contemporaries, who were not silent on the matter – 'it is a subject of deep concern that His Royal Highness should exhibit no taste for the national sports of the Kingdom with which he is so immediately identified'.[49] Despite Prince Albert's neglect, the turf was just able to hold its own until the Prince of Wales, the future Edward VII, and succeeding generations of royalty once again brought their patronage to horse-racing and were a guarantee of its eventual orderliness.

Still more remarkable was the part played by royal princes in the history of prize-fighting, a sport that was an offence against the king's peace and a violation of his laws! The Duke of Cumberland – 'Butcher' Cumberland after his slaughter of the Highlanders at the end of the '45 rebellion – was first a leading supporter and then became its persecutor after he lost heavily on a fight. His three nephews, the sons of George III, proved more constant and they were the social mainstays of the ring during the thirty years or so of its greatest prosperity from the late 1780s onwards.[50] It was the youngest of them, the Duke of Clarence (later William IV), who was the steadiest protector of the sport over many years – between 1805 and 1824 the neighbourhood of his house, Bushey Park, to the immediate west of London, provided a safe and convenient location for regular contests, until he withdrew his patronage as the prospects of becoming king himself grew stronger.[51]

There are many recent examples of royal sportsmanship arousing the curiosity and interest of the nation, if hardly its mass participation in some of the more esoteric competitive activities which take the royal taste. Polo only becomes news if the Prince of Wales is playing, and carriage-driving would never have surfaced to public consciousness but for the participation of the Duke of Edinburgh. More accessible and influential, in practical terms, was the dinghy-sailing of both, and the duke's foundation of the Award Scheme that bears his name, which has introduced thousands of youngsters to outdoor activities. The popularity of horse-riding was similarly enhanced by the accomplishments of Princess Anne, the Princess Royal, who went on to give pragmatic support to women's equality in sport by her success as a jockey.

Today, the activities of royalty belong only to the political margins of sport. In the wider social context, the existence of both royalty and a hereditary aristocracy, whether of wealth or title or both, certainly favours the cause of the more elitist sports whose hallmarks are their demands on time and money. More tangibly, such effects as the royal family now have upon sport come through their status, shared with

44

television actors, pop stars, chat show hosts, and some sports performers themselves, as media personalities. At the everyday level, they
have been transposed from the politics of sport into the ranks of
newsworthy entertainers.

Until the Victorian age it was otherwise. Whatever the Glorious
Revolution of 1688 may have said about the respective powers of Crown
and Parliament, the monarch remained near the centre of the political
stage. So when Colin Moynihan or any of his successors stands up in
Parliament to pronounce on the government's sporting policies, he is
wearing not only the cloak of elected authority, but also that of past
kings and princes. He is Richard II banning 'all playing at tennis,
football, . . . and such other importune games', Henry IV threatening town
mayors with a twenty shillings fine if they allow illegal sports, Henry VIII
reviving the spectacle of the tourney, the Prince Regent playing cricket,
and Edward VII racing his horses and his yachts. He is, too, the
continuing voice of a Parliament which has, in its time, said what games
might or might not be played, laid down the occasions for them, and
even voted funds for various recreational and sporting purposes.

Ever since human beings began to live in organized communities,
politics and play have been irresistibly entangled. Man the sporting
animal is coeval with man the political animal. Any government which
ceases to be mindful of its deep and inevitable involvement in its
country's sporting life does so at its eventual peril. Victorian ministers
always had the Hyde Park riots of 1855, over restrictions on Sunday
entertainment, to remind them of the dangers of undue constraints on
the people's recreation. By comparison, most of today's troubles with
sporting crowds are minor, or are the result – as with the Hillsborough
tragedy of April 1989 – of the traditional problem of inadequate facilities,
which have made grandstand collapses a recurring event in British
sporting history.[52]

In a complex world where sport has become a universal means of
expression, there is a deep need to discover what any rioting fans are
really saying, and it is as likely to be a message about the state of society
as about the state of sport. History suggests that, to succeed, purely
negative policies of suppression demand measures of policing which in
the end themselves prove unacceptable. Government policies have to be
in the context of recognizing sport's new and total function in the later-
twentieth-century world, of both its domestic significance and its
international force. It is no easy task for government. It means managing
a new phenomenon that we are still fumbling to understand. It
demands resources of time and thought, as well as money. Unless these
are brought to bear, unless there is this awareness of the centrality of
sport in contemporary experience and it is not treated as a merely
peripheral issue, the solutions to present problems will remain elusive.

# 4

# Money matters

For some three centuries sport had to compete for time with the capitalist economy. In the twentieth, the two have become reconciled, and sport itself has become part of the financial world. Leisure has given rise to a wide-ranging industry, within which sport has to contend for its share of the market.

One corner of England can illustrate in miniature how this market has grown and changed.

Weymouth sits comfortably on its splendid bay on the south coast. A few miles inland is the market and county town of Dorchester, small, bustling, and attractive. A quarter of a century ago south Dorset offered visitors little beyond the sea, the coast and the country, and ubiquitous memories of Thomas Hardy. Weymouth had its summer theatres and the cinema, its long-established sailing clubs, and a football team which hovered just below full League status. In Dorchester there were the museums, one regimental, the other still heavy with the marks of its Victorian foundation by the local Natural History and Archaeological Society. The minor counties cricket played occasionally in both places created little stir. The only hint of what might come was the growing tank museum of the Royal Armoured Corps, a few miles away at Bovington, where Lawrence of Arabia's cottage had been acquired by the National Trust.

Now, in the late 1980s, the leisure picture has changed beyond all recognition – except so far as the older organized sports are concerned. Over a dozen historic houses and castles within easy reach are open to the paying public, and there is an almost equal number of accessible museums. Dorchester has its Dinosaur Museum and its exhibition of Tutankhamen replicas, both recently opened, and its County Museum has been enlivened and modernized into one of the country's finest. Weymouth has a Diving Musem, two town museums, a sea-life centre, a butterfly farm, and so forth. The range of sports has grown to include water-skiing, sailboarding, scuba-diving, indoor swimming, and all the activities that sports halls can provide. The locality, in fact, presents a microcosm of the explosion of commercially based leisure pursuits that has taken place over much of the world.

It reflects, too, the way in which the old relationships between sport and leisure have changed dramatically, within a single lifetime. There is much more deliberate exploitation of leisure in south Dorset than ever there was in the past, but the traditional sports, football and cricket in particular, stand much where they did thirty years ago. While sport has never, of course, enjoyed a monopoly of leisure, its competitors have grown enormously in number and diversity during the present century. The long-standing national pastimes of pre-war days – reading, religion, the public house, the occasional train trip, the theatre or the circus – have been joined by the automobile, the package holiday, television, videos, and a wholesale widening of horizons and opportunities. The spectator sports have responded by embracing the commercial world themselves, with greater or less determination, and with greater or less success. They have recognized, often with reluctance, that they are subject to the same forces as the rest of industry, that they are in business as well as in play.

Capitalism and sport, in fact, draw closer and closer together as their common interests increase. It is an experience that is comparatively new to both. Capital was the implacable enemy of leisure, and so of its major obvious components, sport and recreation. The greater the scale of the sporting activity, and particularly the greater its frequency, the louder would be the opposition from the masters of trade and industry. And if the sports of the workers were the main targets for attack, the idle pursuits of the gentry could not always be sure of immunity – for their bad example and their waste of time and money that could be put to better profit. Then sporting time was legitimized, and sport gradually revealed itself as a potential source of financial gain to a growing range of interested parties from sponsors to landowners and from bus companies to press barons. The reconciliation made sport economically respectable.

Nor were the consequences solely economic. Certainly, the people's play had been an immediate day to day irritant to employers, but its offence ran more deeply than that. The resistance of popular sport to changing economic practice, no less than its religious and social offence, made it appear to many as an obstacle to national progress. Virtually all innovating and reformist movements from the Middle Ages onwards found popular sport resistant to the changes they sought. The allegiance to traditional leisure patterns could seem even more difficult to shift than inherited habits of labour. Only in the later Victorian age did this substantially change. Only then did sport cease to appear as the inevitable hurdle on the road to public betterment. Today, sport may not yet always be ranked with the angels, but at least it is no longer, in capitalist eyes, irretrievably in league with the devil. Its transformation from economic vice to economic virtue is at the centre of the sporting story of the twentieth century.

## THE CONFINING OF LEISURE

The tap-root of the antagonism between capitalism and sport reached down, like so much in later belief and attitudes, to Puritanism, which, laid such stress on the spiritual worth of hard, honest work. Labour became a duty for all, 'Godly thrift' and 'Christian gaining' became virtues, and idleness a conspicuous sin.[1] It was an inspiring message for the manufacturer and the merchant, heralding the changed attitudes towards the ethics of money-making that marked the sixteenth and seventeenth centuries and subsequently giving R. H. Tawney the dominant theme for his *Religion and the Rise of Capitalism*.[2] With work a spiritual necessity and fair profit-making a reputable pursuit, frivolous interference with steady labour could have no place. 'Diligent labour' was not only worthy in its own right but also held temptation and sin at bay – it 'mortifieth the flesh, and keepeth under its luxurious inclinations, and subdueth that pride and lust, and brutish sensuality which is cherished by an idle life'.[3] It was yet another perspective from which all sport and recreation came to bear the tinge of evil. Play was 'an exercise of profaneness', attracting 'hundreds, and sometimes thousands, of rude and vile persons' to be 'idle in their callings'.[4]

The religious call to the loom and the last was the mainspring of the Protestant work ethic. In time, the pursuit of financial gain became more single-minded and less principled. Honesty in business was then prompted less by high moral purpose than by its success in the accounts book, but the change did nothing to restore sport to favour. Increased capitalization, on the contrary, brought even louder complaints than before when the workers' zest for amusement called them away to race meetings, prize-fights, bull-baits, fairs, and wakes, while costly plant lay idle. What had begun as a religious duty had become a social problem. The behaviour of 'rude and vile persons' who put amusement before their economic duty became a prime excuse for the limiting of play in all directions during the eighteenth century. The enclosure of Lincoln's Inn Fields was justified on the grounds that 'many wicked and disorderly persons have frequently met together therein, using unlawful sports and games and drawing in ... young persons into gaming and idleness'.[5] The idle and their rougher sports might be the first targets, but no recreational activity could escape the prior demands of the workshop. Prize-fights, for instance, with their crowds and their illegality,

48

were always suspect. Even the sympathetic *Sporting Magazine*, at the height of the sport's aristocratic standing, found them 'blameable for the profligacy and the waste of time and money they occasion in the lower classes',[6] and (a few months later) 'productive of idleness, riot and immorality, amongst thousands of the lower classes of our countrymen',[7] Earlier, gentry cricketers had been taken to task for attracting 'thousands of spectators at the expense of their duty and honesty',[8] while the 1740 Act to regulate horse-racing was in large measure designed to reduce the loss of time and labour from the proliferation of minor race meetings. As with much sporting legislation, it soon lapsed, but the motivation was clear.[9] And if these relatively spasmodic interruptions of the working week gave offence, the more predictable breaks for fairs and feasts were put under even heavier pressure.[10]

Disciplining a work force long accustomed to irregular recreational habits loomed as a distinct social and economic problem. Its spiritual dimension faded, even with many of the clergy. One anonymous divine in 1766 asserted that 'the lesser time for idleness any trade allowed, the better it was'. George Augustus Lee claimed, 'Nothing is more favourable to morals than habits of early subordination, industry and regularity',[11] and ten Manchester clergymen voiced their collective view that the 1800 famine was 'one of the judgments of the Almighty sent to punish and reclaim a wicked and impenitent people'.[12] As always, the successes and benefits of the economic system stemmed from its inherent virtues and the worthiness of its exponents, but its disasters were put down to the sins and shortcomings of the workers. What was certain was that lower orders had to be kept to their employment, and their play kept within the sternest limits.

When religion did find a caring voice for the masses through the Methodists and Evangelicals, it was to rescue their souls, not to resurrect their play. John Wesley's uniqueness, for his time, lay in his belief that all humanity was redeemable, a belief which he put into practice by taking his preaching into even the roughest areas, to those often thought of as beyond the reach of religion, and once described by a Worcestershire churchwarden as 'very mean and simple people which few take notice of'.[13] Wesley and the Methodists, like most of the Evangelists who followed them, proved no friends to popular recreation. They saw it as part of the crude and regardless way of life out of which they sought to raise their converts. Their adherence to the work ethic might be more subdued than that of their Puritan forebears, and part of their stress on the proper stewardship of God-given talents, but it still left little room for sport and recreation. Wesley himself condemned horse-racing as one of the cruel sports,[14] and the movement frowned even on wakes, feasts, and fairs.[15] Methodism, indeed, found itself resorting to a discipline not dissimilar to that of the factory owners

49

themselves, with expulsion for such vague offences as 'lightness' and 'carelessness', one of its own historians acknowledging this as a necessity given the uncouthness of many of its newly won members.[16]

'Back-sliding', in fact, had always presented the reforming religions with problems akin to those presented by absenteeism to the employer.[17] Even the mild and understanding nonconformist minister, James Clegg, himself not averse to a game of bowls and a day's hunting, complained annually in his diary of the defection of his congregation to neighbouring wakes, for which his haymakers also 'neglected their business'.[18]

Theories abounded on how to make the labourer give more of his time to work and less to play. Low wages were, it seemed, an obvious remedy, but the laws of supply and demand refused to be flouted. Until the end of the Napoleonic Wars at least, landowners in the Midlands and the North had to have some regard to the better wages that nearby factories offered their workers. Better policing to control the idle poor was an answer propounded by Joseph Townsend, who sought to compel them to 'labour six days for the same sum they now earn in four days'.[19] Others favoured a direct attack on the counter-attractions facing labour – the banning of fairs, wakes, and other out-dated celebrations (a course often successfully followed) or even the imposition of taxes on all sports and entertainments. These, said Josiah Tucker, would include cricket matches, race meetings, cudgel-playing, five courts, billiard tables, skittle alleys, bowling greens, and cock-pits.[20] In the end, though, it was the combined effects of post-war economic slump and rapid changes in methods of production that did most to discipline the work force. Hunger, a surplus of labour on the land as a result of more efficient cultivation, and a widespread uprooting of the population from its old locations and old habits all played their part. The traditional recreational practices were hard to transplant into urban settings and the workers began to be held more securely to the cotton frame and the work-bench. The triumph of capitalistic production over the urge for recreation appeared to be at hand.

However, the loss of sporting time did not herald the dawn of a contented psalm-singing theocracy envisaged by the Puritans two centuries earlier. Accepting the regime of the factory as the least painful of several hard alternatives, the migrants to the industrial centres moved between sullen acquiescence and occasional joyful escape. The sporadic local foot-race or prize-fight was still likely to half-empty the mill for the day,[21] but it was a rarity, and poor compensation for the pay that had been lost. The factory system was not dominant, even in the manufacturing industries, but it was widely sensed that this was the salient in which the decisive battle of the wider war between work and play would be fought. For the factory owners, continuous production was so important that they were reluctant to acknowledge even the Sunday

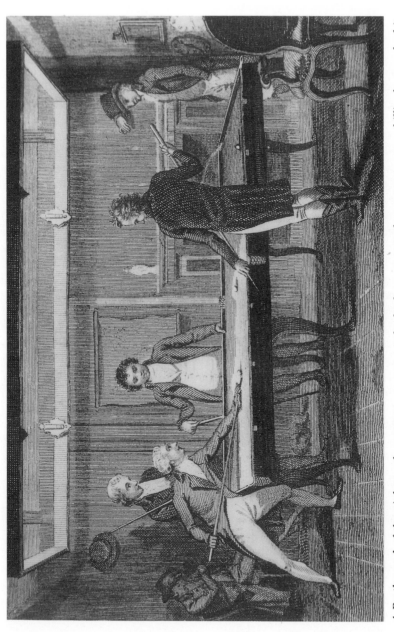

4 By the end of the eighteenth century some sports had taken on a modern appearance – billiards even had its overhead lighting. (Engraving by Mr Scot from an original by Mr Satchwell. Frontispiece, *Sporting Magazine*, November 1798)

break. The machines often shut down only at a few minutes before midnight on Saturday and started up again with the last twelve o'clock chimes of the Sabbath. Desperate for cheap and tractable labour, they took their hands from wherever they could get them, and 7-year-old children from the workhouses and the homes of the poor could be working fourteen hours a day, six days a week.[22] Observers from outside the factory system, and a few within it such as Robert Owen, began to show concern over its personal and social consequences. The dullness and lack of spirit in the work force worried some, like Lord John Manners,[23] while the lurking potential for rebellion prompted others to look for schemes of 'Rational Recreation' as alternatives to Chartism.[24]

It was the workers themselves who saw that the key to the betterment of their conditions lay in *time*. Their first organized efforts were directed to the shortening of the working week, modest enough proposals, with recreation rarely mentioned as a motive for their ambitions. The legislators, when they did eventually intervene, took up the same theme by setting limits on hours of work. The factory children were the first to benefit, followed by the women workers. The gradual reduction of working hours, and the gradual extension of the Acts over the whole factory work force, partial and imperfect in their application as they initially might be, did set the country's social policy on a course which would, after many tortuous years, produce a reconciliation of the conflict between work and recreation.

The Factory Acts, with little original intention of doing so, began the process of separating leisure from labour. By defining hours of work they also, inadvertently, began to define free time as well. Leisure time began to achieve some recognizable status and once there was enough of it the way was open for play to spread its wings again, without economic offence. And when the working week began to take on a new shape, with earlier closing of the mills on Saturday evenings, and then Saturday afternoons, the opportunity came for sport itself to begin to find a firm place in the capitalist world.

It did not, of course, look like that at the time. There were many battles to be fought still before there was any armistice to the conflict between work and recreation. The struggle to achieve a free Saturday afternoon was to reach into the twentieth century, often fought out town by town and trade by trade.[25] Apprentices would still be corrected with a month or two's hard labour in prison for persistent absenteeism,[26] and there were whole areas of the country where the battle had hardly been joined. Birmingham had no large-scale factory production before the 1860s, and the workshops were often silent as the grave on Mondays, only a little noisier on Tuesdays and then ringing with feverish activity for the rest of the week until late on Saturday night. The countryside, too, was little influenced as yet. Even a journal as dedicated to the landowning classes as the *Sporting Magazine* was commenting, in 1852, that the rural worker was as much a slave as if born captive,[27] while Joseph Arch, the farm workers' trade unionist, could still towards the end of the century quote his carter's complaint that 'my wages are twelve shillings but I have no perquisites. I have to work fourteen hours a day six days out of seven, and on Sunday I have to put in half a day's labour'.[28]

Whatever the many hurdles that remained to be surmounted, though, in the striving for an assured modicum of leisure, the relationships between sport and capitalism could begin to take on new forms. Sport could, in its financial dimension, become part of the economic system and no longer be seen only as its implacable enemy.

## THE FINANCING OF SPORT

Not all sport is commercial – play is financed in an infinite variety of forms. Amateur teams, at their most modest, own virtually no equipment as a body, hire their grounds or premises by the match, and rely entirely on their players' own financial contributions. Lesser professional football clubs lean much more heavily on their supporters' clubs and competition profits than upon their gate money. Golf clubs and county cricket depend heavily on members' annual subscriptions, and most individual pursuits are now privately financed. At the crowd-pulling level, though, the financing of spectator sport has become overwhelmingly capitalistic.[29]

Both the investment and the opportunities for profit are extensive at the leading edges of the major sports, though Britain has lagged in providing enough of the one to maximize the other. No major stadium has been built since Wembley, in the mid-1920s, and many football grounds in particular still carry the signs of their late Victorian origins, both in their siting and their facilities. The occasional use for one sport alone cannot produce the money needed for the dramatic improvements which the late twentieth century calls for. Whether they have any substantial future in their present locations must be a matter of doubt; they are cramped for space, often with no car parking, and modelled more on the cattle market than the open-air theatre. A select few will inevitably be brought to bargain their valuably placed existing property for a new green-field site and a multi-sport stadium more in keeping with contemporary expectations.

The capital investment required is certainly huge, involving sums which British sport is usually only prepared to lay out on star players. As with other aspects of British sport today, its economic structures still bear the marks of its past. Attitudes towards the administration and financing of sport are slow to change and there is sometimes even a reluctance to recognize that sport has become a business. Hard-nosed entrepreneurs, when they become chairmen of football clubs, are likely to treat them affectionately as loss-making subsidiaries, and commercial success in the football market-place is never greeted with wholesale approval. When television fees, advertising revenue, and sponsorship flow more freely to the popular and already wealthy clubs than to others, it is inclined to be regarded as unfair, and minds are set against the economic inevitability of a future super league of not more than a dozen or so clubs.

Money and sport still sit uneasily together on such issues. Even after sport itself achieved respectability in late Victorian Britain, its commercial elements gave rise to persistent unease and complaint, hence the obsession with distinguishing between the amateur and the professional, and the mean facilities provided for paying spectators as against club members. These distinctions were, of course, social and even moral, as well as economic. Play, as an ideal pursuit, should not be sullied by any financial considerations. It was a distant reaction against sport's old dependence on stake money and gambling, acceptable now only where horses and not men were concerned. The commercialization of sport appeared to be a new phenomenon, to be kept at arm's length for decades before its eventual acknowledgement.

Yet it was not sport's commercial nature that was new, but the prominence it began to achieve in the national life. To suppose that sport, in the ages before industrialization, had existed in some non-material world is naïve. Play never took place in an idyllic economic vacuum, and by the early nineteenth century it was more than ready to begin its steady march into the full-blown business market. As far back as the early Middle Ages sport had had its financial connotations, even if they went no further than the local alehouse keeper as he felt a warm glow at the approach of the annual football match and its carousing players. His successors had become sports promoters in their own right by the seventeenth century, when the Halifax publicans were mounting foot-races 'to gather the country to drink their ale'.[30] It became common practice for them to initiate a whole variety of sporting and recreational activities, from dancing and bowling to cricket and (more speculatively) minor horse-races.[31] Full justice has yet to be done to the part played by the tavern and its landlord in the shaping of sport. Advertisements from the West Midlands press in the first half of the nineteenth century give some insight into the range of sporting attractions the inn could provide – bowling greens, fives courts, skittles and quoits grounds – even near the centre of Birmingham.[32]

The notice of the sale of the Bowling Green Tavern, though, in 1848 indicated the effects that the pressures on urban land were having on

5 Sport and the publican. The Cricketers Arms, Wimborne, Dorset, is adjacent
to the cricket field which gave it its name (Author's collection)

sports facilities – it was advertised now as possessing the only green
near the centre of the city.[33] It was a foretaste of the movement which
has left many a Bowling Green Inn and many a Bowling Green Lane on
the street maps of towns and cities, but with not a blade of grass
anywhere near them. Some hostelries, often on the Victorian edge of
cities, did manage to hold on to their sports facility. William Clarke's
cricket ground, separated from the dense housing of Nottingham's
Meadows district by the River Trent, soon became more famous than his
Trent Bridge Inn to which it was attached. The game was one in which
publicans had had a strong vested interest since its early-eighteenth-
century days, and they had regularly invited sportsmen to find time for
its pursuit by providing not only the field but also bats and balls, as well
as refreshment, both solid and liquid.[34] Even where play took place out
in the country, away from his premises, there would often be a publican
on hand ready to sustain players and spectators, and after the inn lost its
own playing area it still continued to be a sporting venue as the regular
headquarters and meeting place for clubs of all sorts. It was the base for
county race meetings, where entries were made and booth sites booked,
for cricket and football teams, and it came to house a whole family of

6 An example, in Dorchester, of the numerous imprints left on our street maps by sport (Author's collection)

indoor competitions from darts to cribbage. Brewers and innkeepers were always alert to changes in sporting fashion, and ready to help them along by sponsorship if they promised to boost the takings. This shrewdness made them leading promoters of Sunday amateur football after the end of the 1939 – 45 war, so promoting a significant extension of the sporting calendar. If energetic young men were to be denied their morning tipple by the Sunday licensing hours, they could still spend the time profitably working up a good thirst on the nearest football ground until opening time!

Others looked with some envy at the alehouse's profit from sport and celebration, even in the Middle Ages. To ensure maximum sales for the great church ale at the annual parish feast, other brewing was often banned in the preceding weeks.[35] By the Elizabethan age individual pioneers were beginning to provide sports for paying spectators and before the eighteenth century was out enterprising businessmen were actually sponsoring sports events as an aid to their own sales. An outstanding early example was the provision of prizes for both rowing and sailing contests on the Thames by the proprietors of the Vauxhall Gardens, from where, of course, the best views of the day's excitements were available.[36]

56

The success of mainly small-scale promoters in providing sporting entertainment was one of the irritants to the establishment in the early nineteenth century. A growing awareness of the limits that new working practices had imposed upon popular recreation was matched by suspicion over the direction taken by much of what remained. When the workers were being seduced away from their labours it was not to some healthy exercise on the green, but to the new enclosed running grounds appearing in every city, to prize-fights great and small, to the cock-pit, and the dog fights and rat-catching in the back rooms of seedy taverns. So much of the new sporting enterprise seemed to be in the hands of men at the less reputable end of the business world. Prize-fighting, largely deserted by the gentry, was being organized by a miscellaneous band of publicans, ex-pugs, and minor financiers (few of them Jewish, in spite of George Borrow's fierce accusations in *Lavengro!*).[37] Even cricket seemed to be in danger of a take-over by professionals, with the founding of the All-England touring team which was bringing them much greater financial reward than they had enjoyed from the match fees of the past. It was a time when every innkeeper, especially those in the expanding cities, had his eye to the main sporting chance. Liverpool, for instance, as well as being the effective national headquarters for pugilism around 1830, while Jem Ward held the championship, also saw heady competition between landlords to provide sporting attractions for their customers. According to local iron merchant John Finch, they instituted clubs of all sorts,

> and also get up what they call in the country wakes; and once in the year, bull-baiting is also resorted to, for the purpose of increasing the sale of intoxicating liquors; also quoit-playing, bowling, wrestling, running, boxing, horse-racing, gaming, card-playing, &c.[38]

It had certainly been obvious for centuries that there was money to be made by providing spectators with sporting excitement. Public fencing contests in Elizabethan London were estimated by one critical contemporary to bring in £2,000 annually from inn-yard performances alone, apart from the income in more formal theatre settings.[39] The grandstand at the Paris Garden was evidently packed with paying spectators for the bull-baiting when it collapsed in 1583, and there is other interesting if oblique evidence of the profitability of public sports. The queen granted a licence to one Powlter[40] to organize games in Middlesex on nine summer Sundays. The contemporary fame of the grant came from its Sabbath desecration – its present economic interest is that it was seen as an assured money-making opportunity, since it was made on account of the man's poverty, with four small children to support.[41]

Government was also prepared to take its own profit from sport. There was a petition to the Crown for a patent licence to manufacture tennis balls in 1591,[42] and a monopoly sold for making golf balls – no minor transaction at a time when, according to James Graham's accounts, they were selling at five shillings each.[43] The original licence was for twenty-one years and when it expired the worthy burghers of Aberdeen, not to be outdone by the court, granted John Dickson of Leith the right to make and sell golf balls there.[44] The licensing of bowling alleys was also made subject to a monopoly right in 1620, again doubtless a valuable privilege as over thirty licences were soon issued, but it was in effect little more than a state-sponsored protection racket since the alleys already operated, if in a state of dubious legality.[45]

Once Parliament had control of the national purse-strings it showed less eagerness to make money out of sport than the impecunious monarchy. Local administrators, though, had no such reticence. They found race meetings particularly lucrative, where they could control the letting of sites for booths and refreshment stalls. By 1603, a relatively minor county meeting such as Blandford, in Dorset, was recording profits of £82 16s.3d. for the borough from the town's races, and these were augmented by £11 7s.0d. in receipts from a play performed during the meeting.[46] Personal account books from the eighteenth century show regular entries for expenses at races, and from quite modest spenders, unlikely to be much given to gambling. There was the Essex farmer whose day out in 1787 cost him £1 5s.6d., and Dorset's Mrs Ridout who, a dozen years earlier, had first spent £2 15s.2d. at Blandford races and then, in a fortnight's time, £2 15s. 2d. at the Salisbury meeting.[47] While such sums represent more than the average worker's weekly wage, they pale into insignificance when compared with what the great owners and gamblers of their day and later were accustomed to handle.[48] They were, though, the staple income which kept the country race meeting healthy for well over two centuries, and helped to ensure its continuing place in the calendar.

Doncaster's racing history during the first half of the nineteenth century provides a good illustration of local government involvement with the sport's economics. By the 1820s Doncaster races had achieved high popularity and were making excellent profits. In 1821 they presented 'a most brilliant display of beauty and fashion'; in the next year there were 1,200 spectators in the stand and visitors from the south were smitten with 'astonishment and admiration'.[49] Doncaster was becoming known as the 'Northern Newmarket' and was denuding Newmarket's First October Meeting of most of its usual patrons.[50] Its civic leaders responded, but not well enough. The grandstand was enlarged and new betting rooms were opened, 'their magnificient chandeliers lighted up',[51] and the course itself was improved to remedy the chaotic starts which had characterized the St Leger, with its vast fields. There were, though, complaints that everything was expensive. Local government reform was bringing in a new breed of councillors in the 1830s and their enthusiasm for the racing was limited to the income it could bring in. They were faced, too, by evangelical clerics, so opposed to the sins of the turf that they were prepared to use false rumours of cholera in the town to warn off visitors.[52]

However, this was no village feast, which brought profit only to the handful of stall-holders, who were easily driven off the street.[53] Its races were important in Doncaster's economy. They had gradually slumped during the 1830s, and the corporation then made some amends for past meanness with a grant of £1,000, only to see it wasted by an inefficient clerk of the course. There were more clerical prophecies of the meeting's final and speedy destruction,[54] but in 1849 a new clerk was appointed, racing profits were protected by being placed in a separate fund, and revival was assured.[55]

The majority of race meetings had a fluctuating history, many of them, indeed, an intermittent one.[56] There was every commercial advantage to be gained by maintaining them. They brought in visitors who, in the pre-railway days, would often lodge there for a full week of assemblies, dinners, and balls, augmenting the direct income from the course itself. The greater the profit, the more likely they were to survive the moral and religious opposition, and the investment in them was a strong buttress of their place in the sporting calendar. Many corporations gave active support to their courses – York, for instance, redesigned Knavesmire in the mid-eighteenth century, and Lincoln gave £500 for improvements in 1805 – and the commercial consequences could spread over a whole neighbourhood. In a single year, 1787, Newmarket racing was not merely filling Tattersall's betting rooms at Hyde Park Corner for the twelve months. There was also a print of Newmarket Heath advertised for sale at Huntingdon, available for the October meeting;[57] at Chesterford, the last horse-change on the road from London, up to forty pairs of post-horses would be handled on the Sunday before a race week, giving casual work to the local farm labourers,[58] and then there was Bury St Edmund's Fair, social occasion as much as folk festival, sitting neatly in the week between the two October meetings and attracting considerable numbers of racing nobility and gentry.[59]

Clearly, horse-racing was already a heavily financed business. Its economic importance gave strength to its claims on sporting time and rested its defence on something firmer than mere amusement. The breeding, buying, and selling of racehorses was a serious matter, with the services of stallions at stud well advertised both in the general press and in the annual *Racing Calendar*.[60] The export of thoroughbreds had become a significant trade by the early nineteenth century. English horses were frequent runners on European courses and there were regular announcements of shipments overseas.[61] It was potential damage to this bloodstock business that lay behind much of the opposition to so-called 'cocktail' races, where thoroughbred and half-bred horses raced against each other, the latter being given a weight allowance. The prospect of prize money encouraged the unscrupulous to pass off pedigrees as half-bred, so making a nonsense of the Stud Book.[62] Prize money itself was important. There are some examples of horses being walked, in the coaching days, from one meeting to another through most of the summer, picking up £1,000 or more in winnings, and all at the modest cost of entry fees, the keep of the horse, and the wages of the groom-cum-jockey.[63]

The one element of modern commercial sport that was missing from pre-Victorian racing was gate money. While grandstands could be a fruitful source of income, there was no means of charging the general run of racegoers as courses were only temporary sporting grounds, usually on common land to which access could not be easily controlled. One notable experiment in enclosed racing, at the Hippodrome in Bayswater in the middle of the century, failed for a whole variety of reasons – the land was marshy, the arena was over-used (its many offerings included ostrich-racing!), the arrangements did not please jockeys,[64] and, above all, there was fierce opposition from middle-class neighbours. This focused conveniently on problems over a right of way through the site, and after a dozen or so troubled years the Hippodrome closed. The country had to wait until the 1870s, when a shrewder band of proprietors founded the new 'park' courses, easily accessible from the big cities.[65] The ability to collect gate money was the final piece of the financial jig-saw. Once it was in place, by the end of the century, racing had become, in the words of its most perceptive historian, 'as much a part of the economic as the social scene: it was an industry as well as a sport'.[66] Its progress was underlined by the rewards the best jockeys enjoyed, unrivalled by those going to any other sportsmen of the day.

Spectator sports which could be played on more compact spaces than the broad acres of racecourses had been able to profit much earlier from enclosure. London's premier cricket venue, the Artillery Ground, was fenced in and charging for admission by the middle of the eighteenth century, though there were ambivalent attitudes towards the presence of paying spectators. Only the providers of the facilities saw them as essential, and there were even attempts to limit their numbers. At the Artillery Ground, it was decided to upgrade the provision by installing seats and to raise the entrance charge from tuppence to sixpence to reduce numbers and raise the social tone. The episode peculiarly foreshadows the late-twentieth-century debate over football ground facilities. In this case, the experiment proved all too successful for the owner's liking, and within a few years the prices dropped back to their old level.[67] However doubtful the gentlemen cricketers might be over interference by the crowd, and however critical magistrates might be over its criminal tendencies, the proprietor needed his profits. When Thomas Lord opened his first cricket ground in 1787 (with its 'high batten fence' to prevent free viewing) he was soon reaping the benefits – he was handed £500 from the takings of one early three-day match, and that after the professionals had been paid their fees and travelling expenses.[68] The original financial supports of the game – stake money, wagers, and the purses of wealthy sponsors – were beginning to give way to the new, the admission money paid by spectators. By the 1830s several witnesses from the northern cities were making it clear to Members of Parliament that their cricket grounds were essentially commercial places of entertainment. At Sheffield, for example, the pitch was surrounded by high walls, the entrance charges were equally steep, and it was 'rather a theatre for seeing cricket and other games, than a place of general exercise'.[69]

Patronage had faded and stake money was disappearing from the game. Skilled cricketers were now usually hired by the match, not taken on to the estate staffs of wealthy sponsors. It had become apparent that good bowlers were not necessarily efficient gamekeepers and that privileges such as Thomas Aylward's control of the catering at Sir Thomas Mann's home matches could have perceptible effects on a player's performance on the field.[70] Stake money, where it remained, was becoming little more than a gesture of habit, a legacy of the notion that a game inevitably involved gaming. Charity could dispense with it altogether, as when Radcliffe-upon-Trent beat Carlton in 1819 and the winners returned the ten shillings a man to the losers, hearing that they were 'for the most part poor workmen out of employ'.[71] The new financial structure of cricket as a growing spectator sport was more apparent in such episodes as that at Brighton, where the promoter, Mr Ireland, was unable to mount a promised match on his new ground and 'in consequence had to compensate many would-be spectators'.[72] Within a generation, William Clarke would be leaving his spouse to look after the Trent Bridge Inn while he led his touring professionals up and down the country to please the paying crowds. Cricket had become, at the highest levels, a thoroughly commercial enterprise.

The transfer of both horse-racing and cricket into the capitalist economy was long, gradual, and not without its doubts and difficulties. The increasing investment and growing opportunities for profit in these activities were significant adjuncts to the survival and growth of sport through some of its most difficult years. Those who saw pecuniary advantage from sport would ensure that it was on offer, and when it was on offer spectators would contrive the time to attend.

7 One aspect of sporting capitalism. Other sports soon followed cricket during the later years of the nineteenth century

Money alone, though, could not provide the key to survival. Neither horse-racing nor cricket had to change its basic nature as a sporting contest to win through. By contrast, the two other sports which were already attracting large crowds by the end of the eighteenth century could only accommodate themselves to the new economic and social order by undergoing major surgery. Prize-fighting was damned to ultimate demise by both its illegality and its cruelty. Pedestrianism was pushed into the background by its corruption and unpredictability. Initially, pugilism had held considerable economic promise when it operated in the covered emporia in London. It rivalled the theatre as a paying indoor entertainment, with entrance charges of at least a shilling, rising to up to a guinea for championship fights.[73] Once the sport was driven out of doors, the collection of gate money became a much more doubtful venture. Controlling access to the site was often impossible, the credentials of the collectors often dubious, and the amount of money finishing up with the fighters or the sponsors usually minimal. The wagons which ex-pugilists were in the habit of bringing to fights to provide grandstand views were a more reliable source of funds, but until the organizers began to use specially hired steam transport,

*8* Tom Belcher, a star of the Regency prize-ring, whose Castle Inn, Holborn, was the unofficial headquarters of the sport during its last days of comparative respectability (From H.D. Miles's *Pugilistica*, vol. I, Edinburgh, John Grant, 1906)

spectators could be as much a hindrance as a help. Their numbers attracted both attention and opposition, without the compensation of assured financial benefit. When the patronage of the wealthy disappeared from the ring, and even more drastically than it did from the cricket field, there was no reliable paying audience to take its place. Pugilism had to depend increasingly on the incidental proceeds that came from sparring exhibitions, the ritualistic handing over of instalments of stake money at one favoured tavern after another, and the doubtful support of minor financiers, often those barred, for one reason or another, from more legitimate commercial enterprise.[74] In economic terms, the sport tended to regress rather than move forward into the world of organized and publicized matches, with regular and remunerative customers. It had to find a legal form before it could seek entrance to the modern economic world with any confidence, and it was not until the present century that it was, in Britain, able to do so.

Pedestrianism, in one sense, presents a more interesting commercial history. If the prize-ring's financial failure was due to its inability to come to terms with new conditions, pedestrianism, it can be argued, adapted itself all too readily and too thoroughly to the play of market forces. Stake money and gambling were always intrinsic to the sport – as late as 1868 *Bell's Life* was holding £15,000 a year in stakes[75] – but spectators had already become the central element in its financing. Although the history of pedestrianism is much less systematically researched than that of cricket, the two sports do appear to have run parallel in their introduction of enclosed grounds and exploitation of paying customers. At much the same time as the Artillery Ground was distracting mid-eighteenth-century apprentices, Belsize was mounting well publicized athletic events, and there are frequent other references to grounds that were at least 'roped in',[76] By the time *Bell's Life* published its first annual 'Chronology of Pedestrianism' in 1838, there were any number of enclosed grounds, some of them primarily cricket venues but others given over mainly to athletics. This first annual review clearly demonstrated one aspect of the opportunism of pedestrianism's promoters – of its 60 listed events, 49 were located in the growing industrial areas of the Midlands and the North.[77] The same alertness to changing leisure opportunities made pedestrianism the first spectator sport to mount large numbers of its events on Saturday afternoons. In early Victorian sporting circles, the Borough Gardens at Salford, the Hyde Park Ground at Sheffield, Hackney Wick Grounds and Old Brompton in London were as familiar names as Lord's and Trent Bridge.

They did not, though, share in cricket's elevation to respectability. Powerful upper- and middle-class control eventually reduced gambling in cricket and made it more or less honest on the turf. Pedestrianism lacked any central organization and was entirely in the hands of individual small-scale entrepreneurs for whom there were no hindrances to the attractions of quick profit, at whatever cost to fair and open competition. It became more and more a purely working-class sport, surviving largely in the absence of any sporting alternatives elsewhere. It became associated with the near-criminal edges of urban life through its crooked gambling, fixed matches, and general dishonesty. To become part of the later Victorian sporting pantheon, the athletic sports of running, jumping, and throwing had to take on a new mantle of amateurism, socially acceptable but economically of little account until well into the twentieth century. Meanwhile, it played its considerable part in asserting the demands for sporting time being made by a considerable part of the country's population.

Other sports whose roots were in the past were soon to find their places in the ordered economics of recreational provision. Leisure was being both defined and authorized. It wanted only the emergence of some suitable activities to fill the vacuum of the winter Saturday afternoon for the new pattern to reach completion. Sport, which had drifted out of the economic mainstream as the social structures and labour practices inherited from the Midde Ages slowly disintegrated, had once more made its way on to the edges of the financial stage. It was becoming free once more to participate to the full in the central concerns of society.

It was, of course, more than just a simple economic evolution that sport had undergone. The attention given to the moral and social rehabilitation of later nineteenth-century sport has tended to over-shadow the long period of friction that existed between sport and recreation and capitalistic theory and practice. This also needed resolution before athleticism could raise its flag on the ramparts of virtue. After all, the ideals of amateurism embodied in athleticism only had substance when set against the professionalism, the paying crowds, and the growing sports industry of late Victorian and Edwardian Britain. Without them, athleticism would have been neither necessary nor possible – its whiteness would have had no shadows against which to shine.

The twin themes of time and continuity are again inescapable. The sporting revolution of the 1870s was no blazing phoenix, arising fully fledged out of the ashes of folk play. It was, in its all-important economic aspect, a culmination of a movement in sport which reached back into Tudor England and had been recognizably 'modern' in some of its elements for more than a hundred years. Some pathways of the past had petered out, overrun by the brambles of social change – patronage, stake money, dependence on gambling – but others had steadily flourished, such as the taking of gate money, the increasing capitalization of sport through specialized facilities, the growth of a sports equipment and supplies industry, and the wide emergence of paid players. And central to sport's restoration to favour was the solution to the problem of labour and leisure, in the emergence of validated time to play. When it came, gradually, through the latter three-quarters of the nineteenth century, it did not come as some gratuitous offering from the capitalist gods. The annals of labour history tell of the systematic hemming in of leisure and the denial of recreation. The complaints of employers tell of constant absenteeism and worker ill-discipline. The sporting record of the Industrial Revolution, still largely unwritten, tells of a flourishing sporting life, and of an unofficial, unauthorized leisure calendar, without whose survival the defined holidays of a later age would have been much the harder and taken a great deal longer to come by.

# 5

# Sports out of time

Sport has to find both its occasions and its duration. All sports have their boundaries of time, as well as those of space, and each is susceptible to change. The day-long, country-ranging contest of one age becomes the contained two-hour competition of another. While the history of the sporting encounter, in terms of its time span, has generally been one of intensification and contraction, this has by no means been a continuous movement, shared at all times by all sports. And in the television age, even if the individual contest has remained within its set bounds, the greedy cameras have been contributors to longer tournaments and extended seasons.

The time that society has been prepared to allocate – or allow – to sport has been a significant element in its historical shaping, and sport's capacity, at any given time, to fit into its ration of hours has equally been a major factor in its acceptability or otherwise. The 'When?' of sport and the 'How long?' have been two of its most frequently recurring questions.

## A LONG DAY'S PLAY

Through the 1980s British television faced a dilemma over the presentation of American baseball, and it revolved in no small measure around various questions of time. Channel 4 built up a mass audience for American professional football, and the suspicion is that there could be similar potential viewing figures for the summer game. But no one has found out how to do it.

Some of the problems lie within the game itself. American football can make an obvious and immediate appeal from both its apparent simplicity and its combative violence. By contrast, the subtleties of baseball are initially lost on an audience whose only points of reference are to rounders – essentially perceived as a schoolgirls' game – and to cricket.

The British spectator tends to overlook the limitations of a slim, rounded bat, and the awesome possibilities of speed and movement from a ball that is thrown, not bowled. He sees the absence of risk from the bounce of the ball, and fielders who wear enormous gloves. Over and above these inbuilt inhibitions, though, there are the constraints of translation into television viewing – primarily the constraints of time. How are programme planners to schedule a match that might last anything between two and a half and five hours? The method used with cricket, encapsulating a day's play into half an hour or so of recorded highlights, hardly succeeds with an unfamiliar game with its own strange rhythms and conventions. When the spectator sees a parade of tumbling wickets and boundaries on the screen, he or she sees them against a broad awareness of cricket's inner motions and a sense of the andante passages that lie between the moments of drama. Without such background, a truncated presentation of baseball misses much of its repeated interplay between offence and defence, and all of its tempo.

The complications of timing for British broadcasters become most acute at the very peak of the Major League season, with its pennant play-offs and the World Series. Here is a pre-eminent sporting event of international interest and yet, until almost the eve of the games themselves, it is often impossible to say who will be playing, where, and at what time. In a country where television programme journals are printed some three weeks in advance, programme planners are in a quandary. How far dare they risk changing programmes for what at first is bound to be a minority viewing audience? They do not even know how many games there are going to be – in both 1987 and 1988 Channel 4 reserved three-hour slots for live cover of game seven of the World Series, only to find it wrapped up before then. The difficulties make the game a prime candidate for surrender to new satellite channels.

In North America, of course, there are no such problems. There, baseball reigns, and the World Series is a long-established part of the national calendar. It was once such a marker, before the pennant play-offs extended the season, that the end of the World Series signalled the start of the political campaigning season. Even now, television debates between presidential candidates and the October matches have to be timed to avoid clashes. A flexible approach by television and radio to the baseball finals is not only accepted – it is recognized as inevitable.

This American experience might argue that it is the nature, scope, and timing of sport which dictates popular leisure requirements. Post-season baseball, though, far from illustrating the usual relationship between the span of sport and the availability of leisure, provides a rare example of a suspension of the normal rules. The games have become a national festival, and have risen above the customary rules dictating free time. Hence the difficulty of transferring the celebrations to a society where the World Series has no such status, and where, indeed, purely sporting invasions of the accepted working week have largely disappeared. Test matches against the Australians had many of the same characteristics of national involvement in England during cricket's heyday, and Derby Day still echoes with memories of times when the classic horse-races, run in midweek, could hold the normal leisure rules in temporary abeyance. But these are rare intrusions.

The generally ruling principle is that sport has had to find the shape that suits the time available for it. Post-season baseball, even as an exception, is so only in part. It is no accident that the gradual extension of the October games in recent decades, first by splitting the two leagues into East and West divisions and then stretching the league play-offs to seven games, has coincided with the growing prevalence of night play, eagerly supported by television. The suspension of the leisure norms has not been stretched further – it has just pushed more and more of the sport to the end of the working day.

The history of sport is the recurring story of the accommodation of play forms to the time left free for them. Sport seeks to conform to the changing opportunities for recreation which current economic and social forces allow. Where it finds an exact fit, as football did on Saturday afternoons in the first half of this century and one-day cricket has come close to in the second half, the way to sporting prosperity lies open. When, by contrast, the requirements of contemporary sport are at odds with the approved bounds of leisure, the scene is set for collision. The clashes may be minor, and relatively easily resolved. It was so, for instance, in the austere post-war years in Britain, when the need for uninterrupted weekday labour was thought to be threatened by the major horse-races. They were, for the most part (with the Derby an inviolate exception), removed from their midweek spots to Saturdays, and harmony was restored. Other conflicts, though, have been chronic, deep-seated, and for decades appeared to be irreconcilable. One such governed the growing years of modern spectator sports in the later eighteenth and early nineteenth centuries. Some perspectives of this conflict have already made their appearance – its religious element, and the simple struggle between capital and labour, a continuing clash that has been well described so far as the growing restraints on recreation are concerned.[1] Beneath this open and obvious competition between sport and sanctioned leisure time, there were movements taking place in the extent and timing of sports themselves, developments that have so far gone largely unnoticed.

The forms of modern sports have often been influenced by the difficulties they had to meet in their adolescent years, when they were increasingly at odds with officially authorized leisure opportunities. The first spectator sports were born under one set of economic and cultural circumstances and then, as they were about to flex their growing limbs, they found themselves moving into a quite different world and having either to adapt to changing time requirements or to find the means to defy them.

Leisure life in the eighteenth century was still relatively open. There was a considerable wealthy class, which felt no moral or social objection to spending time, money, and energy on play. The new spectator sports were also able to build up a mass following – and the size of many crowds justifies the description, given a population one-tenth of today's – because the majority could adjust their work patterns to find time for enjoyment. The cost might be a fifteen-hour working day at other times, but the freedom was there. The nature of the leisure that each class could find for itself had important consequences for the shaping of the growing sports. For sponsors, players, and spectators alike, all the pointers were to day-long amusement. For one group there were no bounds to be observed, and for the other the loss of working time justified nothing less than a whole day's pleasure. From this it followed that if one contest, or even one sport, would not fill the day, then others tended to be added to it. The age's sporting days, as often as not, became multi-sport occasions.

The most significant temporal feature of the early spectator sports is their expansiveness. They all tended to occupy at least one full day and would often, as with horse-racing and cricket, extend beyond that. The quoting of individual sports, though, at once draws attention to the fact that sports had their specific elements as well as their common features. They all composed their own variations on the common theme.

Horse-racing, the longest established nationally of them all, led the way in filling its days, extending beyond the single day, and diversifying both the social and the sporting entertainments that were on offer. Racing crowds were always hard to estimate before the coming of enclosed courses, and some of the early figures are doubtless unreliable – 100,000 on Epsom Downs for the Derby around 1800 is within the bounds of possibility, but the same figure for Manchester suggests some flights of imagination.[2] What is beyond question is the popularity of race meetings. At many country venues, such as Blandford in Dorset, Stockbridge in Hampshire, Bridgnorth in Shropshire, and Catterick Bridge in Yorkshire, attendances would regularly be greater than the town's normal population, such was the attraction over a wide catchment area.

These major interruptions of the working cycle could survive because they were occasional. For a town to have more than one meeting a year was highly exceptional. The races laid claims to antiquity and established practice, sometimes real, sometimes spurious, but none the less firmly held. They had in some places taken on the seasonal festive celebrations of the old church wakes, and they shared with the old feasts a tendency to spread themselves. The suggestion that eighteenth-century race meetings were normally one-day events[3] is quickly dispelled by a glance at the *Racing Calendar*. Of the 96 meetings reported in the 1773 edition, for instance, (and excluding the special case of Newmarket) only 8 were confined to a single day, 31 took two days, and 46 had lengthened to three.[4] They did certainly fluctuate, along with the varying prosperity of horse-racing generally or according to local enthusiasm. A list of 'races dropped in fifty years past' published at the end of the century named 48 meetings, a few of them like Tothill Fields and the Artillery Ground obvious victims of urban expansion, but others which were to enjoy future healthy revivals, such as Ludlow, Towcester, and Stockton.[5]

The success of meetings did not depend entirely on the quality – or the quantity – of the racing alone. Meetings could and did survive on as little as one race a day, though it would usually be run in heats – two if both produced the same winner, three if a decider was necessary, and exceptionally four. There might be only a handful of horses engaged in the whole meeting, as at Worcester, in 1798, which saw just one contest on each of its three days. Out of the four horses running on the first day, a different one won each of the first three heats, and so it was one of those rare occasions when a fourth had to be run off. It meant, incidentally, that the horses each raced sixteen miles on the day. On the second day, just two horses ran two heats, and on the third four starters completed three heats.[6] Even so, a ten-horse meeting such as this could seem well endowed compared with the three-day event at Peterborough in the same year, when there were only four horses in all, two of them competing twice on separate days.[7]

The meetings (and the word itself is significant) were, in fact, far more than just horse-races. They were, of all the early spectator sports events, occasions in the local social calendar, anticipated with eagerness by all classes. The wealthy and aspiring looked to the balls, the assemblies, and the dinners that always accompanied them, the rest looked to the holiday they could risk taking, to the free excitement of the races themselves, to the display, and to the booths and entertainments on the course. They were one of the climactic moments of the county year, when all its affairs tended to come together. As Thackeray noted in *Pendennis*, 'there were assizes, races, and the entertainment and flux of company consequent upon them'.[8]

Assizes would sometimes present a ghoulish parallel to the extended attractions of the race weeks – after the Norwich Spring Assizes in 1787 there was a hanging on the Friday, a public dissection of the body on Saturday, and an anatomical lecture on Sunday.[9] The racing celebrations usually managed to be more light-hearted, but it was in the harsh nature of the times that they should often be stained with the blood of either men or animals. The meeting was often the occasion for prize-fights, and other combat sports, for cock-fighting and sporadic bull-baiting. The turf and the prize-ring shared much the same clientele – at the turn of the century at least half of pugilism's main sponsors were also racehorse owners – and there would usually be a few fighting men on hand at race meetings ready to put their fists up if a purse could be collected after the day's racing. In the counties these would be minor affairs between local heroes, but around London they could involve well-known fighters,[10] and at Epsom and Ascot, in front of the crowded 'betting stand', they provided the customary postscript to the day's amusements.[11]

For the most part, post-race prize-fighting was only a subsidiary element to the main activities of the ring, though courses often provided convenient locations for contests outside their racing season. With cock-fighting it was another matter. Race meetings and major cocking matches were virtually synonymous with each other. They provided the occasion – the matches usually lasted three days – the place, and the mood. A sizeable proportion of the racegoers would spend the first half of their day in the cockpit, whether in Carlisle or Newcastle upon Tyne in the far north, Norwich or Peterborough in the east, Worcester or Bridgnorth in the west. Moreover, since race meetings, like quarter sessions and assizes, were essentially county gatherings, it is unsurprising that cock-fighting matches came to be made on a county basis. There is, indeed, an uncanny resemblance between the cock-fighting fixtures and arrangements of the first quarter of the nineteenth century and the county cricket programme of the last quarter, and it is hardly without significance that as the one faded out the other began to come into its own. Many of the matches still have a familiar ring to them – Lancashire v. Nottinghamshire, Leicestershire v. Northamptonshire, Middlesex v. Gloucestershire, and Worcestershire v. Warwickshire – there were few counties which did not participate. Only along the south coast and in the far west did other combat sports take pride of place over cocking, though the Home Counties did tend to take their matches to one of the London pits rather than to local races.[12] Wessex, by contrast, was the lingering home of swordplay and singlestick fighting. Salisbury races often saw both,[13] and they flourished broadly in Wiltshire, Somerset, and Hampshire, aside from race meetings.

There were other local variants on the theme in more distant parts of Britain, reflecting particular regional enthusiasms. In the Scottish borders and the far west country it was likely to be wrestling – at Kelso races there were over a hundred competitors in the wrestling competition in 1823.[14] Bull-baiting, which was being pushed into the coarser areas of most towns and cities, and becoming associated with the less reputable popular celebrations, still managed to find a place at the races in some of

9 The popular Wessex sport of cudgel-playing, typically mounted outside a local inn. Note the construction of the stage (Etching by Mr Hewitt, *Sporting Magazine*, October 1799)

these more remote regions. It was still, along with cock-fighting, a feature of Totnes races in Devon in the early 1820s.[15] Even when notions of sporting respectability began to change, the race meeting still retained its multi-sport nature. Reforming sportsmen of Monmouthshire promised, 'to such as have a predilection for these diversions', horse-racing followed by pedestrianism and pugilism in succession.[16] Foot-races became increasingly popular accompaniments to horse-racing, and other more esoteric events began also to appear, such as Mr Sadler's balloon ascents which enlivened several Yorkshire meetings in the summer of 1814.[17]

The race meeting, by its very antiquity and by its widespread nature, inevitably influenced the patterns followed by other growing sports. Cricket was particularly suited to extension, first by building up teams to at least eleven a side (and often more) and then by adding a second innings. Cricket might never attract the massive numbers of some racecourse crowds, but matches could draw four-figure attendances.[18] Even while the game was still recovering from its depression during the Napoleonic Wars, when more immediately aggressive sports had been the fashion, crowds could still run into thousands, and at widely spread venues.[19] The game was expanding rapidly out of the southeast and its few Midland pockets to become almost a national sport by the middle of the nineteenth century. The long, hot summer of 1822 'afforded abundant opportunities to the lovers of the excellent game' and saw it leap convincingly at last, for instance, over the barrier of the New Forest to become 'very popular' in Dorset.[20] It was the same over much of the kingdom with 'this manly and now fashionable game'.[21]

Cricket followed the eighteenth-century sporting trend by stretching itself in time as well as expanding geographically. By the last quarter of the century it had become common to begin play at 10 or 11 a.m. rather than having an afternoon start, though even in the earlier days the entertainment, at least for the players, was likely to begin earlier, to judge from one advertisement of a match in 1743. The players were to meet at the White Lion at 10.00 a.m. and to begin playing by 1.00 p.m., presumably assuming that they would still be in a state to do so![22] Matches, even between villages, began more often to last over several days. Examples abound – a match at West Bridgford took Bingham and Newark into a third day,[23] and a Southampton match against the Isle of Wight also ran to three days.[24] Again, although cricket offered more continuous entertainment than horse-racing, it was not averse to sharing its fare with other attractions, sporting or otherwise. In its time, even the august precincts of Lord's saw events as diverse as pedestrianism, lacrosse, baseball, hockey, a balloon ascent, and (in 1844) exhibitions of archery and dancing from a group of Iowa Indians who camped on the now hallowed turf.[25]

Cricket's multi-sport tradition, now faded, was established early in the game's public history. The *Penny London Advertiser* of 11 June 1744 sought to bring in the crowds by promising a ladies' race for a holland smock, and this, together with other pedestrian events, became quite common at matches. So were calmer accompaniments to the play, such as the Yalding Band which was to provide music 'for the amusement of the company and to enliven the day' when West Farley met Barming in the serene Kent countryside during the early years of the nineteenth century. Sometimes it was cricket itself which formed the secondary entertainment. This could happen at race meetings, as at Bishopbourne, in Kent, unusual in 1780 for the advanced state of its spectator provision for a village, with admission to 'the Great Stand' costing a shilling.[26] Here, incidentally, as on many racecourses, cricket was also played as a separate sport outside race weeks. Stamford,[27] Lichfield,[28] Wincanton,[29] and York's great multi-sport venue, Knavesmire,[30] were among those which had an early tradition of housing cricket clubs as well as racing, a co-partnership that went unchallenged until the demand for golf courses in the present century. Other occasions also, civil and military alike, were likely to be rounded off with a game of cricket – whether it was a review of a regiment of dragoons[31] or the lingering observance of the summer solstice at Bradwell in Essex and its uncommon conjunction of Midsummer Day football with cricket on the day following.[32]

Enlightened opinion in the eighteenth century was reluctant to find virtue in any popular sport, and it frowned on the enthusiasms which attached to it. Cricket, though, apart from reservations about the numbers flocking to matches, and somewhat less concern over its gambling element, did seem slightly less objectionable than the rest, with its memories of the pastoral idyll. By the beginning of the Victorian age, partly through its own tentative attempts at internal reform and partly by contrast with the increasing corruption of its rivals, cricket had even begun to try on the mantle of respectability. It was the wide tolerance which it enjoyed that gave the game its licence to expand at the very time when opportunities for sanctioned enjoyment were being so steadily suppressed.

Its fortunes contrasted sharply with the third great sport of the age, prize-fighting. The illegality of the ring did little to reduce its appeal and, indeed, added a certain spice to the proceedings, especially as prosecutions were rare. For the big fights, there could be crowds of over 25,000, the estimated attendance at the Neat/Hickman fight so graphically described by Hazlitt.[33] Changing tastes and falling standards undermined the ring's upper-class support from the mid-1820s, but crowds could still be impressive. It was the nature and make-up of the sport's following that changed, as fights came to be organized in the provinces and not based primarily on London. Some 25,000 still assembled

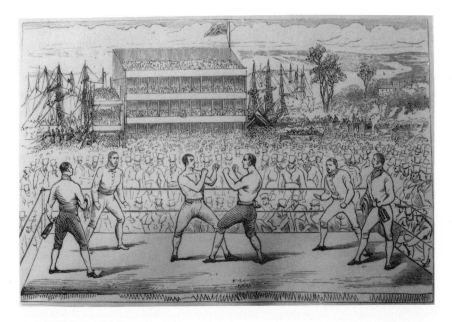

10 Spring v. Langan, for the Championship, Worcester racecourse, January 1824. Vast crowds could be attracted to major sporting events in the 1820s (Frontispiece to H.D. Miles's *Pugilistica*, vol. II)

in the West Midlands for Brown's fight with Sampson in 1828,[34] and the overall attendance at prize-fights, taking the country as a whole, probably increased rather than diminished until the later 1840s. The common assumption that boxing depended solely on the joint amorality of the richest and the poorest is also an over-simplification. The serious-minded of all classes largely rejected the sport – and the middling ranks of society tended to have a greater proportion of such – but the ring always had its substantial support from tradesmen, licensees, lawyers, students, theatricals, and the like. Even in the 1840s, one boxing crowd in Lincolnshire was described as consisting of gentry, yeomen, labourers, and Midland 'sporting men'.[35]

As a proscribed activity, pugilism might have been expected to be an exception to the general tendency to expansion, and to develop a hurried approach to its proceedings. Not so. Whenever there was some assurance of non-interference – particularly under powerful patronage – a programme of three or four fights would be arranged, to provide a full day's fare. The main contest always took place first, but this was a practice which had originated in the covered emporia, in the early legal days, and was not inspired by haste. It proved convenient, of course, once the sport was threatened by the law. The use of river steamers gave another opportunity to mount two or more fights at a time,[36] and even when the ring was under pressure and no second fight had been pre-arranged, there were always pugilists standing by, eager for a pick-up fight for any purse that could be collected on the spot.

The pugilistic day operated within its own well-known parameters. The site had to be far enough away from London to be reasonably secluded, but near enough for the keen rider or driver, rising early, to get back home at night for a late dinner. In the days before steam transport, venues to the south and west of the capital were the most popular – travel over the cobbled streets of the East End to Essex or north Kent would put off all but the most ardent. The fights were usually due to start between noon and 1.00 p.m. The articles setting up the contest were rarely more precise than that, and there would often be delays from having to trek across the country to find a safe site so that darkness brought more and more fights to an end. This was all the more likely since, in its heyday, pugilism (race meeting fights apart) was predominantly a winter sport, its backers having other sporting interests to divert them during the summer months.[37]

Like cock-fighting, the ring had strong associations with the turf. The racecourse, when and where it could be used in safety, was the ideal boxing venue. It would be outside the town, and have its grandstand, however rudimentary, for the better heeled supporters. Barnet, Ascot Heath, Maidenhead, and – under royal protection from the Prince of Wales – Newmarket and Brighton all housed racecourse fights in the closing years of the eighteenth century, while there was another brief flowering of racecourse contests in the Midlands in the 1820s. The most notable was the Spring/Langan fight for the championship at Worcester in January 1824, and the most remarkable, for an illegal sport, that between Hudson and Cannon at Warwick in the same year, when the fighters used the jockeys' changing rooms under the stand and the local militia was mustered to keep good order in the crowd![38] More effective policing and changing public preferences meant, though, that such major pugilistic events were soon impossible to mount so openly, and racecourse fights reverted to pick-up contests at the end of the day's turf entertainment. As the Mayor of Warwick said, when he reluctantly turned away the Ward/Cannon fight a year later, he could not afford the reputation of being 'a fighting mayor'![39]

As prize-fighting became more fugitive, it could offer few additional attractions beyond hurriedly set up gaming tables. Earlier, minor fights in notorious spots around London and other urban centres were often associated with bull-baiting. Tothill Fields, near the City, was still managing to mount one of the famous Belchers' fights in 1804, but here it was the baiting which was the regular fixture, and the fighting an extra possibility at the end of the day. Gentry spectators were certainly no strangers to such events,[40] but essentially these were gatherings of the coarser devotees of violence, and were gradually suppressed. The paucity of other sporting entertainment was doubtless one of the promptings behind the city worker's willingness to endure the hardships that faced the foot-followers of prize-fighting – walking through the night, sleeping under hedgerows, and with a strong likelihood that they would be left behind altogether in a rush to an alternative venue. It was an excursion that, for them, was likely to run to three days rather than one.

It is little wonder that wrestling assumed some of pugilism's popularity and moved more regularly from its Celtic fringes to London in the mid-1820s, as the metropolitan ring went into decline. The sporting press noted a veritable burst of wrestling enthusiasm in 1826. In a single month, the *Sporting Magazine* was reporting 'a great number of matches' at 'various grounds in the neighbourhood of London', and while the performers were mainly Cumberland and Devon men, at least one meeting was confined to 'London mechanics', and it was predicted that 'we may expect to see the science cultivated near home'.[41] So it turned out. Soon the Eyre Tavern, in St John's Wood, and Thomas Rous at the Eagle Tavern, were offering regular wrestling bills. Crowds at the London taverns never reached the 20,000 levels reported from the Lake District and the West Country, and it was probably physically impossible for them to do so, though attendances did run to several thousands.[42]

The rise of wrestling reflected a thirst for sporting entertainment in an age when it was scarce rather than a long-term and widespread interest. The one sport which did rise steadily in its attraction, coming to rival horse-racing in its country-wide appeal, was pedestrianism, the customary title for the endless variety of foot-racing performances that were eventually to be formalized as track athletics. The sport's range was catholic in the extreme, including everything from straightforward flat races to wagers on hopping backwards, trundling wheels and barrows, and even picking up potatoes by mouth and retrieving them.[43] By the 1830s its less esoteric events were being reported from such far-flung venues as Taunton and Preston, Chichester and Bradford, Maidstone and Scarborough.[44] In June 1813, 10,000 folk gathered on Scarborough sands to see the four-mile race between the celebrated Harry Atkinson and Knaggs, and a 'vast concourse' of several thousands at Wakefield watched the equally famous local runner, Woods, perform in his specialized dress – 'a light jacket, and short trowsers, scarcely reaching to the knee, his arms, legs, and feet being naked'. Pedestrianism played a leading role in bringing competitive spectator sport to the growing towns and cities. By the late 1830s its predominantly urban nature was being reflected by its frequency in such places as Derby, Nottingham, Huddersfield, Walsall, Leeds, Manchester, Wednesbury, and Barnsley.[45]

Pedestrianism, in fact, was flourishing. What emerges from any survey of records and reports from the late eighteenth and early nineteenth centuries is a continuing story of the unsurprising human relish for entertainment, and the major role played by sport in satisfying that urge. It is a story of frequent, widespread events, drawing in large crowds, and with an inbuilt tendency for their play to extend itself over at least one full day, and longer if it could. There is, too, an air of festival about many of the sporting occasions, an almost ancestral sense of celebration. A dubious Joseph Strutt, whose classical analysis of *The Sports and Pastimes of the People of England* in 1801 unduly influenced later historians, was much more alive to the decline of the traditional rural sports than he was to the emergence of the new,[46] but the old spirit of play, if not many of its forms, continued to thrive. It may have been transfigured and often, according to the rising standards of the age, coarsened, and polluted by cash considerations, but it was still vibrant and pulsating, in defiance of the pressures it encountered. It was a spirit of enjoyment and suspense which entered into a whole miscellany of crowd occasions, sporting and otherwise. If what pleased the crowds involved a cruelty to animals which would soon seem repulsive, it was matched by harsh public cruelty to transgressors of their own human kind, with judicial whippings a frequent punishment and the quarterly hanging days at Tyburn an acknowledged holiday for many Londoners. On such days the whole neighbourhood was packed with booths and stalls, for all the world like a fair or a race ground, householders renting out rooms with good views of the gruesome proceedings and, in spite of the moral lessons the events were meant to teach, a rich occasion for thieves and pickpockets.[47] Nor was it only a London phenomenon. In Nottingham, for instance, the last public whipping was not until 1830, and the last public hanging a year later.[48]

Whenever there was a day for amusement, people sought to fill it to the brim. Even regattas, themselves only as old as the last quarter of the eighteenth century, were not content to confine themselves to the water. Ramsgate ended its 1829 regatta with pony- and donkey-races on the sands.[49] Conversely, if water was on hand, it gave an added dimension to the dry-land jollifications. At another Kentish festival, a generation earlier, the sports at Sandgate began at 11.00 a.m. with a pony race, followed by a smock race for ladies and then a competition for four-oared cutters which started along the coast at Hythe harbour. And this was just the pre-dinner fare. Afterwards there was a horse-race for Kentish hunters, a sack race, a scamper after a well-greased pig which took two hours, and a concluding cock-fighting tournament for a flitch of bacon.[50]

This, though, was at Easter. It was the one universally sanctioned holiday, other than Christmas and Whitsuntide, to survive the tightening of the Protestant work ethic. Such 'rustic sports' – and this common contemporary description of them is significant – were strongly associated with established holidays, national or, in the case of fairs and parish feasts, local. They were exposed to the many pressures that threatened the inherited social and sporting life of the past. The traditional Harlesden Green Fair may well have been held with its 'wonted splendour' on the outskirts of London in June 1811, with its pony-racing, its 'jumping in sacks', its women's race for 'an inner garment of virgin purity', and lads with their hands tied behind their backs trying to eat suspended rolls soaked in treacle.[51] The question was how long it would withstand the criticisms of evangelical parsons and changing views of what constituted legitimate amusement.

There were other sports taking place during that same month of June 1811. There was commercially sponsored rowing on the Thames, for a boat provided by Astley's circus;[52] cricket was reported as thriving again in Essex;[53] the values of swimming were being enunciated, and young Tom Belcher was fighting Siverthorne on Crawley Downs.[54] The liberty to attend Harlesden Green Fair had some legitimacy about it, some claim from the past, however tenuous and weakening. These other attractions, most of them aimed at spectators, had little sanction in any leisure calendar, little time that they could confidently call their own. How then did they, and the other well-attended sports, manage not just to survive but even to flourish, in a period when free time was under constant pressure?

## ALTERNATIVE LEISURE

The Bank of England closed on more than forty days in 1800. By 1834 its holidays had been reduced to a mere four.[55] This was symptomatic of the wholesale limitation of leisure time that characterized the early nineteenth century. In spite of it, and when all allowances have been made for reporting extravagances, the crowds at sporting events were regularly large, even by today's standards, and often immense by the size of the population as a whole. How could so many find such frequent time for their sports? How did they manage to lighten the gathering darkness that has been so often and so well described?[56]

The obvious starting point is to examine *when* these popular spectator events took place. Quite clearly, they would be arranged for when the customers were most likely to attend, and their distribution through the week must give irrefutable clues to the patterns of available, if unofficial, leisure.[57]

The evidence from the oldest sport, horse-racing, is partly valid and partly misleading. The unique shape of race meetings has already been noted – their tendency, as annual events, to occupy much of a full week.

Taking meetings across the country as a whole, the peak days for racing were consistently those at the middle of the week. The timing, though, was dictated more by the nature of the sport itself than by the regular availability of leisure to its followers. In the days before the railway, the only means of getting horses from one course to another was to walk them there. Specially built vans to transport the horses were very occasionally used, but these rare juggernauts were still horse-drawn themselves, and all they did was to rest the racer's legs, not speed its transit. Since Sunday racing was out of the question, all the pointers were to using the weekend for the movement of horses, and it had to be an extended weekend, given the distances that still remained between courses even when the season's programme had settled itself into roughly regional circuits. There were these practical reasons for meetings to begin on either Tuesday or Wednesday, as they overwhelmingly did throughout the eighteenth century, and usually to peter out by Friday. Friday racing was only occasional, Saturday meetings were rare, and Sunday events nonexistent. This time-honoured shape to the racing week remained unchanged until the rail transport of horses became feasible from the 1840s onwards.[58]

The similar avoidance of weekend play by cricketers and the promoters of prize-fights must, though, have been for different reasons. A substantial majority of eighteenth-century cricket matches of which there are records began on either Monday or Tuesday, with Monday the favourite day of the two.[59] While it is not always easy to be certain how long games lasted, it is clear that Saturday play was unpopular, so much so that it was sometimes deliberately avoided. The Hambledon v. Emsworth match in 1802, for instance, was played on Thursday and Friday, 9 and 10 September, and then adjourned until later in the month.[60] There are other similar cases, and if a club did make a practice of playing on that particular day it thought it worth making the distinction in its name – hence the Montpelier Saturday Club.[61] Certainly, fewer than 10 per cent of games had Saturday play, and again the pattern remained relatively unchanged in the first decades of the nineteenth century. Its only variation came from the tendency for more matches to extend themselves over three days, and for more clubs to play two matches a week on occasion, the combined effect of which was to spread the popular playing days more evenly towards midweek, as new games overlapped with those that had begun on Monday. This first weekday remained the most common time for beginning play.

Prize-fighting might, as an illegal sport, have been expected to have little regard for the current conventions of the sporting calendar. However, here as elsewhere, the sport showed its usual deference to law and custom.[62] In spite of the embarrassments they sometimes caused, spectators were a potential if unreliable source of income, so the ring, too, looked for times when they would be available. Again it turned out to be the first two days of the week. The interesting peculiarity in the timing of prize-fights is the marked change in preference from Monday (which had seen some 50 per cent of former fights) to Tuesday from about 1805.[63] The change was clear and, for a sport where habits died hard, relatively sudden. The only explanation that readily presents itself is that a more than usually vigorous drive against the sport by local justices was forcing major fights further and further away from London so making travel on the day before the fight a more frequent necessity. The change may also have been partly aimed at reducing the numbers of the less profitable foot-followers, since the further the sport was pushed into the working week, the fewer of the poorest could afford to attend. While such attempts at explanation are tentative, what is certain is that Tuesday became *the* fighting day, and remained so almost to the end of the prize-ring's existence. In 1843, for instance, over half the contests reported in *Bell's Life* took place on that day.[64] Equally clearly, Saturday was one of the least popular days for the sport.

Early statistics from other popular spectator sports are too elusive for firm conclusions to be drawn, but all the indications confirm the concentration of crowd-pulling events on the first two weekdays, and the avoidance of both Saturday and, to a lesser degree, Friday. Pedestrianism, for instance, once composite figures begin to be readily available in the 1830s, shows itself as overwhelmingly a Monday sport, with half of all its events taking place then. The significance of the general absence of sport from Saturdays, if not the preference for Mondays, was made clear by comments on the Randall v. Turner fight in December 1818. It was postponed from its intended date because of the queen's death: a further example, incidentally, of the ring's deference to decency and decorum! Exceptionally, it then took place on Saturday, 5 December, and there was surprise expressed at the size of the crowd that still turned out, 'Saturday being a day of business in town'.[65]

It was, in fact, *the* working day above all others. Only a minority of workers were yet subject to the disciplines of the factory system. In most manufacturing industries they still had a large measure of control over their own working hours, operating as they did on batch production in small teams, if not individually, and paid simply for what they produced. Saturday was pay day, and payment was customarily late on Saturday night at that. There was much concern from reformers over this time-honoured practice, which kept the town streets noisy with drinking and bargaining well into the early hours of Sunday morning. It was certainly no day to try to tempt people away from the work bench to the sports field. Saturday saw the sharpest awareness of the size of the week's wage packet and of the need to be there to collect it at the end of the day.

Both employers and employees were engaged in settling the week's account, and Saturday was an inauspicious day for matters other than business. The relative unpopularity of Friday was for similar reasons – the demands of the week's quota bore down ever more urgently as the day of reckoning approached.

On the other hand, Monday was the nearest weekday to the last wage packet, when a few shillings still jingled in the pocket, and it was the day furthest away from the next pay-out. If the official working week allowed no respite for play, then Monday was the day for unofficial holidaying. It had become, in ironic recognition of its replacement of the old lapsed feasts, 'St Monday', and was followed, by those who could contrive to extend their observance further, by 'Holy Tuesday'. The new free days seem to have been seized upon almost as soon as the original holy days became eroded. As early as the mid-seventeenth century the tendency to enjoy Monday as a day of rest from labour was celebrated in the rhyme that 'Monday is Sunday's brother'.[66] For the next 200 years it was to be the bane of economists, socal reformers, employers, and governments alike. Framework knitters were spending most of the first two days of the week at alehouses or ninepins in 1683.[67] Weavers and shoemakers were doing the same. In the early nineteenth century, a plea for sober Sunday recreation was backed by the argument that it would make men readier for their weekday labours – instead, 'Saint Monday, Holy Tuesday, and oftentimes more days that should be devoted to work, are wasted in the skittle-ground'.[68] It was, though, not just the tavern and the skittle alley that profited from these early week holidays – it was also the rising spectator sports. St Monday observance, moreover, was not just confined to the rough and tumble working classes – a Birmingham ditty claimed that

> ... people of all ranks, at times, obey
> The festive orgies of this jocund day.[69]

Modern sports were, therefore, able to expand because there existed an unofficial, unauthorized leisure calendar, one that was quite at odds with society's formal notions of the timing of holidays, of their length and their frequency. Concentration on the disappearance of traditional feast days and festivals, and the folk play associated with them, has tended to mask the persistence, even the strengthening, of unapproved and often even more regular leisure. The underlying conflict of the period was less one between leisure and work than between the official and unofficial leisure calendars. It was this alternative pattern of holidays, with its comparative predictability, its flexibility, and its urban emphasis – there was little scope for it on the land – that allowed crowd-seeking sports to find their place. The one supported the other. Some workers would take Monday off as a matter of course, as in the

Birmingham workshops and in the Potteries,[70] but others, like the Warwickshire miners, would choose their occasions, only laying down their picks if there was an attractive prize-fight, race meeting, or the like to draw them away.[71] The confirmation that the sporting calendar depended on working practices comes from the one area where these practices did not apply – the public schools. By the early nineteenth century, although inter-school cricket matches were still relatively few, they had already settled firmly into what is still their prevailing pattern – of Wednesday and Saturday play.

The operation of the alternative leisure could not but be noted by concerned contemporaries. Its relationship to the rise of spectator sport was less clearly perceived, and has been largely ignored since. Looked at from above, as it usually was, and by non-participants, popular recreation presented a 'problem', and a multi-faceted problem at that. The concern began with the always underlying apprehension regarding all large gatherings, was augmented by the interference with steady labour, and seemed to be justified by leisure behaviour that often fell short of rising social and moral expectations. The only means of keeping popular recreation under control appeared to be through suppression – of traditional holidays and their 'primitive' celebrations – and a denial, intentional or otherwise, of access to customary playing areas through urban expansion or enclosure. Yet, as the old play was squeezed out, these new sporting activities would force themselves ever further forward; and as the old holidays went by the board the inclination to take a Monday break grew ever stronger. Suppression did little to solve the issue of accommodating the people's play to their licensed leisure time. They took their own free time, and little could be done to stop them until the hardest poverty took a hand. From the viewpoint of the middle and upper classes, whose own sports began to separate out more distinctly from the pleasures of the masses, purely negative measures were not succeeding. The ways and the times of popular play continued to give offence. As Cunningham has rightly pointed out, the criticism is itself a recognition of the importance and strength of the new, often commercially organized play.[72]

Articulate sportsmen would defend their activities in the specialist press.[73] For the rest, most of the voices raised were antagonistic. Sport seldom lent itself to serious deliberation in the hard transitional decades of the early nineteenth century. Debates such as that on the merits and demerits of prize-fighting at Jeremy Bentham's Society for Mutual Improvement in 1820 were rarities.[74] The result was that those who had the keenest appreciation of the drift in popular sporting habits were not the thinkers or the social commentators, but the profit-seeking sponsors and promoters, who responded primarily to the twitchings of the purse-strings. A miscellany of opportunists, they were men of the neighbouring world of the theatre, they were proprietors of pleasure gardens and running grounds, they were stall-holders and stablemen with a vested interest in the local races. They were occasionally business men of more substance than probity, like Birmingham's Mr John Beardsworth, from the horse and carriage trade;[75] they were small-time financiers, often denied the conventional routes to profit, and above all they were publicans from every corner of the country, still hanging on to the field behind their tavern, and mounting every diversion from cricket to rat-catching and from bowls to horse-races.

As far as they were concerned, the provision of sporting entertainment was in happy and profitable harmony with the leisure time that their customers could contrive for themselves. The problem of leisure was not their problem. The underlying tension between the scope of sport and the extent of leisure was there, all the same. Its surest indications come from within sport itself. The more appropriate they felt it was to keep up with changing attitudes, the more they began to sharpen their own timing. A new sense of pace and efficiency began to emerge. Racing programmes became fuller, younger horses began to race over shorter distances, and there were complaints over the dilatoriness of the day's proceedings. The meal, taken in the middle of the programme, could last for up to four hours, according to one critic of the 1831 Ludlow meeting. Local sponsors insisted that racegoers should have to eat in town, but it could result in races still being run at 9.00 or 10.00 p.m.[76] There were similar grumbles over the tardiness of cricketers. An anonymous correspondent – of some influence, if the effect of his proposals on subsequent practice is anything to go by – was recommending in 1828 that there should be earlier starts, one inch or more added to the height of the wickets, six- or even eight-ball overs instead of four, only two minutes allowed for new batsmen and fifteen between innings.[77] Cricketers had to be constantly cajoled to abide by the clock, and complaints over late starts continued until the 1880s.[78] Only sports with other more pressing preoccupations with sheer survival, such as the ring or traditional football contests, failed to respond to the new sense of urgency that had at last begun to impinge on sport itself.

The solution to the conflict between what society was prepared to allow by way of free time and the demands on time of popular sport was to come by way of compromise. At first it would be an awkward and almost accidental settlement, producing a revised leisure shape that was strange to most sports, and to which they adapted with what was often, even for an activity steeped in conservatism, surprising slowness. When at length they did so, however, the people's sporting activities then took the form that they were to keep to with little fundamental change for well over half a century. The adolescent years of popular spectator sports, though, still retained a permanent hold on their ultimate character. The expansiveness is often still there, even today. People still go for 'a *day's* racing', and evening meetings, even though the long summer evenings leave plenty of time for them, have never become really popular. Crowds may flock to one-day, limited-over cricket, but for most this is just the sweetmeat compared with the full five-day meal of the real game in test matches – the feeling remains for 'proper' cricket, even if few actually turn up to watch it after the first three days! Boxing, once it was released from its legal restraints, was quick to revive and garnish its old rituals and ceremonials, the challenge and the response, the public weigh-in, the fanfared entrance of the gladiators, and the post-fight congratulations and recriminations – all is extended as far as it will stretch.

The inheritance that British sport still carries from its early days in those first decades of the Industrial Revolution is perhaps best illustrated by again looking across the Atlantic at the differences between the British and the American sporting experience. Apart from the horse-racing and hunting that expatriates had brought to the antebellum South, some cricket, and embryonic prize-fighting, the organizing of American sport came too late to enjoy the elbow room, the sense of extension, that characterized the early days of spectator play in Britain. When the organization and exploitation came, the whole tempo and direction of American society worked against open-endedness in time, just as it worked against the indecision of the drawn game.

Baseball emphasizes the differences wrought by separate histories and changed expectations. For all its theoretical timelessness, its tempo is quite unlike that of cricket. Its leisure lies in the pauses between the action. The action itself is much more consistently explosive. It is essentially a high-risk game which can be turned upside-down by the final pitch of the contest, and its potential for sudden reverses is far greater than that of cricket. It is melodrama as against tragi-comedy. Its pastoral dream fades even more quickly than cricket's, as it loses both grass and sky. Those of us who find it a great game have to acknowledge that it derives from a separate sporting tradition, that there are inevitable and historical hurdles in accommodating it to British notions of the nature and scope of sport, notions that began to be formed long before Abner Doubleday was even thought of.

# 6

# The pace of play

World-wide leagues in the major sports lie only a decade or so in the future. Already there are the World Cups, regularly or occasionally competed for, and the capacity to organize continuous fixture lists covering clubs in five continents is almost with us. It only needs an extension of supersonic travel and the assurance of financial rewards from satellite television to make the appeal irresistible. Even now, with a game that commands very uncertain live audiences, cricket teams can find it worthwhile to cross the world to play just a handful of matches. American football teams cross the Atlantic for warm-up exhibition games, and oil-rich Arab states fly out the best British soccer teams, often for a single game. Murmurings about a European Association Football League are bound to grow louder and eventually overcome the resistance of national ruling bodies – the geographical constraints are no greater than those already overcome in many North American competitions.

Faster travel has opened many sporting doors. The wagon and the stage coach lifted sport from being local into a regional activity. The railway made it national, and the steamship and the aeroplane have spread its tentacles across the world. Once it was travel out of the home parish for play that was deemed inappropriate[1] – now trips to watch England play test matches in the West Indies are arranged as a matter of course. Jet travel is completing the process of internationalizing sport, but it was the power of steam that brought the first great steps in making the world's sports into one.

Its use in the manufacturing industries has often made steam seem the enemy of recreation and leisure. It did, indeed, release the mills from their clusters in the river valleys and tie down their workers all the more firmly to the unfailing factory hooter and the unremitting demands of production. There was no chance of a few days summer idleness when the water in the mill stream fell too low to turn the wheels, and there were undoubted pains and agonies in these early steam decades, particularly so far as the more defenceless were concerned, the women workers and the children. Yet it is still arguable that the new technologies of the early nineteenth century, and steam power most of all, did, in the not too long run, bring more benefits than trials to most of the population. This was certainly so with their sport and recreation. Throughout the history of play humanity has exploited material advances for its amusement as well as for its survival. Both the nature and the dimensions of sport have changed as man has created new artefacts and assumed more and more management of his environment.

It was so from the beginning, as new materials and symbolism went hand in hand to displace some of play's primitive origins. Gruesome legends recall that Scots warriors used the skulls of their victims for their first games of bowls,[2] and the football was the substitute for the blood-dripping head of the slain enemy, fought over to enrich the victors' fields.[3] More surely, before metal-working skills had improved enough to displace them, early skates were often the shoulder-blades of sheep.[4] What is certain is that whenever the material world has changed, man has sought to exploit the change to enhance his sporting possibilities. Cricket flourished before the cricket bat willow was discovered,[5] but it was that tree's strong and resilient wood that did much to alter the nature of the game. Bowls ran more truly once the native boxwood gave way to African hardwood,[6] and the bullock hide, tied with thongs and stuffed with hay – the 'solid orb' of one early sporting verse[7] – was displaced first by the inflated bladder in the stitched leather case, and then by the plastic coating, so that the football became all the while lighter, more predictable, and giving greater scope for the development of skills.[8]

Well before the age of electronics and the microchip, technological progress consistently brought about major changes in sports – in equipment, in facilities for players and spectators, in the spread of information about games, and in the modes and timing of travel to them. As sporting guns became more reliable in the eighteenth century, fowling went out of fashion;[9] as metal-working skills became more accessible the first iron golf clubs appeared (initially as an aid to lifting balls out of depressions), and the discovery of rubber for making balls spelled the end of the top hat full of feathers stuffed into a sewn cowhide, and all the vagaries that could entail.[10] The popularity of games with small balls in late Victorian Britain owed much to the rubber ball – it is more than mere accident that the All-England Tennis and Croquet Club at Wimbledon took its name at the very time that the first rubber seeds smuggled out of Brazil were beginning to sprout a few miles away at Kew Gardens, and a new industry was about to be born with their transportation to Malaya and Ceylon.

The key to the initial spread of spectator sports lay in the improvement in communications during their infant years. To thrive consistently they needed more than repeated local competition. To achieve this, they needed agreed rules and practices, not games that varied from place to place. Time had to be condensed, so that the hurdles of distance could be surmounted. Communication, between people and of information, was vital to the diffusion and organization of public sports. Sporting intelligence, as *The Times* called it, had to be transmitted – it was essential to promote uniformity, to arouse popular interest, and to spread the news of fixtures and results. Most of all, as time pressures increased, more rapid transit was needed, for players and spectators alike. Cunningham has described the railway as 'the great technical breakthrough in the history of leisure',[11] and it certainly was so in the history of modern sport. But the railway was no more than the consummation of the movement into a heightened tempo of life and play that transformed the leisured habits of one mid-century into the brisk time-tabled schedules of the next.

The sporting rhythms of the eighteenth century were typified by the Hambledon cricketers' great horse-drawn caravan, lumbering over the south-eastern corner of England.[12] Those of a hundred years later were of the touring professional cricketers, some of them, like Richard Daft, often playing six days a week.[13] Yet even in those earlier years, people were very aware that their world was speeding up, with the newly metalled roads and the lighter, swifter stage coaches – well before the railway age they had cut the journey from London to Birmingham from a two-day expedition to under ten hours.[14] The trek to a boxing match could still seem idyllic – a 'truly delightful scene', with the 'string of carriages for miles winding round the road – the horsemen galloping and leaping over the hedges; the pedestrians all on the trot, and the anxiety displayed on every countenance to arrive in time'.[15] The February reality of 1822 was, as so often, quite different. There was a seven-mile shift to a new site in the sweeping rain. The cavalcade at one point crossed the Surrey Hounds in full cry and some would-be spectators, mounted on hunters, found themselves carried off, willy-nilly, after the fox! The 'toddlers', as so often, were hard put to keep up with the carriages, 'gigs shivered to pieces', post-chaises sank deep into the clay, and hats were lost in the wind. Little wonder that when the fight at last started, at 4.45 p.m., in the gathering gloom, it was before 'the select and few'.[16] All the time, though, there was a feeling of social progress. The 1820 view that Hounslow Heath – the present site of Heathrow airport – had become as safe for stage-coaches as St James's Park[17] was just one of many signs of optimism, as well as being a reminder of the still rural nature of the suroundings of London. By the 1830s there were forty coaches a week on the Bath run and over 50,000

11 'Returning from the Intended Fight': the stampeding chaos and peril of prize-fight crowds in pre-railway days (Etching from *Sporting Magazine*, October 1801)

passengers a year were taking the road between Brighton and London, impressive figures to contemporaries, but grossly misleading as predictors of likely numbers of railway travellers.[18]

A keener awareness of the impact already made by river steamers would have led to more accurate forecasts. These had opened up the recreational life of the Londoner and the Glaswegian beyond anything that had been known before. The growth of the traffic to Margate and Ramsgate, for instance, was phenomenal – 17,000 in 1812/13, 21,900 in 1815/16, 43,000 in 1820/1, 98,000 in 1830/1 and 105,000 in 1835/6.[19] Other convenient rivers, and especially the Clyde with its grand scenic attractions, shared in the explosion of steam travel. Sportsmen, though, seem to have been slow to take advantage of the new form of transport for their own specific purposes. A few more boxing matches than in the past began to be mounted on the Kent and Essex banks of the Thames, but these seem to have been more a response to added police vigilance than a resort to the new form of transport. Indeed, to one group of sportsmen, the oarsmen, the increased river traffic was a hazard rather than a benefit, according to a letter in *Bell's Life*. Paddle boats were making rowing on the Thames exceedingly difficult, with the result that the numbers of skiffs and wherries there had been much reduced.[20]

The pressure to find new means of mounting their events was felt most keenly by boxing promoters. The new local authority police forces, operating with increasing effect from the mid-1830s, would no longer tolerate the massive cavalcades of horsemen, carriages, and pedestrians which advertised what was an unlawful gathering. More discreet means of bringing about contests had to be found, if the sport was to survive. The inspiration came from a source which showed little intentional friendship towards sport in general or pugilism in particular, namely the Temperance Movement. Thomas Cook broke new ground when he hired a special train to run his own excursion trip for local abstainers in 1836. Within a few years, the pugilists were following suit, chartering both trains and steamers to take fighters and spectators to the usually undisclosed site of the match.

Steam transport brought a new lease of life to the sport. Its promoters resorted to river and rail at much the same time, from 1839.[21] Each had its advantages and drawbacks. The river steamer gave the best chance of avoiding the law since, unlike the railway, it was not served by the new-fangled electric telegraph which could pass warnings of the coming throng to police forces down the line. Tickets for both train and steamer could be sold in advance, giving the assured income from spectators that the ring had always lacked, and numbers could, it was always hoped, be controlled by price and space. The river had the advantage of taking the crowd right up to the site of the fight, which was usually close by the landing stage, whereas railway fights could often not come off immediately adjoining the line, so that *all* the passengers then found themselves reduced to the ranks of foot soldiers. It did, though, all look more straightforward than it usually turned out in practice. The sport was riddled with subterfuge, disorder, and sheer greed, which ensured that all manner of mishaps and connivances would upset the apparently simple plans. They failed, for instance, in their hopes of exclusivity. East-enders soon got wind both of intended fights and of any exceptional river traffic. They then followed the 'official' fighting boat downstream in anything from tugs to coal barges, at a fraction of the cost. When the sponsors tried to cater for a wider range of customers by hiring two vessels, one first class and one second, there could be confusion about where they were to rendezvous,[22] and when pirate boats sought to follow on down-river they could sometimes come to grief in their haste.[23] Then there was the problem of the return journey, often slow because it was against the tide and the prevailing wind, in a boat more heavily loaded than it had been on the outward journey because of the 'cheapsiders' who had found their way on board. On the other hand, it could well depart immediately after the main fight, the only one in which the organizers had any interest, so leaving stranded those who wanted to see any supporting bouts.

Landing at the chosen site could also have its perils. There was no English disaster comparable with that in Australia at the intended fight between MacLaren and Carstairs, when several were drowned in trying to wade ashore.[24] It could still, though, be a wet and muddy business, enough to deter all but the ardent and imprudent. There were still plenty of these, though the ring sank deeper and deeper into the social mire. The 2,000 or more who travelled down from London every Tuesday in the early 1850s for fights on the Dartford Marshes were described as 'the very scum and refuse' of the metropolis. Others took the North Kent Railway, leaving no room for the respectable, even had they been prepared to brave the unlit hazards of the Blackheath tunnel in such company.[25]

The railway was, for over a quarter of a century, more or less friendly towards boxing, though the various companies varied in their enthusiasm. The Eastern Counties and the South Western companies were the most co-operative. The Kent and Sussex lines were difficult,[26] and the Great Western would take the money without being very forthcoming in helping the fight to actually take place.[27] At first, the fight parties used scheduled trains, but this soon proved too public, their destination too predictable, and the trains themselves, with their frequent stops, too slow.[28] A changing world could also take its toll – the spectators arriving at Wolverton station, and then forced to move several miles into the next county to avoid the law, found only a handful of carriages there, and this at a spot which a few years before had seen some of the busiest coach traffic in the country, on the Birmingham–London run.[29]

From the late 1830s the answer lay with the specially hired train, the tickets cryptically printed for just 'there and back'. In the early excursion days, matters could be quite relaxed. When the Ward v. Bailey fight was turned away from Wiltshire, the returning South Western Railway train stopped conveniently in a cutting near Woking and the crowd swarmed up the bank for the encounter to take place on the local common, one of the traditional fighting grounds. Initially, too, the railway special was a means of excluding the near-criminal elements who came to make up a large part of the ring's following. Gradually, though, the roughnecks gathered in growing numbers at the London termini when it was known that a fight train was due to leave. They picked pockets, harassed, jostled, stole tickets, and created general mayhem. Attempts at secrecy seldom did much to keep them at bay.[30]

The writing was already on the wall when the last great rail trek to a prize-fight took place – to the Sayers v. Heenan fight in 1860. This much-heralded contest, seen as for the Championship of the World, was between the London hero, Tom Sayers, and the American, John Heenan. The spectators filled three special trains. The fight was an honourable draw.[31] Sayers announced his retirement, and the curtain began its slow fall on bareknuckle fighting as a national sport. The insertion of a clause in the Regulation of Railways Act of 1868 forbidding the provision of trains for prize-fights was by then just adding a legal seal to a closed chapter of railway and sporting history.[32]

Pugilism was, in fact, virtually doomed by the time the railway age began. So many of its characteristics went against changing social tastes and could not adjust to the new sporting expectations that stemmed from these broader shifts in attitudes. Its inherent brutality went against rising humanitarianism. Its remorseless battering of the defeated went against the refinement that was slowly coming into sports and games, while its continuing association with the least orderly sections of urban life condemned it to a dying future as a pursuit of working-class ghettos and unscrupulous sharpers. It speaks wonders for the powers of steam transport that it could still keep major contests on the ring's agenda for over a quarter of a century, though it did so not by bringing the ring into harmony with the contemporary world, but by keeping it apart. The special excursion brought to the sport such elements of modernization as it was capable of assimilating – the fight became more contained, in both space and time, the whole proceedings were speeded up, and its conflict with the working week was more narrowly confined. But it was essentially a dying sport.

If the railway could breathe some life into a moribund prize-ring, what could it not do for those sports which were already flourishing in the days of coach and sail? There were, of course, the usual doubts over whether trains could do anything for anybody, sportsman or not. After a steam coach run to Henley in 1830, one correspondent, while allowing the value of steam 'for modern machinery, or on the wide ocean', could never see it as 'desirable for land travelling',[33] while another, eight years later, still had his doubts over railways, claiming that 'it must be a long time, if ever, before they become general'.[34] Already, though, there were a thousand miles of track and the number of passengers was rising annually. Already, too, the railway was making its contribution to legitimate sport, with extra trains from Vauxhall for that same year's Derby, 'to that point of the railway south of Kingston which is nearest Epsom'.[35]

The railway had begun its transformation of horse-racing. Within a generation it had become a main factor in determining the success or failure of individual meetings. Long-established fixtures, like Blandford, could quickly disappear if the early railways passed them by. Others could take on new life from the railway connection, often with direct support from the railway company itself. For Liverpool, for instance, it was the happiest of coincidences that its line to Birmingham and London and its Grand National Steeplechase appeared almost together in the late 1830s. The effects of the railway on the nature of meetings were also dramatic. The races had been one of the great social occasions of the year, with the town full of visitors lodging there. Now the trains brought many of the spectators in daily, and returned them home after the racing, and the balls, dinners, and assemblies of the past soon faded away. Apart from a few exceptional meetings which retained their status in the social calendar – such as Ascot and Goodwood – the races lost much of their old communal significance. What had been a social event, albeit with strong economic undertones, tended to become a predominantly commercial sporting entertainment.

Horses themselves were soon being transported by rail from one meeting to another. The regional circuits, loosely arranged, which had allowed horses to be walked from one engagement to the next, began to be overtaken by national arrangements, dependent upon the railway network. The sport was in a state of flux and transition. The racing world retained its fixed points – Newmarket, Epsom, Ascot, Doncaster, and York, all varying from time to time in brilliance – but the rest of its map was always changing. This was never more so than in the middle decades of the century. The same fever for opening up new territories that fired the railway companies also inspired the promoters of race meetings. The companies became important sponsors – the 'South Western Railway Stakes' at Salisbury in the 1850s was typical of their investment – but the sport became more speculative. It needed higher ground rents for booths and refreshment tents, and increased attendances, to produce the competitive prize money that would attract owners to the meeting. The choice of where to race a horse in the past had been largely dictated by where it happened to be the week before. Now the railway made more deliberate selection possible. The new economics of the turf was reflected in the volatile state of meetings – of the ninety-nine new ventures started in the 1860s, for instance, only a quarter survived for more than a decade.[36] The association between the successful racecourse and the railway was then further strengthened either by building a station (and sometimes a short branch line) adjacent to the race ground itself, or by siting new commercial courses alongside existing busy routes.[37]

The railway made two other important contributions to the reshaping of nineteenth-century life. It brought standardized time, and it brought the need to observe timings more exactly. Time had always followed the local rising and setting of the sun, so that Bristol was ten minutes behind London, Manchester nine minutes, and Glasgow sixteen. Railways could not operate with such variations and, after a few years during which provincial clocks sported *two* minute hands, all towns by the early 1850s were using 'Railway Time' or 'London Time'. Nor was it merely that time became standardized. The railway encouraged a sharper sense of promptness, a greater emphasis on precision in all life's comings and goings. It was not a change which sport could afford to ignore. Not only were the demands of the steam trains more insistent and inflexible than those of the stage, they were also carrying a much higher proportion of the paying spectators. Races, for once, had to start on time. Fuller programmes demanded much tighter control, and the last race had to be run as promptly as the first, so that passengers could catch the train home. The speeding up of events may have been urged by critics,[38] but it was affected by the time-table demands of the railway. A similar quickening of life was generated by the electric telegraph. Soon its instant conveying of results and news was sustaining a burgeoning sporting press. In 1831 the Sevenoaks cricketers were still taking pigeons to away matches to have their results relayed home quickly.[39] Within a few years, sports results were on the London streets within the hour. No longer could there be the frantic gallops such as occurred in 1819 when Sultan, St Leger favourite, pulled up in training, and those in the know sped hot-foot to the betting rooms in Doncaster, Nottingham, and Sheffield to hedge their wagers before the news became generally known.[40] The possibility of telegraphing bets, incidentally, gave a further urgency to the standardization of time and the precision of race starts.

Such was the growth, the speed, and the accessibility of rail travel that no part of the country's recreational life could remain untouched. In the coaching days, the average travelling, by transport of some kind, over the whole population amounted to no more than 13 miles a year, at 5d. a mile, and at 9 miles an hour. By the Jubilee year of 1877, the average annual journeying had risen to 148 miles, at 1¼d. per mile, and at 25 to 30 miles an hour. How much of this movement about the country was connected with sport is impossible to say, but certainly there was an enormous increase in recreational travel. The Lancashire and Yorkshire Railway was promising sea bathing to its excursionists in the 1850s,[41] cricket matches became a common feature of works' railway outings, and even a trip to Ashby de la Zouch held out the additional prospect of cricket, archery, skittles, and quoits.[42] By the third quarter of the century the long-standing special trains to the races had been joined by other sporting excursions. When the Players met the touring Australian cricketers in 1880, for instance, the special from Dover stopped at Penge for spectators making for Crystal Palace and the match, and then went on to Victoria for the non-sporting, and all for 5s. third-class return.[43]

Cricket, like horse-racing, had virtually become a national sport without the aid of the railway. Its last pockets were just being colonized at the time the railway network spread over the country. What the railway did achieve for cricket was a speeding up of its standardization, and a more rapid evening out of skill levels. Other parts of the country could hold their own with the southeast. In the coaching days it was a comparative rarity for teams to travel any great distance, and the game was subject to local variations and idiosyncratic umpires. In 1819 a formal match was still said to be a rarity in Bristol, so 'we have seldom had an opportunity of witnessing the game played in strict conformity with the rules'.[44] All sport tended to become much more provincial and London's domination lessened. Neither the process itself, nor the railway's contribution to it, has had the prominence it deserves. It was marked strongly in pugilism, where all the champions of the 1830s and 1840s were from the industrial Midlands. Newmarket went into temporary eclipse, at the expense particularly of Doncaster which now, it was noted in 1852, was only four and a half hours from London by the Great Northern Railway.[45] The domination of pedestrianism by the Midlands and the North grew even stronger and the progress of cricket there was greatly accelerated. In 1817 it had taken XXII of Nottingham to match an All-England XI. By 1837, a North v. South match had become the obvious means of celebrating the MCC's fiftieth anniversary, and within a few more years the balance of the game's strength had moved firmly in the provinces' direction.

There were few sports which resisted the unifying influence of the new communications system. A notable exception was football, still only emerging from its long embryonic stage as folk play and children's game. It had no central institution such as the Jockey Club or the MCC which could exert some more or less accepted authority, nor had it a basic code of rules such as Broughton had given to pugilism. Those who sought to organize an agreed pattern for the game were so fiercely loyal to the rules they had played to at their schools that to arrive eventually at even two codes was a slow and argumentative business, which has already been well described.[46] The public schools themselves, though, participated to the full in the consolidation of cricket – by the 1860s virtually all of them were travelling to play 'foreign' games against other schools,[47] and the annual Eton and Harrow game at Lord's had become one of the age's more surprising sporting attractions.

If the impact of steam travel on sporting progress is clearly demonstrable in the United Kingdom, the process was even more sharply etched in the United States. Steam brought immigrants across the ocean and steam spread them over the new continent. The railroad became an important element in the creation of the country itself. It became the essential link in the development of its organized sport, which was for the most part a post-Civil War phenomenon. After the conflict was over, baseball in particular leapt in popularity; rapid rail communication kept the game unified, and made possible the first national league in any team sport anywhere in 1876, some dozen years before the founding of the Football League in England.[48] Baseball's 'National League' could, of course, only be national to the extent that railway travel then allowed, and it took the aeroplane to bring the Pacific coast into a regular countrywide sporting programme.

Faster travel, particularly over the oceans, gave impetus to international exchange and competition. Apart from the discomforts of a long voyage by sail, the time that it consumed and its uncertainties were considerable barriers to sporting contacts between different countries. Even so, the days of coach and sail had already seen an international dimension in sport – racehorses were sent from Persia for the Prince Regent, and trotting horses were imported from the United States, balancing the considerable trade in thoroughbreds in the other direction and to the Continent, where more and more British owners also raced their own horses. Sportsmen had frequently crossed the Atlantic. Among pugilists alone, these included Molyneux, Richmond, and Freeman, who travelled eastwards, and William Fuller and others who had sailed from the old world to the new.[49] These, though, were all one-way journeys. Sporting visits of any frequency had to await the regular steam service, which began in 1841. Ben Caunt, the current British boxing champion, promptly boarded the Cunard Line's *Britannia* at Liverpool on one of its first trips to Boston.[50] He was the first of a whole string of fighting men to try his luck in the United States, where the prospects for the sport were generally more open than they had become in Britain. The interchange was such that the ring could soon conceive of a World Championship, the first sport to do so.

12 *and* 13  Two of the first international professional sportsmen. Tom Molyneux (*left*) came to Britain from New York and twice fought Tom Cribb for the Championship, in 1810 and 1811. Benjamin Caunt (*right*) was the first of many boxers to cross the Atlantic in the other direction to seek his fortune. (From H. D. Miles's *Pugilistica*, vols I and III respectively

Travel by individuals, whether men or horses, was easier to envisage than the wholesale movements of teams from country to country. The success of touring cricket teams at home, though, began to prompt a lifting of the sights and before long they were on the high seas. The first touring team from Britain to America sailed in 1859, attracting a crowd of 24,000 at Hoboken, New Jersey, but generally winning their games too easily to make the trip an unqualified success.[51] In the 1870s and 1880s, overseas touring became a regular feature of the cricket scene. Americans – baseball players, cricketers, even players ready to play both games – came to Britain, and then, after the opening of the Suez Canal, and relatively speedy travel to Australia, the exchange of teams between the opposite ends of the world was a possibility. W. G. Grace was in Australia in 1873/4 and the first Australian cricketers (apart from an earlier Aboriginal party) were in England in 1878. Thereafter tours were frequent, sometimes too frequent – commercial sport, no less than other commodities, could over-supply its market. There were two English teams in Australia in 1886/7, one led by Lord Hawke and the other by Alfred Shaw, and they both ran at a loss.[52] The international boundaries of the game were further extended in the 1880s when the first Indian team came to Britain. Little more than fifty years earlier it had been rare for any team to travel as far as a hundred miles for a match. Now they would cover many thousands. Steam, which had helped sport cover the

*14* A carefully posed group of early international sporting travellers, including W. G. Grace. English cricketers at Montreal, 1872

15 W. G. Grace again dominated the scene, as he did the cricket field – and the tour's expenses sheet! Lord Sheffield's Australian touring team, 1891/2, in Adelaide Botanical Gardens

nation, now helped it cover the world, for where cricket led the way, other sports would follow.

The expansion had been remarkable. As the coaching days drew to their close, few could have predicted the sweeping effects of the new modes of transport, and even fewer would have predicted that sport would be one of the major beneficiaries. If they had done so, there would have been little widespread pleasure in the prediction. Sport in the 1830s was still more frowned upon than blessed. Apart from the objections to both its nature and its clientele, there was still the apparently insuperable problem of finding occasions which would not add to the offence. There may have been some awareness among the more business-like sportsmen of the need to speed up their entertainments, to contract them more smartly into available time, but the question remained. When could acceptable occasions be found?

Surprisingly, the railway had a part in the eventual answer.

The Monday sports day[53] might be well established, but it was totally unauthorized. It was associated with a rhythm of labour feasible to the workshop but alien to the demands of the factory and the mill. The weekly pattern (which we have already noted in Chapter 5) of an easygoing start, a quickening pace in the middle, mounting to a climax on Saturday and the night's pay-out – all this went against the need for regular labour and continuous production. And it brought a riot of late-night shopping and drinking that went on into the early hours of Sunday, so bringing the growing forces of Sabbatarianism into alliance with those already seeking to alter the balance of the working week.

The movement towards a free Saturday afternoon was, at first, scarcely even a conscious one. Its origins lay in historical survivals rather than in innovation. An early Saturday afternoon finish had persisted in the original centre of the woollen industry in the southwest, where it was a relic of the medieval observance of the eve of holy days.[54] Work often ended there at 2.00 p.m.[55] Elsewhere in the textile trades, and especially where the usual daily hours were at their longest, there was also some tendency to earlier Saturday closing – in some Lancashire mills it had become no later than 6.00 p.m., or even up to two hours earlier than that.[56] It was against this background that, in the mid-1840s, there was an appreciable leap forward in the Saturday freedom gained by workers. In February 1846, London engineers secured a 4.00 p.m. Saturday finish. A year later, and for reasons which are still not wholly clear, Manchester accepted 1.00 p.m. closing, a pioneering agreement in that it affected all trades.[57] The 1850 Factory Act closed all textile mills at 2.00 p.m., and the Sheffield trades had secured similar general concessions.[58] The advance towards a free Saturday afternoon, begun almost accidentally, was gathering the momentum that would make it universal first in industry and then in commerce over the next half-century.

The timing of the advances in industrial leisure and the spread of the main line railway system is an almost exact match. During the second half of the 1840s, when Saturday freedom first began to extend, the railway mileage rose from 2,000 to 6,000.[59] Wages rose, production soared ahead on the back of mechanization and greater efficiency, and exports expanded rapidly. It was an economic climate in which some relaxation on just one day of the working week became more conceivable, particularly if it could secure some added regularity elsewhere. An aspect of the country's added efficiency appeared to lie in its growing smartness of pace, as life itself became more time-tabled, more delineated as between one type of activity and another. The prevailing mood, shared by both sides of industry, inclined towards a sharper demarcation between work and leisure, and the hours appropriate to each. There was no sudden free Saturday afternoon for all workers over the whole country, nor was there an immediate end to the observance of St Monday, but the process of change had begun. Town by town, and even trade by trade, the bargaining went on, often involving the trading off of traditional holidays which the workers were in the habit of taking. In Nottingham, for instance, most hosiery manufacturers had replaced the special holidays for Goose Fair, the races, and so on, for a regular Saturday half-day in 1861, but the lace workers had no early Saturday before 1870. Retail trades did not generally win a comparable midweek half-holiday until the new century, but the Nottingham shops managed to do so in the early 1880s.[60]

The gradual changes in the work and leisure patterns are reflected in the varying fortunes of the railway excursion. The excursion usually depended on a full day's freedom from work. Its heyday was in the 1850s, when many occasional days could still be taken. Frequently and inevitably, Monday was the favourite day for such outings – of the twenty-two rail excursions advertised from Birmingham in 1846, only six were *not* on a Monday.[61] The decline in the number of excursion trains in the later 1860s doubtless owed something to their reputation for rough conditions and equally rough company, but a telling factor was also the reduction in the number of free full-day holidays. The early Saturday afternoon might be regular and assured, but it gave little opportunity for train trips. Excursion trains became mainly confined to Sundays, fixed holidays, and such events as race meetings.[62] It was a pattern of change shared by Birmingham, where attendance figures at the Botanical Gardens tell the same story. Between 1854 and 1857 the average Monday attendance was 40,450. Between 1869 and 1873, this had dropped to 20,600, with most of that concentrated on the two holiday Mondays at Easter and Whitsuntide.[63]

The wholesale reshaping of the week's working and leisure was well on its way to completion. The changes in the organization and timing of sports, initiated in no small way by steam transport, had happened gradually and their significance had often gone unnoticed. Sportsmen – like those prize-fight followers stranded at Wolverton station – could be as keenly aware of the drawbacks of change as of its benefits. Even sports promoters, usually the most acute of innovators where profit promised, were often slow to appreciate the new possibilities opening to them from the new shape of the leisure calendar. The coming of the later Victorian sporting weekend constituted one of the most decisive events in the growth of modern sport, and in the determination of the forms which it would assume over the next hundred years. It set the time span of games, the scale of their appeal, and the availability of an ever-growing spectatorship. It established a pattern of weekend leisure behaviour which was to have its own internal modifications, but which would remain basically unaltered into the second half of the twentieth century – the sporting Saturday afternoon followed by a night at the music hall, the public house, or the chapel concert, or, in later days, at the Palais de Dance or joining the long Saturday queue to see Valentino, Clark Gable, or Greta Garbo. For whole generations, the advent of the free Saturday afternoon initiated a scheme of weekend leisure and recreation which became woven into the fabric of life itself.

The fact that it came about so imperceptibly prompts one of the eternal questions that has to puzzle the historian. What is it that we do today – or fail to do – which will bemuse our successors? What is happening, too, in our sporting lives that we fail to appreciate, in the nature and timing of our sports? It would be presumptuous to suppose that, with all our analyses, models, and social sciences, we are immune from the past's proneness to ignorance about itself. What are the still unrealized implications of what is happening to today's sports? What that looks reasonable to us will, to succeeding generations, appear the most arrant nonsense? The idea that the Olympic Games might spread universal peace and the spirit of fair play among the sportsmen of the world might well be a high candidate in the nonsense stakes – it could well look from the vantage point of the future to have the same unreality as Dover's Cotswold Games. The lingering concept of amateurism in some spectator sports is already so transparent that it hardly merits serious consideration, as does the notion that sport can somehow be separated from politics. There are more searching questions than these that our successors may ask. Are we, as we accept sport as an effective substitute for working out national rivalries, allowing into sport the same ruthlessness and deceit that characterized actual warfare? At the domestic level, are we at the start of the process – in America, well on the way – of taking sport out of the stadia, even out of the astrodome, to make it primarily an experience for the living room? Is its future to be on a vast televised wall in our parlour? And will the offside decisions, or the verdict on whether it was a ball or a strike, be made not by some referee but by the instantaneous pressing of a million television interaction buttons?

Such ideas are certainly no more fanciful than a national competition in a team sport would have seemed to even the most forward looking sports fan of the 1830s, no more outlandish than the notion of teams of players travelling the oceans to compete against each other, and, on the local plane, no more absurd than the notion that Saturday afternoon, of all times, would become the favoured occasion for sportsmen to make their matches, and for hundreds of thousands of folk to pay to watch them.

# 7

# The sporting weekend

'Thank God it's Friday!'

The lapel badge said it all – it even became the name of an American bistro chain. The weekend beckoned, a thankful two-day relief from the nagging demands of the working week. As both concept and fact, it became embedded in the life styles of western men and women. The weekend has been tied in with numerous images of leisure – the weekend house parties of an upper-class past, now reserved in nostalgic crime fiction; the weekend leave of the wartime serviceman, celebrated sentimentally in popular song; and now the travel-sellers' weekend breaks, which can even stretch across the Atlantic. The weekend empties the big cities on Friday evenings, heralds different eating habits, invents brunch for late risers, and demands modes of dress far removed from the working-day formality. It is still one of the most certain punctuation marks in our working and playing lives.

The weekend, though, is always changing. Once a time for dressing up, it is now a time for dressing down. It has a persisting tendency to expand, like the old parish feasts once did. Already it is much less sharply defined and compartmentalized than it was. Shorter working lives – whether through under-employment, earlier retirement, or ageing populations – have often blurred the once sharp division between working days and free days. Self-employment and home occupations have contributed to the same process, even if most people, whatever their circumstances, retain some differences between their midweek and weekend life patterns. Even for the fully employed, the weekly shape is often changing. As well as flexible hours, there are growing numbers of fortnightly or even longer shift patterns, giving long but relatively random breaks in the working cycle. In many occupations, too, Friday afternoon is undergoing the same erosion that Saturday afternoon saw in the nineteenth century, and the weekend exodus starts earlier and earlier in the day.

The notion of the weekend, though, remains indelible, even if its separateness is becoming, in practice, less distinct. There is little acknowledgement generally made of its comparatively brief history, and equally little of the discovery of Saturday by Victorian sport.

## SATURDAY PLAY

Saturday sport, looked at over the broad span of the centuries, was a novelty. Its contribution to the late Victorian sporting revolution was far-reaching. The reconstructed leisure time-table, of which the free Saturday afternoon became the dominant feature, altered more than the simple timing of play. It modified the sports themselves, urging upon them a new compactness and order.

Saturday sport came slowly. It found its place gradually, over some forty years, varying from sport to sport and from town to town. Newly organized sports, such as football and athletics, not bound by any existing calendar ties, quickly seized upon the new free afternoon, while the older spectator sports moved more slowly, except where alert commercial interests produced a response to the customers' changed leisure time. The staggered arrival of the Saturday afternoon closure also had important influences on the geographical shape of spectator sport, some of them still traceable in today's provision.[1]

It was a Bradfordian who, in the late nineteenth century, claimed that Saturday afternoon had become, 'as it were, part of our religion'.[2] The comment had historical and theological echoes beyond its intentions. It has already been noted that Saturday early closing was not a Victorian discovery, but the resuscitation of what had once been the observance of the eves of holy days.[3] In parallel with Jewish practice, the weekly holy day was often regarded as running from evening to evening, rather than from midnight to midnight.[4] Victorian churchmen, though, for all their keen awareness of the ill-effects of late Saturday working on Sabbath morning peace, were slow to give formal support to the free afternoon. The Early Closing Association, which became something of a force in the 1840s, was predominantly secular in both its membership and motives, and the Lord's Day Observance Society itself did not give its full blessing to the early Saturday until 1860.[5] By then, the movement towards a free Saturday afternoon was being carried along by the widespread preference for shorter hours over higher wages that characterized the whole period (and affected all classes) between 1840 and 1870.[6] It was encouraged, too, by the general prosperity which pushed up real wages by an average of some 20 per cent in the 1860s and early 1870s.[7]

There were hopeful predictions about what the workers would do with their newly won free time. Giving any of it to sport figured in very few of them. After the modest reduction of working hours under the

Ten Hours Act of 1849, January Searle claimed that there was now 'leisure enough for the working classes to get wisdom and understanding'.[8] Within the workers' own campaigns for shorter hours, sport, if it was mentioned at all, sat awkwardly in a limbo between apology and defiance. Thus the Pudsey reformers in 1836 sought 'Time for Rest and for play – yes, for play – for Fireside Improvement, Literary Advancement by Evening Schools, and, above all, for Religious Instruction for Factory Workers'.[9] Up to a point these ambitions were realized – Lancashire probably had the highest level of general literacy in the country in the 1840s[10] – but it was only up to a point. The growth of leisure in the middle years of the century coincided with tightening restrictions on how that leisure could be used. The old sports were harassed by an increasingly efficient police force, betting was banned from public houses, and these, more often than not, lost the space they once had for outdoor sports and games. Urban land was at a premium, and leisure activities were pushed more and more exclusively to within the walls of the tavern itself, where the old noise and boisterous activity of the streets was contained in singing schools and embryonic music halls. Lord Shaftesbury might well claim to the prime minister that the Manchester operatives had been both 'morally and physically improved' by their early Saturday finishing,[11] but *The Times* found another scene in a typical Lancashire town in the early 1860s:

> The working classes of Blackburn and its neighbourhood have few amusements. ... They run to foolish singing rooms ... where depravity prevails and morality is at a low ebb; after which both parents and children retire to the beer-shop, and thus spend their hard-earned weekly wages.[12]

In a little over twenty years Blackburn Rovers would win the Football Association Cup, taking it north for the first time. Sport would be well on its way to filling much of the Saturday vacuum. The speed with which it did so depended on any number of factors, national and local. Some were related to the nature and organization of a particular sport, others were dependent on the timing or sequence of Saturday afternoon release for different groups of workers. The different experiences of Birmingham and Liverpool provide a useful illustration of local influences. In Liverpool, the elite sections of the work force secured the half-day around 1860, other skilled workers followed in the early 1870s, but the bulk of the industrial population only succeeded in the late 1880s. The majority of Birmingham workers, by contrast, enjoyed the half-day by the early 1870s. On the assumption that cricket generally made its appeal somewhat further up the employment scale than football, the differences in the timing of the half-day can account for the early growth of the former in Liverpool (with over 200 teams in 1870, as against Birmingham's 60), and the equally early development of football in Birmingham – in the 1878/9 season there were more than 880 games reported in the Birmingham local press, and only 2 in the Liverpool newspapers.[13] There were other factors, such as the late arrival of public parks in Birmingham, by which time it had become the fashion to provide football pitches in association with them, as against the purely decorative open spaces of an earlier generation, but the differing Saturday closing patterns were highly significant. The inspiration for the Football League itself came from Birmingham, through Aston Villa, while it was not until the competition's second season that Liverpool's flag was raised at all, with the arrival of Everton.[14]

The transition from the old leisure calendar to the new, and the modification of former sporting habits, were usually gradual, as well as being uneven in their spread. The two traditions often existed side by side for several decades. In Sheffield where many workers secured the half-day before 1850, cricket was well established, and football strong enough for there to be matches against both Nottingham and London in the mid-1860s. Yet the operatives continued to run their own pack of hounds, in the old style, and the Hallamshire Volunteers were still objecting to having Saturday as a drill day in 1863 – Monday was said to be much better, to avoid loss of pay.[15] Elsewhere there were many examples of Monday events that still drew large crowds, such as the 15,000 at the Hackney Wick Grounds for the eight-mile race between the American, Deerfoot, and Mills in December 1861.[16]

This was, of course, a commercial venture, and in the most financially keen of all spectator sports. It came at the mid-point in the quite rapid transition which pedestrianism made to exploit the new Saturday freedom. Fixtures reported in *Bell's Life* spell out the change with a greater clarity than that found in any other existing spectator sport. In 1856 it was still overwhelmingly a Monday activity, with nearly 200 of the 260 matches over one three-month period taking place then. Within a decade its emphasis had moved decisively to Saturday. In 1867 half the contests were taking place at the weekend, and less than a third remained with Monday.[17] Rising commercial pressures on horse-racing also brought Saturday events to the turf, in what had been essentially a midweek sport. Long-standing meetings usually retained their old places in the calendar. As occasional events, and unable to benefit directly from larger crowds by collecting entrance money, the more flourishing of them could survive the change in leisure patterns. The new commercial courses, though, set up in the 1870s, enclosed, and charging for admission, soon moved to the free weekend afternoon. While there were still only 26 days of Saturday racing in 1888 (out of a total of some 220), their locations are revealing. There were three at each of the new courses – Sandown Park, Alexandra Park, Hurst Park, and

Kempton Park – three at Manchester, and others at industrial centres such as Nottingham, Leicester, Derby, and Liverpool.[18]

The manual worker was the first beneficiary of the free half-day, but the fashion spread. The Saturday afternoon closing of Lloyds in the mid-1850s[19] was a typical sign of the new relaxation coming to the commercial and professional classes. The austere mood of the early industrial days was undergoing a certain softening. The middle classes began to discover an enthusiasm for leisure activities in general and sport in particular, and to look for legitimate opportunities for both. Their increased involvement in organized play became a major contribution to the shaping of the sporting weekend since, as active sportsmen, they took their contests, whether in new sports or old, almost exclusively to their authorized leisure time on Saturday afternoon. Quite apart from its legitimacy, the habit of Saturday afternoon play was one that growing numbers of them had become accustomed to at their public schools.[20]

Cricket, for instance, saw several strands of interest at work in its timing of play. The first-class game might ignore the changes in working hours, dependent as it was as much on members' subscriptions as on gate money, and finding their membership lists growing rapidly.[21] The matches continued to start predominantly on Mondays and Thursdays, allowing for two games a week, but leaving the Saturday afternoon fare wholly to chance. There could be an exciting finish, a tame draw, or no play at all if the contest finished early. This last outcome was one that professionals were very alive to if they chose a Thursday game as their benefit match, and a scratch game would be hurriedly arranged to bring in the Saturday crowd.[22] For the club cricketer, though, it was legitimate opportunity, not financial consideration, which pointed to Saturday afternoon play. By the early 1860s, the number of clubs and fixtures was expanding rapidly, and the movement away from unofficial midweek holidays to Saturdays was already marked. Within twenty years, the great majority of games were taking place at the weekend.[23]

Football followed the same pattern, but even more decisively. The southern clubs, who made the running in the early organization of the game, had no alternative calendar tradition to compete with and played on Saturdays from the beginning. Of sixty-two matches notified by *Bell's Life* in the winter of 1867/8, all but seven were on the weekend half-day.[24] It was a habit which went from strength to strength. In the month of October 1875, for instance, only one out of forty fixtures was on a day other than Saturday,[25] and by this time *Bell's Life* had its 'Football notes', which were reporting that 'there is every evidence that the game is steadily asserting itself and rapidly becoming the most popular of winter pastimes'.[26] The other new and growing middle-class sport, athletics – aggressively amateur, to distance itself from the ill-repute of professional

*16 Midland Athlete*, title page, 1 October 1879. The advertisements indicate the considerable, but not yet complete, displacement of sporting events from Monday to Saturday (National Centre for Athletics Literature) pedestrianism – was also overwhelmingly a weekend sport from the start, and not, incidentally, by any means only a summer activity. There were fifty-six meetings advertised in the first three months of 1879, all but three of them on Saturdays, and virtually all classed as 'ordinary' runs, that is, not competitions designed for spectators.[27]

Sport was clearly not merely changing its occasions. It was changing its nature, developing a whole range of emphases, not all of them in harmony with each other. The interaction between sporting time and sporting style was to have far-reaching consequences.

## THE RESHAPING OF SPORT

The principal agents in the movement of sport to Saturday afternoons were, on the one hand, the entrepreneurs and promoters who saw a potentially profitable audience, as yet uncatered for, and, on the other, the newly released middle-class players presented with a sanctioned playing time. The mismatch between the two main progenitors of the movement of sports to the weekend was bound, in an acutely class-conscious age, to bring its difficulties.

For most of the century the sporting activities of the working class had been steadily deserted by those with pretensions to respectability.[28] The rising business and professional men found little time or inclination for forms of play that smacked of idleness, disorder, and the feckless speculations of gaming. The aristocracy, sensing the new climate of seriousness, chose either withdrawal or discretion. Hunts became more exclusive, and Newmarket more and more isolated from the general racing scene. Even cricket, the one game which, through the early Victorian years, preserved both a degree of acceptability and broad social participation, retained its own class consciousness. There were the leaders and the led, the gentleman batsman and the journeyman bowler. None the less, the cricket field remained the one playing arena where the classes were likely to contend regularly both with and against each other. Apart from the absence of real will to bring the classes together (and in spite of the praise for the few organizations, like the National Rifle Association, that did so)[29] there was no assured leisure occasion on which the meeting could regularly and legitimately take place. If the white-collared classes chose to take a day away from their ledgers and their bargains, no one weekday was better or worse than another. Club cricket fixtures, for instance, in the pre-weekend days were spread fairly evenly through the week.[30] Any worship of St Monday was lukewarm.

As the diverse social groups now began to share a common and regular free time for play, it seemed necessary to define how they should play together – or how they should play apart. Some sports

110

chose to draw formal distinctions between one player and another, but within the same game. Others simply barred one section of society in their rules, or achieved the same result through their organization in closed clubs.

The crude response of some middle-class sportsmen was just to exclude working men by their rules. Competition with the plebs was seen to hold dangers – particularly that of loss of face by defeat. The privileged classes were not content to rely solely upon their better life-long nutrition, larger frames, and greater leisure chances. There was even a certain reasonableness in deciding that a man who earned his living rowing a boat, and spent all his working life doing so, could not compete on fair terms with a gentleman rower for whom this was an occasional recreation. There was, too, long historical precedent – boatmen and amateur rowers had always had their separate races for a century past. It was not, though, left at that. The bar was extended to cover all who had ever done manual work or had worked for wages. It was the strictest possible distinction between the professional and the gentleman amateur, and it had its appeal for other sports.[31] Not that formal delineations were always necessary. The social order could be equally well preserved by exclusion – on grounds of cost, class, or caste. The new sports of croquet, lawn tennis, golf, and (initially, while machines were still expensive) cycling, lent themselves to the formation of self-regulating clubs, where the like-minded could protect their play from unsuitable social contamination.

They were neat answers to one side of the 'problem' of popular recreation. It was not a problem created by the free Saturday afternoon – indeed the free afternoon eventually provided a reasonably acceptable outlet for popular sporting passions – but the availability of leisure time common to all classes brought it to a head. The consequences have remained with us. In rowing itself, the extreme definition of amateurism continued undiluted until 1937, and 'professionalism' was only limited to those who had actually raced boats for money in 1956.[32] It was a form of sporting apartheid that was bedevilled with contradictions, which made, for instance, a post office clerk an amateur but a postman a professional. It excluded J. P. Kelly, the future American ambassador to London and father of Princess Grace of Monaco, from the 1920 Henley Regatta – and when he was already the Olympic sculling champion![33] Such contradictions in the rules and practices relating to amateurism involve, even in the same sport, differences between one country and another, as well as between different sports. Mid-Victorian cricketers complained that Australian 'amateurs' on tours made more out of them than they did, and it was certainly more costly to take a team of amateurs to Australia than it was to take professionals.[34]

The professional cricketer was a familiar sporting figure. Occasionally he could, like Arthur Shrewsbury, be a highly successful business man, but the professional was generally kept firmly in his place by his employer. It was not uncommon, even in the 1930s, to hear on some county cricket ground a young amateur order a test-playing professional to bowl at him in the nets, or even fetch his gear. When football became commercial, and the choice was between professionalism and schism, the association game adopted the former road, taking its model of player control from cricket. Rugby split into the Union and League codes – and the split was not over paying players to actually *play*, but over compensation for working *time* lost by playing. The interplay between work patterns and the sporting calendar continued to reveal new dimensions.

The case for acknowledging all sport as open is now unanswerable. At the international level there can be few sports which are truly amateur and of these – particularly some women's sports – they are so usually from necessity rather than choice. Otherwise, only an unworthy fiction keeps up the pretence of amateurism. Athletes receive five-figure sums just to appear at meetings, on the thin argument that they will not have the benefit of it (apart from such essentials as luxury cars and vastly expensive houses) until their competing days are over. Rugby Union is a rich sport, and remains more nearly honest than most, but even sympathetic commentators have acknowledged that in Wales at least it smacks of professionalism.[35] Twelve-metre ocean-going yachts are laughingly said within the sport itself to be sailed 'by the best amateurs money can buy', while in show jumping it is the horses who are the professionals – they win the money, not the riders!

The pro/am question was just one issue brought to a head by the coming of the shared sporting Saturday afternoon. The free half-day did much more than reflect changing employment needs – it confirmed and hastened changes which were already taking place in the nature of sport itself. New expectations from sport had been making themselves gradually more apparent over the past half-century, and the half-day holiday suited these developing themes. The only wonder is that the process was so lengthy, and that awareness of what was happening was so incomplete at the time. Even as the FA Cup was being launched, an editorial in *Bell's Life* on 'Winter amusements for the people' was lamenting the absence of any winter sport.[36] Certainly, with the cockpits closed, pugilism at its last fugitive gasp, and play hounded from the streets by the police, the city-dweller was left for several decades with only poverty-stricken leisure choices. With no history of regular daytime winter leisure, there was no tradition of acceptable winter play to draw upon. It was inevitable that the people's winter sport would have to find a new form, simply because there was no existing alternative.

Unfavourable contrasts have been made between the sport that emerged in later Victorian years and the earlier, pre-industrial play.[37] Its

112

constriction in time and space, its confinement to fixed occasions, and its sharp separation from work have tended to be seen as the simple consequences of the changed shape of leisure time. The transitional years were certainly years of sporting deprivation for many, but the new pattern of half-day weekend leisure was, in fact, in long-term harmony with changes that had already been taking place in many popular sports themselves, and over several past decades.

Popular play in Victorian Britain resists easy analysis. More than at any other time, there was not one working class, but many. The range of tastes, ambitions, and achievements among the workers became wider and wider, and the gulf between the skilled man in one of the premier industries and the destitute slum-dweller became increasingly unbridgeable. A letter to the press in 1832 (calling for a Fast Day, to lift the cholera epidemic) is revealing – it argued that 'the sober and industrious workmen of all classes' were probably outnumbered in the capital by 'those who are dissolute and idle', and that the 'difference in habits constitutes one great line of separation which will for ever prevent a cordial union between the careful and the negligent classes'.[38] Subsequently the skilled and semi-skilled benefited disproportionately from rising wages and shorter hours,[39] while the disadvantaged became further depressed and confined. The ranks of the 'sober and industrious' grew in both numbers and aspirations, and it amounted to more than just curtains at the windows, linoleum and rugs on the floor, and possibly even a harmonium in the corner. It involved a wholesale reaching for a more ordered way of life. There was a leaning towards new leisure tastes and new sporting styles. The old pursuits struggled on in the city ghettos or behind the coal tips – dog-fighting, the occasional rough prize-fight between locals, rat-killing, and pitch and toss[40] – but the majority of the working population began to move to more contained, more regulated, and less socially objectionable sporting events.

The former tendency for sport to expand, to stretch itself over a whole day or more, was already under pressure when the Victorian age began. While attacks on free time were prime movers in the change, new sporting expectations were also beginning to play their part. The old characteristics of sport were losing their appeal. Their dependence on strength and stamina more than skill, their acceptance of unequal matching and the remorseless grinding down of the defeated, without constraint of time, their deep and often dubious entanglements with stake money and gambling – all these became less and less satisfying. The growing taste was for more than mere sensationalism. It was for equal competition, unsullied by financial consideration, for speed and skill as much as strength and endurance, and so for shorter, time-limited contests. The long agonies of the vanquished, whether the man who had fought for two hours or the horse that had raced for fifteen miles, became less and less part of sport's appeal.

Two of the long-standing spectator sports, horse-racing and cricket, were already responding to new preferences by the 1830s, and football would take on the new shape from its very beginnings as an organized sport. The turf remained sullied by sharp practice and suspect gambling until well into the second half of the century, but it was moving away from the lumbering long-distance racing which could engage a horse over three heats in a day. Younger horses were running shorter distances, at much greater speeds, and usually with closer finishes. More horses were being raced (the number more than doubled between 1830 and 1865),[41] cards were fuller, and the day's programme was handled with much greater efficiency, with an eye on the time of the last train home. Cricket's transition took on a different sequence. Gambling and cheating began to course less freely through the game's bloodstream, and its early reformation concentrated on these impediments. William Lambert was banned from Lord's for allegedly throwing a match between MCC and Nottinghamshire, and gambling was formally banished from the ground in 1825.[42] Round arm bowling brought new zest and skill to the game in the following seasons,[43] and by the 1840s the timing of first-class matches was becoming more reliable, with play from 11.00 or 11.30 a.m. to 6.00 or 7.00 p.m. Cricketers, though, were never easy servants of the clock, and although the MCC began to fine tardy professionals in 1848, complaints of dilatoriness in starting county matches were still being heard well into the 1870s.[44] The transitional state of the game in mid-century was reflected in the domination of the professional touring sides, travelling up and down the country for games against local teams. Their activities flowed with one sporting tide, the recreational enterprise being shown by the small-scale commercial provider, but went against another, the growing taste for balanced competition. They gave many thousands of spectators a view of the famous, but their visits eventually palled. The enthusiasm of club cricketers to act as chopping blocks for the touring professionals could not be endlessly sustained, nor could that of spectators to watch local stalwarts being beaten out of sight.[45]

Divisions between the professionals themselves (particularly that eternal division between north and south, still never far below any sporting surface) hastened the end of the touring era, but more fundamental was the steadily rising interest in county fixtures. These combined local allegiance with keen competition. Early symptoms of such new expectations among cricket supporters had already come from a surprising quarter – the interest shown in the apparently exclusive sporting contests between the universities of Oxford and Cambridge and, later, and even more esoterically, in the Eton v. Harrow game.

114

Begun in relative obscurity, but played annually from 1838, the university cricket match had become a matter of national interest by the mid-1850s, with attendances of above 2,000 a day. By 1871, when turnstiles were installed at the ground, the crowds were numbering between 8,000 and 12,000 daily, and queues were forming outside the gates from 5.00 a.m. onwards, which, of itself, discounts the view that attendance was merely a social obligation of the elite.[46] Queuing at dawn was not a middle-class habit. People were doubtless drawn to Lord's by the same curiosity that had taken their forebears to the Artillery Ground, to watch the titled and the wealthy at their play. There was, though, more to it than this – what spectators had come to recognize was that here was competition between relatively equal sides, a contest fairly arranged which would, by the standards of the day, be fairly resolved. The keenness of the university matches fed this appetite – there was not a single overwhelming victory for either side between 1855 and 1871, at least half a dozen had close finishes (that in 1871 was won by just two runs), and there was no draw at all.[47]

It was sport in the new mode, shaped by new leisure times and new leisure tastes. That other annual contest between the universities, the Boat Race, particularly began to draw the crowds after the close finish of 1856, when Cambridge won by only half a length. Significantly, the next year's race was moved at short notice from Friday to Saturday, 'in order to prevent disappointment among gentlemen desirous of watching this interesting event',[48] and thousands assembled along the banks of the Thames in spite of the drizzling rain.[49] Here again was an evenly matched contest, free from financial interest as it had been from its first rowing in 1829, when such unstaked events were rare. *The Times* remarked in 1867 on the race's continued avoidance of betting, in spite of its rising popularity.[50]

The late Victorian sporting world was ready for football. Its eventual shape and style were almost predetermined by the new expectations of those it would entertain, either as players or spectators. Football was already a time-limited game, fitted by the schools into their afternoon session. It would be played by teams of equal numbers and would have its set rules to ensure fair play. It would enlist local enthusiasm and local support, interested in victory, but only if the victory was won through keen competition.

The winter Saturday afternoon was there for it to occupy.

## THE SABBATH RAMPARTS

It was, though, only Saturday afternoon that was on offer. There was no intention of opening up the whole weekend for play. Part of the justification for the Saturday half-holiday was, indeed, that it would free the Sabbath from all secular activities, by giving an opportunity for playing, buying, and selling on the previous day.

The ebb and flow of Sunday sport down the ages is a subject which calls for full and separate consideration. The role of play on one whole day of the week, a seventh part of human life and a much greater part of commonly available leisure, has ramifications too diverse to pursue in an overview of the whole leisure calendar. Its significance here lies in the part that Sunday was to have in the new weekend.

From their beginnings, the spectator sports had seldom ventured into Sunday play, and this irrespective of the ban in the 1780 Sunday Observance Act. It would have given unnecessary added offence to activities already dubious in their status. Victorian Sabbatarians saw only occasional danger from the spectator sports and their first leisure targets were traditional amusements such as feasts and fairs which had a long-standing tendency to spill over into Sunday. Lingering Sunday wakes celebrations were put down in piecemeal fashion in the 1840s.[51] Race-week fairs had the habit of setting up their stalls on the Sunday before and these proved more difficult to control, but only Epsom at the start of Derby week was still giving nagging offence by the end of the century.[52] Informal Sunday cricket, of the sort encouraged by the Reverend Edward Pusey, from the reviving traditionalist wing of the church, and impromptu football playing were gradually worn down and by the 1870s, just, incidentally, as the Saturday half-holiday was becoming widespread, the Sabbatarians might well have been tempted to feel that, on the sporting front at least, victory was in their grasp.

There were weaknesses, though, in the Sabbatarian armour. They were much more conscious of what was a dying threat from the old amusements than they were of new sporting attractions which would soon encroach upon the Sabbath. Moreover, their spearhead, the Lord's Day Observance Society (henceforth LDOS), was dedicated to the over-riding Christian obligation to keep Sunday holy and would never accept the modest concessions which could have won wider support for its parliamentary attempts to secure tighter Sunday observance. The LDOS inspired four Bills between 1833 and 1837, all backed up by highly organized petitions from the country at large. They were comprehensive measures, reminiscent more of seventeenth-century Puritanism than of a land in the throes of the Industrial Revolution. Had any of the Bills become law they would have undoubtedly caused contemporary deprivation as well as displeasure – they were popularly dubbed 'Agony Bills', after their promoter, Sir Thomas Agnew – but their long-term effects would not have been drastic. They were essentially backward-looking. Their specific bans on cock-fighting, dog-fighting, baiting, hunting, and shooting, and on fairs and wakes on the Sabbath, do indicate that these activities were still likely to give offence, but the further attempt to leave no leeway for transgression, by barring 'any pastime of public indecorum, inconvenience or nuisance', would have been a weak barrier against the sports of the future. Their characteristics, at least in intention, would be decorum, convenience, and the absence of nuisance.[53]

However, the Bills failed and the LDOS both nationally and through its local branches henceforth worked through individual prosecutions, direct pressure, and well-orchestrated petitioning.[54] There would be no active support from government for new legislation. After the Hyde Park riots of 1855 against the stopping of Sunday band concerts – itself a sign of the poverty of alternative Sabbath recreation – governments were more fearful of the simmering discontent of the populace than of Sabbatarian complaints, and ministers left such dangerous issues alone. Legal restrictions on Sunday behaviour had gone far enough.[55] Railway companies were allowed to operate on Sundays, in spite of every parliamentary attempt to insert limiting clauses in the Acts authorizing them. Sunday rail excursions were soon in vogue, and the London to Brighton Railway even made an early declaration of the coming of the weekend when, in 1857, it offered 'Saturday to Monday' excursion tickets.[56]

As well as the lack of positive government support, another problem for the defenders of Sunday was the changing nature of recreation itself. Sport was becoming respectable. It had been easy enough to ban sport from the Sabbath when its presence on any day of the week was such as to make it more or less objectionable. One of the many elements in sport's rehabilitation was its careful avoidance of Sunday for organized play, but once its reputation was on the road to repair, sportsmen, if they had the means, were prepared to outflank the ramparts of the Sabbath. The LDOS itself had left the door half open for them, since one of the flaws in its moral stance had always been its readiness to accept the Sunday labour of domestic servants and to take no action against the Sunday opening of West End clubs. Now, the middle classes, the very founding fathers of the English Sunday, took advantage of these concessions in their new sporting enclaves – the private clubs for croquet and tennis, and then (more daringly, because it could not be hidden behind high walls or hedges) their golf. No sooner, then, had the Sabbatarians driven most of the remnants of the old recreations from the Lord's Day than they had to meet these new and more insidious sporting incursions, less dramatic and less disturbing of the peace than the old, but moving now with the social tide and the rising leisure preferences, not against them.

It was working-class recreation which suffered and middle-class sport which took the first benefits. The relative purification of the old sports and the rise of new ones, free of inherited taints and now with legitimized occasions, meant that even churchmen could once more feel able to foster the people's play, but the growing urge to extend those occasions was one which the middle classes were much better placed to exploit.

They were, for instance, more exposed to Continental influences, with the surge in European travel.[57] *The Times* might fulminate in its news pages against a Sunday steeplechase near Paris, largely patronized by English visitors,[58] but it always gave the results of French horse-races, identifiable only as Sunday events from their datelines. The less tender readership of *Bell's Life* was left in no doubt that these were Sunday meetings, and the *Racing Calendar* carried a Continental Supplement in which they were unblushingly identified.[59] The general lesson taught by Europe, to all but the most die-hard, was that Sunday sport did not of necessity produce wholesale debauchery in other directions.

At home, the middle classes found new leisure horizons. They were the people best placed, financially or by inclination, to take up the new recreations. Cycling, for instance, leapt into popularity in the 1870s, and given the initial high cost of machines it began as a middle-class pursuit. Cycling clubs mushroomed, and soon weekend tours were regular features of their programmes, tempering their Sabbath intrusion by allowing a space for attendance at morning church.[60] It was – typically – at the popular level, where cycling quickly became a competitive spectator sport, that the LDOS stepped in, tackling the proprietor of the Lilley Bridge Ground when a marathon race extended over the whole weekend.[61] There were 230 cycling clubs in Britain by 1880 for those for whom cycling was a recreation, and the Cyclist's Touring Club's membership of over 20,000 some ten years later was claimed to be the largest athletic association in the world.[62] All the LDOS could muster against the mass weekend excursions were attacks on churchmen who cycled to church themselves, or who fell short in their condemnation of Sunday riding.[63]

Tennis also found the means to grow, and again as the preserve of the middle classes, and with the freedom to choose its occasions. Easily hidden from public view, its clubs soon took Sunday play in their stride, some in the face of local objections, like the All-England Club at Wimbledon which 'declined to sacrifice the convenience of its members to the Sabbatarian prejudices of adjoining occupiers'.[64] Sunday golf, though, was bound to face more systematic opposition. The LDOS always showed more concern over public Sabbath-breaking than over private violations, and it was in the nature of the game that any evil example could not be hidden from view.

Golfers, though, in their private clubs, on their own land, were in a strong position to defend their right to play at will. There was no national governing body to be pressurized, and the LDOS was wisely

118

advised by learned counsel that attempts to prosecute Sunday golfers under the old Caroline Acts would be 'beset with doubt and weakness'.[65] The resort had to be to individual lobbying of the autonomous local clubs, and up to the turn of the century the Sabbatarians probably won rather more of these battles than they lost. Thereafter, with the tide running steadily in favour of Sunday play, and Edwardian Britain prepared to loosen a button or two of its moral waistcoat, more and more golf clubs were opening for the whole of the weekend. By 1909 the LDOS was keeping its spirits up by listing its successes in keeping links closed on Sunday, in a mood quite alien to its earlier expectations of total victory, when it was the occasional set-back which preoccupied its committee.[66]

Where Sunday activity in the newer recreations was kept most effectively at bay was where it had either a commercial element or took place on publicly owned premises. By preventing Sunday play on the West Hampstead Tennis Courts, which could be hired, or on the London County Council's golf courses,[67] the Sabbatarians further underlined the class nature of their pressures, however incidental this might be. The original jibe of Sydney Smith, nearly a century earlier, that such societies were 'for the suppression of vices of persons whose income does not exceed £500 per annum'[68] remained substantially true. Some of the expansion of Sunday pleasure did nevertheless spread more widely across the social spectrum, and some of the prohibitions did affect all classes alike. Sunday angling became increasingly popular from the 1870s, with special trains taking London fishermen down to the Sussex rivers,[69] and rambling shared a similar growth. Sunday, the one full free day, was the time for the town-dweller to rediscover his lost countryside, now accessible by the railway and the bicycle, whose benefits extended, as it became more affordable, to people like Kipps, H. G. Wells's shop assistant. On the other hand, ice-skating, on new commercial rinks, and wide in its social appeal, came under fierce and sustained attack when the rinks opened on Sundays. The proprietors side-stepped the 1780 Act by creating clubs for Sunday skating, only to fail eventually through mismanagement and financial insecurity.[70] The opening of public baths on Sunday mornings was a safer proposition. Cleanliness was, after all, next to godliness, and it was hard to make distinctions between those who chose to wash and those who chose to swim. Many shared the practice of the Hanley Baths in the Potteries, opened in 1873, and available on Sundays from 7.00 to 9.00 a.m.[71] The habit became so deep-seated that an early Sunday morning trip to the corporation baths remained, during a working-class childhood in the 1930s, the sole sporting pleasure the day had to offer.

More broadly, the pattern of the weekend that had been set by 1900 remained substantially unaltered until the 1950s, that is until Saturday became a full day's holiday for most, and Sunday restrictions began to collapse. The weekend, like much of sport itself, had become delineated on class lines. The scope for the full weekend was confined to tennis players, golfers, yachtsmen, and continental travellers. Sabbatarian attacks had driven further nails into the coffins of such dying spectator sports as pedestrianism, driven back in the last decades of the nineteenth century to spectacle and exploitation through gruelling long-distance events at the Agricultural Hall and the 'demoralising exhibition' of women pedestrians performing non-stop over the seven days of the week.[72]

Most of the newer sports entered the twentieth century unscathed by Sabbatarian attacks and enjoying a measure of calendar freedom through the whole weekend. Significantly, it was the one new game which enjoyed mass support that found itself strictly confined to Saturday afternoon. In an age when the visibility of sin tended to give more offence than the sin itself, it was inevitable that football should be kept away from the Sabbath. The new middle-class sports were primarily participatory activities, not yet drawing large crowds, and certainly not with any frequency. It needed the one high point of the tennis year to bring 3,500 spectators on the Southern Railway's special trains to suburban Wimbledon in 1885,[73] when weekly crowds of 10,000 were already flocking into the town centre football grounds. Such invasions were too reminiscent of the urban throngs which had at last been banished from the Sunday streets in their old form. They stood no chance of reappearing in any new. This, though, was not the only reasoning behind the Football Association's Rule 25, with its stark instruction that 'Matches shall not be played on Sundays within the jurisdiction of this Association', a ban which applied not just to Villa Park and Bramall Lane but also to the humblest village ground where the crowd might amount to no more than three men and a dog.

Social control played its part. Football did, after all, rise to popularity at a time when fears of anarchist outrage were fanning the embers of unease among the ruling classes over all mass plebeian gatherings, and there was a general disposition to put it under as many constraints as possible. Restricting its occasions was one such limitation. But there were more immediate and less subterranean reasons for keeping football as a Saturday sport. Players were unlikely to want to play on two successive days, nor, at the commercial level, would the spectators be prepared to pay gate money twice. And if there was to be only one day's play, then, religious considerations apart, the whole tradition from their schooldays led the first Home Counties players to Saturday afternoon. Thereafter, as the industrial areas won their half-day, they eventually found a game near to their own sporting inclinations whose major occasion already coincided with their own free time.

120

There was, too, the force of religion. The churches of all denominations had become widely involved in the new people's game – Wesleyans with Aston Villa, Congregationalists with Everton, and the Church of England with many, from Bolton to Southampton.[74] The links might be little more than nominal, and were often short-lived, but the sport was set from the start on a course which kept it firmly away from Sunday play. If any further guarantee were needed, it came from the character of the men who took over the organization of the game and the concentration of nonconformist sentiment in the regions which soon housed its most illustrious clubs. The administrators were either the products of successful business enterprise in these parts, or stalwarts like A. F. Kinnaird, old Etonian, vigorous player, a leading administrator of the game for over twenty years, and a strong life-long supporter of all Sabbatarian causes.[75]

Thus, football's role in the sporting weekend was strictly rationed. The Football Association's ban on Sunday play was only finally withdrawn in 1981, making it almost as enduring as the statute law restrictions themselves. In this respect the game exemplified the relatively static nature of the English Sunday and the weekend of which it was part. There were considerable extensions of leisure time for all classes between the 1870s and the Second World War – shorter hours, Bank Holidays, and annual holidays, often with pay – but no alteration in the basic shape of the weekend, nor in the type of sporting opportunities it offered. To remain with Association Football – the FA continued to issue strong warnings to its County Associations through the Edwardian years over countenancing Sunday play,[76] and the relaxations of wartime were immediately withdrawn with the return of peace.

There was widespread hope after the ending of the 1914–18 war that the modest concessions over Sunday play would be sustained. They had been poor enough compensation for the general wartime reduction of leisure through long overtime and the loss of holidays, and the relaxations had been mild – football matches in army camps, Sunday meetings of rifle clubs, and Sunday baseball played by and for American troops.[77] The Sunday Games Association, set up in 1919, sought to build on the wartime experience but it enjoyed few successes beyond the opening of the LCC's public golf courses on Sunday (the end of a campaign covering a quarter of a century)[78] and there was an extension of Sunday cricket, though established clubs still often disguised their Sunday teams under another name.[79] Outdoor activities certainly expanded, and increasingly spread over the whole social range – Sunday remained a favourite day for cycling, and for rambling which, as 'hiking', became a major feature of the 'Keep Fit' national campaign of the 1930s. And every town still had its quite unofficial plebeian sports in some unobtrusive corner, like the Sunday whippet-racing on the marshes of north and east London.[80]

Whatever formal progress was being made towards the extension of the sporting weekend came to a halt in the mid-1920s, as the General Strike signalled a change in the national mood. All post-war hopes were finally shelved, including the hope for a full weekend open to sport. The occasional *cause célèbre* of an Eric Liddell or a Dorothy Round highlighted the sustained spiritual strength of Sunday sporting abstinence among a section of the population – the one refusing to run in the 100 yards heats on Sunday in the 1924 Paris Olympics, the other compelling the ladies' final in the French tennis championships of 1934 to be delayed until Monday.[81] Such cases served to stiffen the conservatism of British social and sporting life in the inter-war years. Sunday remained available only to outdoor activities and to those participatory sports which were largely the preserve of the middle classes. The recreational opportunities offered by the weekend in the 1930s showed little advance on those of 1900. Leisure time expanded considerably in other directions, but it was as if the inherent Puritanism of the British establishment, amazed at its nineteenth-century liberality in granting workers an assured ration of regular free time, could not bring itself to increase that particular ration.

The establishment of Saturday afternoon freedom, though, still represented the greatest revolution in the leisure calendar since the loss of Sunday in the late sixteenth and early seventeenth centuries. Sport was given its legitimate space in the week – measured and constricted it might be, but it was guaranteed, and play no longer had to be stolen from the working week. And for all the restrictions that remained, and for all the class distinctions that divided it, the weekend often held a cohesion that was all its own. Sport might be on the rise, and religion on the decline, but the weekend could still embrace both. The crowds on the Kop and the congregations in the chapels and the churches once more enjoyed an overlapping experience, and a sizeable proportion of them were still the same people. The weekend would remain at the centre of the expanded and diversified leisure life that was to come. What would happen to the communal significance of its sports was another matter.

# 8

# The coming of the leisure age

The Bank Holiday Act of 1871 formed a partial bridge between the old leisure world and the new. Most of the free time which it defined had long existed in custom, but had no precise sanction. Only the August Bank Holiday was novel, and this, like the Easter and Whitsuntide holidays, made its passing acknowledgement to tradition – it was located on a Monday, to become the only official marking ever made on the leisure calendar by that old and unsanctified saint's day. Leisure was being measured for its new clothes, more tightly fitting than the old, but of more substantial material, and soon proving capable of being let out, piece by piece. The addition of a Monday break on at least three occasions a year gave added recreational force to the already strengthening weekend. More broadly, the 1871 Act presaged the strong leisure growth that was to characterize the whole coming decade. After the extension of the Saturday half-day to practically the whole of industry, progress began to be made towards a midweek early closing day for shops.[1] The rising influence of trade unions secured widespread reductions in weekly hours of work from over 60 to 55 or 56.[2]

At the most skilled end of the work force, the ability to take a continuous break of several days was extending to the full week's holiday, with all the new horizons which that opened up. It was a process which was to gather momentum throughout the twentieth century, and remains the most potent dimension in the still changing shape of leisure time. That free time has expanded by fits and starts. Both world wars were followed by substantial reductions in working hours, and there was further significant shortening during the 1960s.[3] By the late 1980s, few jobs were demanding more than thirty-eight hours a week at most, often with flexible working. An earlier element in these reductions, especially during the 1960s, had been the disappearance of Saturday morning work, making that a full free day. With the parallel crumbling of restrictions on Sunday play – slower, but just as certain – the whole shape and nature of the leisure weekend began to change, and with it, once more, people's sporting expectations. And again, as in the mid-Victorian age, the providers of sporting entertainment were often slow to react to what was happening to a potential audience. In particular, 'sport for all', for women as well as men, and for the family as a unit, had been a social demand long before it became a campaign slogan.

Fundamental, too, to the changed use of leisure time has been its availability in more continuous form. Some trades had achieved a full week's holiday before 1914, but the great strides came in the 1930s. Even before the practice was given statutory force, many employers were granting the week's holiday with pay[4] – by the mid-1930s it was estimated that about half of London's working population was taking a full week's holiday, and in the northern mill towns, where the old parish wakes had hung on through all the generations of pressure, the wakes weeks, in their new form, were emptying the streets and silencing the cotton frames. It is a movement which has continued strongly in the second half of the century. By the 1950s two weeks' paid holiday had become normal. By the 1980s, four weeks was not unusual.

The nature of sport, throughout its history, has been deeply influenced by the time available to it. The dramatic changes in the access to leisure time during the past century could hardly fail to have sweeping sporting consequences.

## SPORT AND THE ENLARGEMENT OF LEISURE

The expansion of leisure during the first half of the twentieth century was, in both its scope and its style, such as brought benefit to the established spectator sports. They could cope well with the broadening opportunities which it offered. In the second half of the century, while sport and leisure pursuits in general have constantly widened their appeal, they have grown equally in diversity, and the older team games in particular have had to try to come to terms with a greatly changed leisure calendar and a transformed recreational market.

Gone, for instance, is the mass urban population that was once tied permanently, the odd day's excursion apart, to the doorstep of the local football club or the county cricket ground. With time has come mobility. The holiday away from home became an important addition to the ways of spending the increased leisure allowance. At first its effects were not dramatic. In the age of the single week's holiday, the train would take its tens of thousands to Skegness and Cleethorpes, to Margate and Southend, and soon, above all, to Blackpool. Once there, the holiday recreation was that of the rest of the year, but writ large, and given the added spicing of fun-fairs and piers, a summer show every night, the sands, and the sea. For the rest, it was the cinema, the public house, the possibility of a county cricket match during one of the many seaside festival weeks, or a coach trip for the day or half-day. It was all fine for a single week, but it was not likely to satisfy over several weeks, once holidays were extended and new possibilities were revealed through easier travel and added prosperity. Cheaper and faster air travel, and the spread of the package holiday, opened the doors first to Europe and then to the rest of the world. More and more overseas destinations were brought within the average citizen's purse and ambitions – Spain, Portugal, southern France, and Italy, and then further: Greece and the islands, Turkey, and the Seychelles, all with their firmer prospects of hot sunshine than ever the British resorts could supply. Longer vacations also meant that the popular search for winter sunshine began. What had once been the preserve of the wealthy became, in part, the retreat of the pensioner to long-stay, cut-price January holidays on the Costa Brava, avoiding both freezing weather and fuel bills. It became, too, the now widely enjoyed skiing holiday, made accessible through hired equipment and training beforehand at home on dry artificial slopes.

The nature of holiday-making became much more diversified once it no longer all had to be crammed within a single week or fortnight. There are opportunities for both strenuous activity and easy relaxation. The mill-hand of the 1930s was hardly likely to spend his precious week chugging a barge a few miles up and down the Grand Union Canal, though there was already a hint of what might come in the growing popularity of the more organized pleasures of the Norfolk Broads. Now there are few activities of either mind or body which have not been packaged into one sort of holiday or another, from caving to chess playing.

A recurring theme, though, in the history of sport and recreation has been the persistence of old habits in the timing and styles of play. It is too easy to be blinded by the presence of the new. Not only do the traditional wakes weeks often still exist within the holiday patterns of today, but also – and in spite of the travel agents' efforts to persuade otherwise – there is a continuing endurance in some of the older holiday patterns. Only one-third of all holidays are, in fact, taken abroad, some 15 millions out of 48 millions according to 1987 statistics.[5] Blackpool alone, it is worth remembering, still caters for more bed-nights than the whole of Portugal, and although 20 per cent of the population now go away on holiday at least twice a year, many people take no break away from home at all.[6]

Whether taken in Britain or abroad, the long holiday has taken up a considerable share of the added leisure available in the later twentieth century – and the part played in it by the major sports has been relatively insignificant. Sailing and the water sports, walking, rock-climbing, skiing, bowls, tennis, and golf are typical of the sporting activities that have benefited and little of the increased vacation time has gone to cricket, football, or even horse-racing.

The change in recreational styles was hastened, from the 1950s onwards, by the granting of the second instalment of the weekend. Within a decade Saturday morning work had ended in almost every industry, and the opening up of Sunday to sport had made its cautious start. It was a change that proved much more than a simple extension of leisure time. Coinciding as it did with a rapid expansion of car owner-ship and declining national fortunes in the major sports, it ceased to be the sporting weekend of pre-war days, predominantly male, predominantly local in its possibilities, and centred, as often as not, on the local football or cricket club. The weekend became everybody's recreation time. Wives, many more of them now working themselves, asserted their right to share its benefits, as they themselves began to share tasks such as shopping, which supermarkets began to make socially acceptable, even inviting, to men as well as to women.

The new leisure expectations, and the constantly growing number of alternative recreational opportunities, have posed repeated problems for the established spectator sports. They have had to compete for an audience which, for all its added leisure, was not apparently prepared to give any more of its time to spectating for which it has to pay. The audience wanted added sharpness in competition and presentation, especially as it became accustomed to the theatricality of televised play. Nor was it the spectators alone who demanded new satisfactions, as professional players started to seek a fuller share in their sport's profits.

Both football and cricket, the great crowd-pullers of the first half of the century, found the post-war world soon beset with difficulties. The early legislators of football had fitted it admirably into the compact freedom of the Saturday afternoon. The teams had been brought down to eleven apiece, its time had been reduced to the ninety minutes first laid down in Uppingham School in the 1860s,[7] and all in all they had found the archetypal solution to the problem of regular plebeian leisure 'through codifying sporting rules, which saved both time and space'.[8] It would have fitted equally well into the summer weekend as the winter, and did begin as a summer game in Scotland.[9] However, it was a winter game that was called for and cricket, now thoroughly socially acceptable, had too strong a hold on the summer sports calendar to be even questioned. Many soccer clubs, indeed, were founded originally to keep cricketers together and occupied during the winter,[10] and some of the early administrators were deeply involved in the summer game. Notable among them was C. W. Alcock, early Honorary Secretary of the Football Association, who was also Secretary of Surrey County Cricket Club; he became instrumental in drawing up the conditions for professionalism in the game, on the lines which had long applied to cricket.[11] Football was given its strict season, originally from October to March, and only spreading at its edges, through September and April and beyond, as fixtures and competitions increased. Rugby Union, true to its original purity, has resisted most of such extensions.

The near-monopoly of the winter Saturday afternoon enjoyed by soccer for over half a century induced a complacency among its British administrators which is still hard to disturb. As originators of the game, they kept their distance from the rest of the growing football world. As employers, they kept their players under financial control and governed their conditions in a fashion that few Victorian mill-owners could have improved upon. As providers of entertainment, they paid scant regard to the comfort of their customers – Wembley Stadium and Arsenal's Highbury remain practically the only major stadia not to carry substantial reminders still of their pre-1914 origins.

All of which left the game, after the Second World War, in a poor stance to face renewed international opposition. Once the post-war euphoria had passed, and the results of the national teams continued to disappoint, other ways of spending Saturday afternoon came to seem more and more attractive, and the crowds began to drift away. The occasional injection of new interest managed to keep the game alive. The ruthless fitness, iron determination, and simple methods of Ramsey's 1966 team, playing in England, brought success in the World Cup. Then, as the national teams slipped back into their customary second-rate performances, the achievements in European competitions of individual clubs such as Spurs, Celtic, and Liverpool, often with British teams, drawn from all the Home Countries, could still persuade the fans that not all pride was lost.

Further relief to the game came from another calendar change which released it from its heavy dependence on Saturday afternoons. Midweek night matches became a growing feature of the season's programmes. Attempts to play football under lights were almost as old as the game itself,[12] but effective floodlighting had been limited to a few leading clubs in pre-war days and was hardly taken seriously by the authorities. By the 1960s it had become an essential. Floodlit friendly games against leading Continental clubs pioneered the movement – aided by live television, which was kept sternly away from the Saturday games. The entry of British teams into European competitions and the introduction of the English League Cup brought lengthier fixture lists and made midweek games essential. Midweek now had to mean night games. One incidental result of floodlighting was that Saturday kick-off times could be standardized to a predictable 3.00 p.m., and not be brought forward to as early as two o'clock in December and January to catch the midwinter daylight. Another was the disappearance of the midweek afternoon game on the town's early closing day, traditionally the occasion for cup replays. They had seldom been the occasion for high attendances, and now the midweek closing day for shops was itself being eroded, with staff taking staggered full-day breaks, and that minor theme in the sporting calendar slipped quietly away. Monday night was the first favourite for floodlit games, though less out of deference to any pre-industrial tradition than to allay, when most such games were friendlies, persistent Football League doubts over any rivalry to their own competition by giving maximum time for recovery before the all-important Saturday match. As midweek matches became at least as important as any others – and often more so – they moved as near to the middle of the week as possible, to Tuesday or Wednesday, with little variation.

The coming of midweek football was both smooth and rapid compared with the sport's agonies over playing on the other day of the weekend. At first glance, it might seem surprising that the thoroughly establishment game of cricket should be the first major spectator sport to encroach upon the Sabbath, but not only was it following the Victorian middle-class example,[13] it had even more acute sickness to attend to than had football. Cricket had adapted its timings in the past, if usually slowly and belatedly. First-class matches, for instance, did not start on Saturdays until after the First World War, and until then play on the most popular day of the week was always speculative. The Saturday crowds saw some good finishes, but they also saw little or nothing on occasion. By the 1960s the game was in desperate need of resuscitation. Attendances at county matches had slumped from over 2 million in 1949 to a mere three-quarters of a million in 1965.[14] The one glimmer of light for the game was coming from the new one-day knock-out competition for the Gillette Cup, started in 1963. Limited-over cricket, with its assurance of a result, could clearly draw the crowds, and cricket's Sunday response was the same as Aston Villa's Saturday response had been nearly a hundred years before – a league, to provide regular play on the free day. The John Player League (again it was helped by sponsorship) coincided with the repeal of the old Caroline laws on Sunday observance, though this had little relevance beyond its indication of a change in the national mood.[15] Much more pointedly, it fell in with television's interest in covering the Sunday matches that had been played for some years by the touring International Cavaliers.[16] Gradually Sunday was seen to be available for any style of cricket – for County Championship matches and even, from 1981, for test matches, and the one self-denial of not starting before noon, in deference to churchgoers, appeared to be loosening by the late 1980s. It remains, though, the one-day, limited-over match that is the staple of Sunday cricket.

128

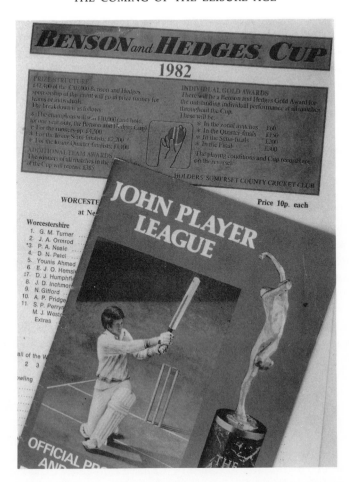

17 John Player League and Benson & Hedges Cup cricket programmes. In the 1980s, sporting sponsorship remained one of the most potent advertising opportunities left open to cigarette manufacturers (Author's collection)

Football showed much greater reluctance to invade the Sabbath. Even when the Football Association brought itself to rescind its Rule 25 to allow the thousands of amateur Sunday clubs into the fold, it had no intention of countenancing Sunday professional play. When Sunday league and cup matches were sanctioned in 1974, it was only as an emergency measure to meet the power crisis. The immediate appearance of success from the change cut no ice with the Football Association or the Football League. Gates for both cup and league games were generally higher, sometimes much higher, than the usual Saturday attendance, and there was a widespread impression that the dyke had

129

been breached. Correspondence in *The Times*, for instance, was heavily weighted in favour of Sunday play,[17] but the football hierarchy, true to its ancestral predilections, withdrew the concession once the industrial crisis was over.

Whether the soccer crock of gold glimpsed at in 1974 would have been turned into reality is hard to estimate. Germany, for instance, has not found any permanent benefit in Sunday play. By the time that it was permanently permitted in Britain in 1981, much had altered, both inside and outside the game. There was much greater competition for Sunday audiences, and football grounds have often become much less safe and attractive places. Other sports, particularly Rugby League in the north, had moved into Sunday afternoon, and by the time football was allowed, a typical Sunday afternoon was offering also Rugby Union, athletics, badminton, canoeing, fencing, hockey, cross-country running, ice hockey, real tennis, road running, and squash rackets.[18] While few of these might attract vast crowds, they do together indicate the wide spectrum of what had become available even in the formal sports, let alone in the growing variety of participatory recreations. Another major event, whose support would be assured, was also about to take up Sunday play – the Wimbledon finals would be played then, though this was hardly announced with the brashness of the club's original move to Sunday play for its own members. Now all was altruism. More people would have the opportunity to view on television, and the extra income would go to the general promotion of the game in the country.

The one sport whose Sunday prospects remained restricted was horse-racing. Newmarket had dipped its toe into the Sabbath waters with a charity meeting on 11 October 1981, which had further defied the weight of history by including on its card the sport's oldest set race, the Newmarket Town Plate, initiated by Charles II in 1665, to be run for on the second Tuesday in October.[19] The law, though, still kept the betting shops closed, and attempts to secure their opening, even on a limited number of Sundays, continued to fail in the late 1980s.[20] Otherwise, the sports grounds are all now effectively open, and open to sports of all sorts. The enfeebled 1780 Act, under which only the Public Prosecutor can take action, may nominally ban paid sport and entertainment from the Sabbath, but it is easily either side-stepped, by selling one-day club membership, or a programme rather than an admission ticket, or totally ignored. Yet the coming of Sunday play has, generally speaking, brought more choice to the people than profit to the administrators and promoters. Its main characteristic up to the late 1980s has been its occasional nature. Of the significant spectator sports, only Rugby League football has become a predominantly Sunday activity. No soccer clubs have moved more than the occasional game to Sunday, although one major game does now switch on most weekends in the interests of television, itself a deterrent against any other widespread Sunday fixtures. Even the Sunday cricket league brings no more than a maximum of eight matches (and usually fewer) to any single county ground in the course of the season, and other crowd-pulling Sunday events are for the most part scattered and irregular. Brands Hatch and Silverstone bring a few noisy weekends; Wimbledon has just two busy Sundays; major football matches are rare events.

Sunday has certainly become part of everybody's sporting weekend, but its fare remains quite different from what is enjoyed on Saturday. Indeed, some of the looked-for opportunities for Sunday play have evaporated, with the failure to capture consistent Sunday audiences for football or for test match cricket. Sunday continues its gradual transformation more through gradual secularization and commercialization than through the incursion of sport, and Sunday retains its distinctive social and domestic habits – the long lie-in, the late breakfast, cleaning the car, and digging the garden. What Sunday has done is widen the options open to the many who choose to take a trip out on Sunday afternoons, but it is more than likely to be a family trip, and the entertainment on offer has to be predominantly family entertainment.

## SPORT FOR ALL

The family nature of much contemporary recreation is a novelty. Not only has the leisure growth of the second half of the twentieth century added something approaching a quarter of all waking time to the area of free choice, it has also included among its beneficiaries the previously deprived half of the population, namely its women. The story of the sporting use of leisure time is largely a male narrative up till some 100 years ago. Stress on domestic virtues as against communal participation, first from the Puritans, and then from Methodists and Evangelicals, had modified the total nature of popular recreation, but their special denial had been directed at women.

The folk play of the Middle Ages had frequently involved both sexes. Both the contemporary evidence – much of it critical, from the reforming friars[21] – and later survivals of medieval calendar customs suggest that women shared with men such limited freedom for play as their lives afforded them. Dancing was universally popular, and like the May games played by youths and maids together, often involving some sort of chase, it was frowned upon for its invitation to carnality. There were, too, many specifically female sports, or sports played separately. Stoolball, shuttlecock, marbles (played by women 'as well as children', according to one account),[22] skipping, and racing were common female pursuits. The medieval woodcuts copied by Strutt to illustrate his history show women engaged in a whole variety of sporting activities –

131

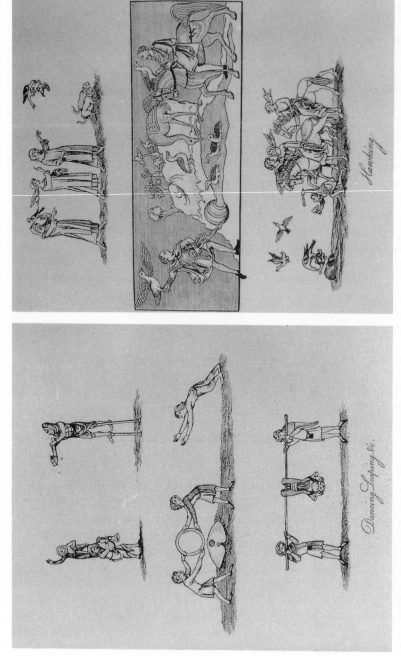

*18 and 19* Strutt's illustrations to his *Sports and Pastimes of the People of England* (1801), taken from manuscript sources, show women's participation in medieval sports hunting with bow and arrow, hawking, playing whip and top and a form of bat and ball, as well as performing acrobatics.[23] They were primarily for the young, but the more mature were not necessarily excluded. There was an old custom at Bury St Edmunds, for instance, at holiday times, for twelve old women to 'side off for a game of trap-and-ball, which is kept up with the greatest spirit and vigour until sunset'.[24]

Puritan attacks on the people's play were all the more furious where women were involved. The Puritans and their successors eventually produced an ambivalent attitude towards female play. It lost its openness and, like sex, moved uncertainly into a hinterland between the claims of purity and the frequent actuality of prurience in its male promoters and spectators. As with male sporting activities, however, it took the hard material demands of the Industrial Revolution, with its economic and social pressures spreading across all classes, to quash most of the female sporting liberties of the past. When it did so, the consequences were sweeping, with women's lives too constrained and their sporting traditions too fragile for them to find the alternative outlets which their menfolk contrived. Nor, by the majority, were such alternatives thought either necessary or desirable. The woman's place was securely in the home – that is, when it was not in the mill or the workshop.

The walls that imprisoned women's receational lives were only built gradually. Shakespeare's women still had their freedom to play bowls with men;[25] Pepys admired the lords and ladies at play together in the bowling alley at Whitehall, 'in brave condition', and his wife and the maid ran races for wagers – and that on a Sunday, too.[26] Eighteenth-century and pre-Victorian Britain abounded with sporting ladies – riding, hunting, shooting, going to races, to cricket matches, and even to prize-fights, while their less well-off sisters ran races for smocks, rowed, occasionally played cricket, and even fought prize-fights of their own. Margaret Evans had the reputation in her native North Wales of being 'the greatest hunter, shooter and fisher of her time', and not only that, but was also an expert violinist and joiner, and such a powerful wrestler that, even at 70, 'few young men dared to try a fall with her'.[27] There was the Countess of Derby, a dashing horsewoman who put the men to shame on the hunting field, taking fences that they baulked at,[28] and the lady sharpshooter from Lancashire who outgunned her expert brother.[29] Then there were the numerous lady archers who found at least local fame, and carried home prizes, for their skill at the butts. One reason, indeed, for the growing popularity of archery in the eighteenth and early nineteenth centuries, and acknowledged as such, was the rare opportunity it still gave for both sexes to enjoy respectable sport together.[30] There were twenty 'principal' companies of archers listed in the 1790s, and the number was growing year by year.[31]

There were few male sports which did not have their female participants at some time or another. Pugilistic contests were by no means rare, and they were often much more serious matters than mere street-corner brawls. They could have many of the trappings of the male ring, with their seconds and shouted odds. At one 'desperate battle' at Stepney, Mrs Ruff of Coleman Street beat the apparently well-known Moll Glass after 30 minutes, in spite of odds of 6–4 against her,[32] and at another, in Bristol in 1813, Charlotte York fought Mary Jones in formal style. They 'disencumbered themselves of most of their habilments and shook hands' before setting to, with 400 women there as spectators.[33] Ladies of the carriage class often watched male contests from a safe distance, and the doings of prize-fighters could be the main topic of conversation 'even amongst the most polite and *tender* circles', as they were before the Painter v. Oliver fight at Norwich in 1818.[34]

Female pugilism appears not to have survived the 1820s, in any formal sense. Their participation in rowing lasted much longer, and they were certainly rowing in regattas until the middle of the century. Women's races were features from their beginnings in the 1790s, highly popular, and often carrying prizes of several pounds. The women were regularly praised for 'their skill and prowess',[35] and while male facetiousness was always likely to break into the reporting,[36] there was the example of Grace Darling's rescue of shipwreck survivors to demonstrate that oarswomen were to be taken seriously. It was as rowing became consciously elitist in the third quarter of the century that women were inevitably squeezed out of competition, just as all but the gentry amateurs among the men were also excluded.[37]

The most sustained female sport was foot-racing. The prize was usually a holland smock,[38] hence their designation as 'smock races'. They were frequent and widespread, again until the mid-nineteenth century. So far as the promoters and the male spectators at these events were concerned, there was, to say the least, ambiguity in their motives. Male runners generally wore little, and women were often expected to do the same, and even at a time when the female breast was a much more public sight than it later became, press comment regularly mentioned the undress of girl competitors. The advertisement for a cricket match in 1744 promised the additional attraction of a smock race between two ladies who were to 'run in drawers only',[39] and reports of later races would refer to runners giving 'a full display of their personal charms',[40] or exposing, 'with their wonted generosity, those beauties which are easier to be imagined than described'.[41] While the interest in these races was not confined to the athletics, the competitors were often congratulated on their speed; the contests were keen, and often taken seriously enough to be run in heats.[42]

The moral ambivalence of smock racing was underlined by the

stipulations for entry when they formed part of feasts and celebrations, and were not specially mounted one-off events. They were commonly described as for 'virgins', or, in the terms of an advertisement for the 1797 Jubilee celebrations in Berkshire, for maidens 'whose characters are unsullied and persons impregnable'.[43] The tests for qualification must have been difficult, and it is not recorded why one of the five entrants for a race in Kent two years later was barred from competing.[44] That particular event was won by a lady well enough known to have the title of 'Folkestone Bess',[45] and there were certainly ladies who took part in more formal pedestrian contests, making wagers similar to those of their male counterparts.[46] When amateur athletics drove its wedge through the history of track and field, it was in professional pedestrianism that women made their first reappearance. There, like the men, they tended to become as much part of circus entertainment as of sport. By the late 1870s, women pedestrians, like the famous Madame Willetts, were undertaking the Barclay Match of 1,000 miles in 1,000 hours before paying spectators; 'demoralising exhibitions', according to the LDOS, particularly in their disregard of the Sabbath.[47]

Pre-Victorian women shared, by and large, in the leisure calendars of the males of their own class. For working-class youngsters of both sexes, childhood was brief, much of its play impromptu and rough and ready until they could join their elders. Even with the better-off, childhood was slow to achieve any distinctive status of its own – eighteenth-century family portraits invariably show the children as just miniature versions of the adults, even down to the clothes they are wearing. In play they were likely to be left to their own devices, or to the company of servants, and it was not until public school sport began to develop that it had any degree of formality or organization. The family at play was a social concept for future generations.

Working-class women, though they might nominally have the same free time as their menfolk, had the harder bargain. The meals still had to be on the table, even on holidays. Wealthier families, by contrast, gave the greater share of leisure to their women, given that there were servants to carry out all the domestic tasks. Jane Austen's females, with little to occupy their time but reading, gossip, and visiting, were well on their way to becoming the child-bearing ornaments of the Victorian bourgeois ideal. The leisure time available to women of all classes did begin to show some easing as the nineteenth century progressed, but it was at the very time when the sporting uses to which that leisure could be put were being all the more curtailed. On the one hand, the popular recreations which working women had shared with their men were being more and more eroded, while middle-class men, if they played at all, were withdrawing into their sports, few of which, apart from archery and possibly riding, were thought suitable for their ladies.

Women, who had been frequent spectators at practically every type of spectator sport, found themselves increasingly left at home. In the past, they had even been involved in organizing sports events on occasion, to little comment – the fact that there was a lady official at Blandford races in the early 1830s only came to light incidentally, by way of an acrimonious correspondence in the *Sporting Magazine* over the quality of the racing there.[48]

By that time, however, more and more complaining voices were being raised against the participation of women in sports, voices that would soon also even diminish their role as spectators. A report that two ladies had ridden round the course at Tiverton races in 1826 was dismissed as a falsehood, in tones which implied its impropriety.[49] Women's cricket, which had usually in the past been described in matter-of-fact style, and even admiringly,[50] began to be frowned upon as disreputable. The *Nottingham Review* in 1833 talked of women at a local feast 'so far forgetting themselves' as 'to enter on a game of cricket', though it does on this occasion appear to have been a somewhat bibulous affair. Even archery, so often praised by Pierce Egan and others for its suitability for both sexes,[51] began to have its critics so far as women marksmen were concerned. One admirer had asked, 'What displays the beautiful form of a female, or the robust frame of man, more than the elegant attitude attached to archery?' He had his short answer from the pseudonymous 'Orlando' who said that the ladies would be better 'playing on the harp, or dancing a minuet'.[52]

It was to such amusements that they were mostly reduced, until croquet and badminton began to rescue them from the drawing room and the parlour in the later part of the century. For more and more Victorian women, their leisure life became more and more confined, in opportunity if not in time. They were pushed further and further into life's margins. The tradesman's wife no longer partnered him in his business, but took on the privileges, and the constraints, of the lady. Domestic service became the fastest growing Victorian occupation,[53] and, as Cunningham has aptly put it, all but working women became 'more the objects than the subjects of leisure',[54] their sporting opportunities extending little further than being paraded at Ascot, or at Lord's for the Eton and Harrow match. The effects of social and economic change on the recreational lives of working-class women are much harder to summarize, as they varied substantially from place to place and from decade to decade. For instance, gangs of women field workers were common in the earlier part of the century, but diminished as farming methods became more efficient and mechanized. And whether income of her own was compensation enough for lost time, and possibly an unemployed husband as one of its consequences, is difficult to estimate. Certainly, having their own money in their purses gave the rough, tough, pit-bank girls of the Black Country, who sorted the coal on the surface, in all weathers, the independence to frequent the Darlaston beer shops, drink their pints, swear and smoke their pipes, and share in such local sports as dog-fighting.[55]

Such freedom as working-class women managed to secure in the nineteenth century – and they shared, for instance, in the benefits of the railway and its family excursions – was always bought at a price. The rising expectations of home comforts and higher living standards, across the whole social range, put an added strain even on the non-employed women, let alone those with both job and house to manage. Each had to fight the grime of industry, battling with litle human or mechanical help to keep the house clean, often struggling to achieve, within her own limits, those standards she had been trained to in domestic service before marriage. It was not until well into the 1950s that housewives widely began to be released from such drudgeries as wash-day, which, with the washing, drying, ironing, and airing, regularly lasted from Monday to Wednesday. It was only then that a real release into measurable leisure became possible.

When women's physical recreation did revive in the later nineteenth century it did so gently and cautiously. When women began to take again to sport, their new play lacked the characteristic female features that had often marked it in the past, when, for instance, stool-ball and shuttlecock were recognized as primarily women's games. Their new play tended to be an imitation of the men's, in whose footsteps they trod, a generation or more behind. The technicolor of the male sporting world became the pastel shades of the female version. The slow general emancipation signalled by the Married Women's Property Act of 1881 was accompanied by the gradual dawning of new leisure freedoms. Walking became respectable, skirts less cumbersome, and even cycling was a possibility, giving not only some physical exercise but also a degree of social release – a lady might even venture out alone.

Inevitably, the more privileged were the first to benefit. As middle-class Victorians rediscovered leisure and play, the rising tide of female ambition was directed towards the sporting amusements closest to home, to such family games as badminton (originally an indoor game for the vast saloons of great houses), archery, croquet, and lawn tennis. Dress, though, remained a barrier to any vigorous exertion – the original women tennis players had to hold the racquet in one hand and the hem of the skirt in the other – and it was not until the early years of the present century when gymnasts began to move into short trousers, lightweight cotton suits, and dance dresses, that physical freedom for women's play became feasible. Hobbling skirts were less of a handicap to energetic players in golf than in most sports. Pioneer lady golfers were playing from the 1860s, but progress was halting and when the

GEORGE and CUMMINGS on the mark for the World 10-Mile Professional Championship, at Aston Lower Grounds, Birmingham, October 2nd, 1886.

George's Trial on the same Ground Ten days before the Race was 49 min. 29 sec.

PETER CANNON,
One of Starters and Mackintosh Keepers.

NATHAN MATHER,
Cummings's Friend and Supporter.

W. CUMMINGS,
Holder of the 10-mile Prof. Record, 1889.
*Time, 51 min. 6 sec.*

W. G. GEORGE,
Holder of the World's Mile Record, 1886.
*Time, 4 min. 12 3/4 sec.*

P. H. SHAW, I.A.C.,
George's Friend and Trainer.

W. SNOOK,
One of George's Supporter. Amateur Opponents.

GEORGE ATKINSON,
Editor *Sporting Life*.

20 *and* 21 Two illustrations of the total male domination of athletics, both professional and amateur, before 1914. (*Above*) World Ten-Mile Professional Championship, October 1886. (*Below*) Birchfield Harriers National Team, 1912 (National Centre for Athletics Literature)

Ladies' Golf Union was founded in 1892 it was estimated that there were fewer than 2,000 women players in Britain as a whole.[56] Competitive golf saw the first women's championships a year later, and women began to be admitted to male clubs, usually given a midweek day on which they had some priority. The male golfers though, where they had asserted their right to Sunday play, seldom shared that with lady members!

The women players, as in most male-dominated sports, had to accept a subordinate role, which they often underlined with an inappropriate conservatism of their own making. It was an attitude not dissimilar from that of the early spectator sports towards Sabbath breaking. They raised enough frowns already, so why should they give avoidable added offence? Such was the mood that prompted the Ladies' Golf Union to 'regret' Miss Gloria Minoprio's departure 'from the normal golfing costume' when she appeared in the 1933 championships impeccably attired in a high-necked sweater and smartly creased trousers.[57] The style soon became fashionable, aided, as was so much sporting freedom for women especially, by wartime conditions. Once peace returned, such dress was commonplace.

Women's golf became professional in its highest reaches, a spectator attraction which can offer rich rewards. It still poses, though, the question that pervades many women's sports. Is it the same as the male game, or a different one altogether, because its dimensions are not the same? Physique produces differences in performance levels even in most of the games played to common rules, such as cricket and tennis. The fact that women international cricketers are of much the same standard as the best male club players may also, in part, be due to lack of early opportunity, but the difference has limited the spectator appeal of the sport. Attempts to make the women's game saleable even started in W. G. Grace's day when the 'Original English Lady Cricketers' at first drew some five-figure crowds,[58] but interest lapsed and the doctor, while allowing that they had not burlesqued the game, could not see cricket as suitable for women. However, his claim that 'they had their day and ceased to be'[59] was true only of the professional venture. Women's cricket flourishes over much of the world as an amateur sport, with its financial ambitions largely limited to raising enough money to pay players' touring expenses.

There were other old-established sports that did bring women more equal opportunities. Bowls, for instance, was never barred to women, other than for the ill-repute it carried with it in some periods of its history, and was an acceptable enough ladies' game by the start of this century for the London County Council to reserve one rink on each of its greens for their use. Women's clubs date from the same time, the first county association (Somerset) was formed in 1928, the English Women's

Bowling Association in 1931, and its Scottish counterpart in 1936.[60] By the 1980s women were proving the equal of men in open competition. Then there is the example of the fearless hunting women of the past to inspire women jockeys to achieve on the turf the same pre-eminence with men that they have for long enjoyed in the show jumping arena. New mechanical sports, such as car racing and rallying, are also without any specific sex advantage and have from their beginnings presented opportunities to women, sometimes taken, often ignored.

Male sport has had a long history of professionalism and audience satisfaction. Such elements in women's sports belong almost exclusively to the latter half of the twentieth century, and have centred particularly on tennis and athletics. In terms of the singles and doubles events open to them, women and men had come to be treated equally in the Wimbledon tennis championships by the time of the First World War. After it came Suzanne Lenglen, as revolutionary in her play as in her costume. In her loose, one-piece, calf-length dress, she served overarm like a man, and dashed around the court with a marvellous aggression. With her, women's tennis moved into the entertainment world; although her own move to professionalism was largely as a result of a misunderstanding with the Wimbledon authorities and the crowd, it pointed the way to the future and her American contract for $100,000 was a promise of the rewards that were to come for women players. Once tennis became an open sport, however, it took more than ten years for women's prizes to match up to those of the men. The American, Billy Jean King, hoisted the reputation of women's tennis when she beat the aging Bobby Riggs out of sight in the Houston Astrodome in answer to his boast that men players were in a different league from the women. This brought nation-wide publicity to the female sporting cause, although all it proved was that a woman champion at the peak of her career was too good for a faded male veteran, and her real achievement was to lead the campaign for equal prize money for women in inter-national tournaments. The women were still meeting objections from the Wimbledon Committee even in the 1980s – on the grounds that they played fewer sets than the men and that, in the earlier rounds, their matches were less popular.[61] She was instrumental, too, in persuading the Phillip-Morris Tobacco Company to sponsor a new all-women's tournament – the Viriginia Slims – which since 1970 has given ladies' tennis a distinctive status of its own, as well as sharing the limelight of the men's game.[62]

The early years of this century saw a rapid expansion of events for women in several sports – skating from 1906, hockey from 1902, and badminton from 1900.[63] It is unsurprising that the Olympic movement, given its usual inbuilt conservatism, did not introduce women's events until the 1928 Amsterdam meeting, and then the British refused to

141

compete as there were only five of them. Some justification might be found in the comparative novelty of organized track and field for women – effectively, on the national scale, women's athletics only emerged in the early 1920s, another of the many consequences of the revolution in both female dress and female manners brought about by the war years. Significantly, one of the notable first women's contests was a 4 × 100 yards relay run by members of the Women's Royal Air Force at Stamford Bridge in September 1918.[64] It has since taken long struggles to bring women's events into parity with men's. Long-distance races were still being excluded up to the 1980s, there is still no steeplechase or triple jump in the Olympics, and, in the sport generally, appearance fees for distinguished women athletes are well below those given to men.

While the extension of the women's role in the spectator sports has made steady progress, particularly after the feminist movements of the 1960s, it is still dogged by anomalies. Women's advances have been more assured in activities which are primarily recreational, and where there is little discrimination, sports such as skiing, on both land and water, horse sports, sailing, scuba-diving, sailboarding, and the like. In sports such as these, the question of sex remains largely unasked, and the extension of opportunities here can reasonably be expected to embrace both sexes in catholic fashion. What does remain a problem for sport in this, one of its major dimensions, is the question of which sports should be classed as unisex, with men and women competing against each other on equal terms, and which demand separate contests. And if the competition is to be separate, why should women slavishly follow game forms which were originally devised by and for men? It is the sort of issue which male sport has had to face within its own confines in the past. Early pugilism made no distinction between large fighters and smaller ones – the classification of boxers by weight came in only gradually throughout the nineteenth century. Closer competition between racehorses was secured by handicapping.

It will doubtless be left to the twenty-first century to see the emergence of a distinctive women's sporting world, equal to that of men, overlapping with it, but with its own characteristic elements and offering something beyond synchronized swimming.[65]

What are the limits to the expansion of leisure time, and to the diversification and development of the sports that can reasonably be expected to fill a sizeable part of it? Daylight, as a requisite for play, has already gone by the board, altering the British sporting calendar in the process. Floodlighting made European club competitions possible in football by providing new night occasions and a simple addition to existing national programmes. The lights revived cricket in Australia in a novel night form which can draw nearly 100,000 spectators to the

Melbourne Oval. The debate is on over whether real grass is necessary for sports whose pitches began as fields, and whether arenas have to be open to the elements. And dispensing with daylight, grass, and weather makes the disappearance of sport's traditional seasons a relatively minor matter.

As time for play has expanded, so distance has contracted. Sport is world sport. A random issue of *The Times*, on what would once have been a quiet day in January, has Sheffield Shield cricket from Australia, Shell Cup one-day games from New Zealand, skiing from France, basketball and ice hockey from the United States (the latter the world junior championships, from Alaska), and tennis from Australia and New Zealand.[66] It is the outward sign of the deep change that has brought sport into everybody's lives, and brought it there largely by television. Sport no longer has to be sought – the greater effort is needed to avoid it. In making the leap, too, sport itself has changed, sometimes fundamentally. For the last two and a half centuries, sport has had its two faces, the actuality of the real competition and the creative picture which reporters have painted around it. The division between the two was pointed out long ago when a defender of the prize-ring noted that actual fights were invariably less violent and bloody than press descriptions of them. Now the reality and the media message come together, sharing the same instant in time, and the two have become fused, perhaps even confused. Sport has become box-shaped, and we have to question where the true reality of it now lies.

# 9

# Instant sport and open season

One of the wonders of the 1930s was the live radio broadcasting of great sporting events. To listen in to the action as it happened made for indelible memories: the penalty that gave Preston North End the FA Cup in the dying seconds of the 1938 final and, earlier, Hedley Verity spinning out the 1934 Australians on a sticky wicket at Lord's. Nor did the wonder stop there. It began to reach across the world, making nonsense of time of day or season. There was the crackling radio commentary on dark winter's mornings telling of test matches in Australia, or, just before the war, Tom Goddard taking a hat trick against the South Africans as families sat down to their Christmas tea parties.

The records show, alas, that the specific cricket memories from the 1930s did not come from live commentaries at all, but from summaries of the play – the BBC reporter was still not even allowed to broadcast from Lord's itself, but had to dash across the road to a makeshift studio in a nearby cellar! The news, though, had the stamp of immediacy, and memories are diligently worked upon by later experience, hence the hazards of oral history. What was important was that the contest and the news of it had come together in time. Through the whole past history of organized sport, the wider audience, away from the direct action, had to wait for its information about the happenings. Now there could be instant participation, instant involvement. The time-lapse between the play itself and the news of it, already nearly bridged in shorthand by the electric telegraph a century before, had been quite eliminated. It only needed the picture to come at the same instant as the sound to utterly eliminate the interval that had always existed between the sporting contest and the mass appreciation of it. Now, with the picture – coloured, concentrated, and dramatized – our sporting lives have taken on a different scale. Instant sport has condensed the whole competitive world into a corner of our living rooms. In destroying time, it has annihilated space as well. There can be darkness, fog, or snow outside, but live bright sunshine and cricket or athletics inside the house.

No less dramatically, sport itself has been changed. It has gradually had to come to terms with television, and increasingly the terms have been those set by the medium, not by sport itself. Sport has had to fit into programme schedules and the demands of advertising, and more than that, it has even had to modify its own nature to fit into the shape of the television screen. It has become more and more box-shaped. And who are now the spectators? What is now the totality of the sporting event? Arguments over the distinction between players and spectators have often been overstated, in so far as sport is considered as a social phenomenon, and not as a possible means to health. Now they pale into insignificance when the vast majority of spectators are watching a screen, miles away from the event itself. Where, even, does the reality of sport now lie? Sport, from one viewpoint, has always belonged to a fantasy world, a world of transposition and imagination. Is what we now see on our televisions the ultimate product of the sports industry, with the live action the lesser reality, the playing-field just the studio floor from which the producer selects and assembles to build the most dramatic story?

It is, after all, only the speeding-up of a long-established process, rendered all the more revolutionary by the potency and immediacy of the new medium. Sports reporting has always interpreted actuality in its own current terms, has stressed what it deemed exciting, has raised expectations in spectators, and taught them to find what they were led to anticipate. The report has often been more gripping than the event itself, as the early nineteenth-century defender of the prize ring noted.[1] The radio commentator shares with the press journalist the same freedom to excite, unhampered by having to match his comments to any visual experience of his listeners. For him no horse-race need be a pale procession, no boxing match a mere maul, no football game a formless chapter of errors. It was a tradition that the television producer was bound to follow, learning how to overcome his visual ties to the event by growing subtlety and sophistication.

The time-lapse between the sporting contest and the public perception of it may have been reduced to the split second of a radio wave, but there is little that is entirely novel in the emphases chosen by its reporters or presenters. A look at a single newspaper in a single year – the *Universal Daily Register*[2] in 1787 – shows how little has changed in method, no matter how much the news has been speeded up. The *Register*'s sports reporting was then generally easy-going. Only where the sport was also a social event did its news appear within forty-eight hours – racing at Newmarket or Ascot, or royal hunting excursions.

When the Prince of Wales was present at the Mendoza v. Martin fight, it was reported two days later, though the usual gap was up to a week.[3] Reports of more distant or less prestigious race meetings could be very slow – Hull after a couple of weeks, Kelso after three, and even nearby Guildford had to wait a week for its results.[4] Cricket, too, was seldom reported until three or four days after the end of the game. Yet there was much in the reporting that foreshadowed the future of sporting journalism. There were advertisements for future events, and the stoking up of interest in them, especially in the Humphries v. Mendoza fight, as the two men went into training. Odds were being quoted for the 1788 Derby, six months away, and sporting gossip was already in fashion – Captain O'Kelly (owner of Eclipse) was moving his stud away from Epsom, and Tring, the boxer, was appointed sedan chairman to his patron, the Prince of Wales.[5] Statistics had hardly gone beyond crowd numbers, stake money, bets, and scores, but sponsorship was already there, for racing on the Thames, and for both professionals and amateurs.[6] There were the perennial problems of crowd control, with the new cricket ground at Marylebone high-fenced to 'keep out improper spectators', disputes over rules in sailing matches, and

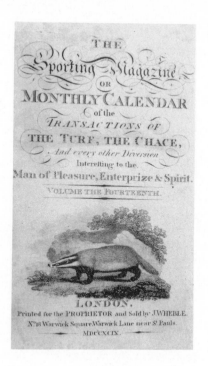

22 The *Sporting Magazine* was one of the earliest specialist sporting publications

suspicions of malpractice in coming prizefights.[7] And there were the usual sporting dramas and disasters, duly coloured in the reporting – the pugilist whose head was 'beaten almost to a jelly', and the almost inevitable collapse of a grandstand, this one at Preston races, where out of 200 injured at least 50 had broken limbs and, though there were no deaths, many were seriously hurt.[8]

Sport and the media were already beginning to thrive on each other. Sport provided copy for the press, and the press coverage in turn fed the appetite for more sport among its readers. By giving space and publicity, the press was, however incidentally, arguing the case for sport and strengthening its claims on time. In 1792 the *Sporting Magazine* was launched, expressing astonishment that among all the journals by then available there was not one 'expressly calculated for the sportsman'.[9] The magazine, whose monthly issues ran to some 20,000 to 30,000 words each, reported the whole gamut of sporting events from archery to bull-baiting, and from singlestick fighting to fives. It gradually discarded the less socially acceptable activities from the 1820s onwards, until by the middle of the century it had become very much the journal

23 The *Sporting Magazine* published its own Racing Calendar, which was often fuller than Weatherby's

of the landed gentleman, concentrating on the breeding and riding of horses, and the killing, in one form or another, of most other creatures. For the first forty years of its history, though, the magazine was a steady defender of popular recreation and sport, and by the time it withdrew into the upper-class preserves, *Bell's Life in London* had long taken over the role of prime reporter and instigator of the country's organized play. Its close-printed pink broadsheets were packed with weekly results, accounts of play, odds and fixtures, gossip, and a spicing of titillating or sensational court reports. Sport, particularly through the pen of its most famed reporter, Pierce Egan, brought a lurid extravagance into the language itself, one that Charles Dickens was to harness and tame to his own ends. Egan gave the sports report an almost independent existence, to the later despair of those who searched for the hard matter through the florid language and personal prejudice. The sporting press was conscious of its influence on sport itself – in his evidence to the Lords' Select Committee on Gaming in 1844, Vincent Dowling, the editor of *Bell's Life*, had neither doubts nor reticence about his paper's role and quoted the case of cricket (a safe game in such company) whose popularity and spread he put down to his reporting of the game and the achievements of its players.[10]

VINCENT DOWLING (EDITOR OF *BELL'S LIFE*).

24 Vincent Dowling, editor of *Bell's Life in London*, was the most influential of the early Victorian sporting journalists (From Henning's *Fights for the Championship*, 1902)

# FOOTBALL ECHO

## and Sports Gazette

No. 843

WEYMOUTH, SATURDAY, SEPTEMBER 8, 1962

PRICE: 2¼d.

# Terras can only blame themselves for defeat

WEYMOUTH ...... 1     BATH CITY ...... 2

WEYMOUTH'S hopes of a near full-strength team for the return Southern League game with Bath suffered a set-back when Cliff Nugent cried off this morning.

but there was no penalty despite appeals.

**CARTER 'BOOKED'**

Then the irrepressible Fogg brilliantly controlled a loose ball, killed it for Bevan, whose drive was inches wide.

Still, despite the shooting disappointment it was stirring stuff for the crowd—although at times feeling crept in and the referee lectured players on both sides.

From a corner by Court, Gill last season's Torquay first-teamer, punched clear from three white-shirted challengers.

Carter voiced his opinion by

after three minutes. Robertson beat three men, hit a low centre into the middle where Hobson deflected it off Langman's foot for a corner.

A minute later it was Bath's turn. A 50-yard free kick by Sheppard was deflected by centre-half MacFarlane and Gill just managed to turn it away for a corner.

From this Fogg nodded into the goalmouth and Dixon, only a yard from goal, missed the ball—and laid himself out by heading the goalpost!

The horrific finishing went on

25 Even relatively small towns could publish a Saturday Football Special edition of their daily evening newspaper, though some, like this from Dorset, failed to survive the television age (*South Dorset Evening Echo*)

The electric telegraph was by then bringing the result of the game to the public much more quickly, and by the closing years of the century the new mass football following had its special Saturday night sports papers (often pink, green, or buff, according to local taste!) appearing on the streets within the hour at the end of play. Many of them remain, but gone are the private telegrams with pre-paid replies that used to be sent to sports grounds by those keenest to keep up with the scores.[11] Sports news, though, was kept in its place in the general press. Only major scandal, usually involving bribery,[12] or an international issue such as the body-line controversy, usually spilled over into the news pages. Even in the sports pages the choice of news could be odd. Few of the readers of the mass-circulation *Daily Express* would, surely, on Friday, 24 January 1936, have been much concerned to know that Keble beat Lincoln 2–1 at soccer, or that Brasenose won 17–3 against Oriel at hockey in Oxford college games, though this information appeared in its brief results section.

Radio's entry into sport was spasmodic. Commentaries on the two major football codes began early – in 1927, H. B. T. Wakelam found himself broadcasting a rugby international one week, and then at Highbury for the soccer match between Arsenal and Sheffield United on the next Saturday, in both cases with an anonymous voice placing the play in a numbered square according to a grid printed in the *Radio Times*.[13] Cricket, where the ball-by-ball commentaries on 'Test Match Special' have since become almost a national institution, was thought too slow for live commentary, and the cricket authorities were equally unenthusiastic. When at last the BBC was granted a commentary point at Lord's it was at square leg, the least appropriate place for seeing what was happening,[14] and rather worse than trying to commentate on baseball from the bleachers. Actual commentaries remained a minor element in sports broadcasting through the 1930s, when it could include such esoteric offerings as fifteen minutes of the final of the Ladies' Individual Darts Championship. Short talks were the staple sporting fare, often of regional interest. Although television had arrived it was limited to small, flickering screens within range of London and its social impact was minimal, as was its sports coverage. In Easter week, 1938, for instance, the only televised offerings were two fifteen-minute judo demonstrations, though the following week fared better with the soccer cup final in full, Herbert Sutcliffe demonstrating to cricketers 'How it's done', and, lest it should be thought that sanity had returned to Broadcasting House, a quarter of an hour of a darts match between the BBC and the Press Club.[15]

Three events marked the spread of television and its influence in Britain. They were the coronation of Elizabeth II, which boosted the sale of receivers, the coming of competition with the launch of Independent

Television, and the introduction of colour in July 1967. Coincidentally, coronation year also saw one of the most exciting of football cup finals, which stirred the sentiments of the country by bringing a winner's medal to one of its best-ever players, the veteran Stanley Matthews, who inspired his team to a gripping second-half victory. Even in black and white, the cup final was drawing over half the population of the British Isles to their screens, and television's sporting revolution was beginning.

Faced with the prospect of commercial competition, both the BBC and the sporting organizations began to realize the value of television rights. Nominal fees – even in some cases just the payment of admission charges for broadcasting staff – became a thing of the past. The BBC set aside a quarter of a million pounds for new contracts, and effectively left Independent Television with little beyond the doubtful delights of professional wrestling.[16] Colour, in its turn, gave television sport a major boost. It made horse-racing intelligible even to the uninitiated who saw the jockeys' colours for the first time, it had the dubious advantage of making snooker a television possibility, and its entrance was celebrated by long coverage of Wimbledon on its first day. The expansion of televised sport and the viewing audience since then, and often on a global scale, is a matter of everyday experience. Ten million viewers for 'Match of the Day' (an abridged soccer telerecording on Saturday nights) was a matter of wonder in the early 1970s,[17] but it pales before the potential 250 million viewing figure across Europe for a live league football game between Arsenal and Liverpool in January 1988, and an actual viewing figure of the same size for the year's Superbowl.

There could be no surer indication of television's power in the diffusion of sport than the presence of American football in the British ratings. This, with a game that was virtually unknown in the country before the 1980s! The demand for instant sport – and, in spite of rising fees, its frequent comparative cheapness – has brought a whole new panoply of activities into the national sporting consciousness – show jumping, ice-skating and winter sports generally, darts, and snooker. Rugby League has been released from its Lancashire and Yorkshire heartlands, while tennis, golf, and athletics are no longer minority interest sports. Until the 1980s, the process of diffusion was a virtual monopoly of the BBC. ITV could see so few opportunities in its early years that it essentially abandoned sports to the other channel – 'sport' does not even appear as a programme category in the *TV Times* until the spring of 1957. Gradually ITV made its way into horse-racing, and pioneered some motor sports such as autocross, but the really innovative sports coverage came from the new commercial Channel 4 in the 1980s, when all possibilities had apparently been already exhausted. By looking particularly to major overseas events, Channel 4 brought

151

a new international dimension to British sporting television. Its conspicuous success with American football has encouraged ventures, with varying success, into Australian Rules football, baseball, volleyball, basketball, handball, and others.

Television has affected sport in many ways, and for both good and ill. It was often seen originally as a threat, undermining the live audience figures, and continues to be looked on with suspicion by football's administrators. Television took most of the blame for the reduction of traditional sporting crowds in the 1960s, though growing recreational choice was probably just as strong a factor. Particular sufferers were horse-racing, where live television found an ally in the legal betting shop just round the corner, while even the 1966 World Cup victory could not save soccer from steady long-term decline. And sport made by television can equally be deserted by it. There are already indications that snooker, and particularly darts, are losing their share of television time. The hypnotic effect of the green baize table with its sequence of coloured balls can disguise the limited possibilities of the one, though these are still infinite compared with the images presented by the other of distinctly unathletic figures attempting to target a treble twenty space about half the size of a postage stamp.

In both sports, the individual performer is the absolute focus of the camera's attention. Televised sport lives off the sporting 'personality'. Cool professional skills from an undemonstrative player can be much less compulsive viewing for the non-expert – and the vast majority must now always be so – than erratic brilliance from an unpredictable one. The cult of the personality has been extended to the team games much more emphatically than in the pre-television days, with one or two individuals becoming the centres of attraction. Their behaviour away from the sport is as newsworthy as that within it. Journalists of all persuasions now hound all major sporting events, no longer leaving them to the sports reporters, who may well find themselves out-numbered by 'investigative' journalists, scandal scrapers, and gossip columnists, with every other specialist imaginable called in for an opinion, from the diplomatic correspondent to discuss the international implications of some incident or other to the medical authority for the latest discourse on drugs. There were more than 8,000 media folk covering the Los Angeles Olympics in 1984, and that was more than ever reported at any of the world's major political events.

It was a reflection of the internationalization of sport produced by television. One of its effects has been that local conditions are no longer the only arbiter of timings, which must take account of viewing audiences over the world. The Mexican World Cup was played in the blazing, breathless afternoon, rather than in the comparative cool of the evening, to cater for prime-time European television, while one of the

MONUMENT TO JOHN JACKSON IN BROMPTON CEMETERY.

Thomas Butler, *Sculptor*, 1847.

Vol. I.

*To face page* 102.

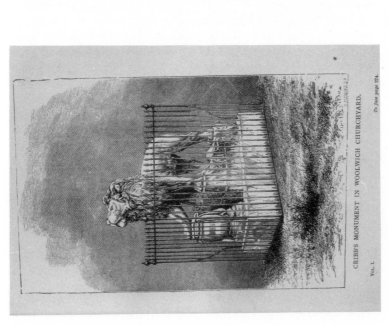

CRIBB'S MONUMENT IN WOOLWICH CHURCHYARD.

Vol. I.

*To face page* 274.

26 *and* 27 The sportsman as hero – the lion image in memorials to prize-fighting champions: (*right*) to John Jackson in Brompton Cemetery and (*left*) to Tom Cribb in Woolwich Churchyard (Etchings by W. Thomas, from H. D. Miles's *Pugilistica*, vol. I)

attractions of the United States as a future world cup venue is the possibility of catching large audiences on both sides of the Atlantic with later afternoon kick-offs. Then, too, there are games which are timed solely and specifically for the television cameras, and kept separate from the regular fixture day – the Monday night football game in the United States, or the Sunday afternoon soccer match in Britain.

The day is significant. The widespread acceptance of Sunday play in sport, for all its continuing technical illegality, owes much to television initiatives. It encouraged proliferation by its promises of coverage, as when the new BBC second channel was looking for Sunday afternoon programming and Sunday League cricket provided it. This came on the full tide of change in Sunday sports coverage in the mid-1960s. In 1964 the programmes were still very restricted with, in the whole month of May, just fifty minutes of recorded rugby from South Africa and a thirty-minute commentary on the French lawn tennis championships. In the same month a year later there could, on occasion, be sporting events on both channels – on 16 May, for instance, there was live international soccer, Sweden v. England on one, and the usual cricket on the other. When the BBC began its Sunday 'Grandstand', a full sports programme, in the early 1980s, it did so without the usual fanfares, and it passed off without protest. It was the signal that Sunday was now as much a sporting day as any other.

Instant sport and the open season are already with us. Is it, though, the same sport that existed in the pre-television days? Has, perhaps, sport itself been destroyed, as some would suggest,[18] by its forced alliance with the camera and the screen?

Certainly television has materially altered many sports, as well as altering the perception of them. This, though, is no novelty – it is the pace and extent of the change that is new, not the process itself. For a century and a half the press exerted important influences on the nature and organization of sports. The concept of a 'world championship' was originally prompted by Regency pressmen at the time of the Cribb v. Molyneux fight; the county cricket championship was only formally set up after several seasons during which the sporting journals had published their own (and sometimes conflicting) rank orders. The term 'test match' was also a product of the imagination of writers and journalists rather than of players or administrators.[19] Television therefore entered a tradition of sports reporting that had already not merely recorded play but had also, in some important respects, modified its development. The new possibilities and the new restraints of the instant moving picture were bound to influence how games were played. The telephoto lens and the instant replay could take the viewer to the heart of the action, and repeatedly so, in slow-motion. On the other hand, the inflexible shape of the screen, and the demands of programme schedules, set their own new limitations.

28  An example of inter-war newspaper sponsorship of sporting events: London to Brighton Relay Race, 1939 (Programme cover, National Centre for Athletics Literature)

The action replay is a powerful weapon for holding the viewer's attention: it is his or her means of reliving triumph or disaster, or of disputing the referee's decision with a greater knowledge than the official's own. The living game in the stadium can even seem less real than that presented by television, unless there is also a large public screen on which to relish immediately the crucial moment. Time is captured, and brought back at a touch, and in American football at least the referees are now prepared to resort to this captured time to check on their own decisions. Generally speaking, though, whether or not the viewer is granted an instant replay is a decision made quite outside the game, by the producer, who in large measure creates the game that is seen on the screen. He or she selects the images, decides where to concentrate attention, what to highlight, and what to omit. It is the television producers and presenters who can make or break a player or a manager – and usually do so under the safe mask of anonymity. The cricketer, Emmot Robinson, once said to that most lyrical of sports writers, Neville Cardus, 'Ah reckon, Mr Cardus, tha's invented me.' The impact of television has been to make such invention – or destruction – commonplace over all the media.

Television is primarily entertainment, and sport, to hold the viewers, must entertain as widely as it can. The old cynical press dictum that no newspaper ever lost money by under-estimating the intelligence of its readers is always in danger of being applied to television, and to televised sport. The camera relishes action, it lingers over it, particularly over violent action. It looks for incident, extravagant personal expression, the head to head confrontation. The man against man conflict of the boxing ring is applied to other sports, whether valid or not, and made the essence of the competition – the bowler against the batsman, the pitcher against the striker, and, less realistically, pitcher against pitcher, captain against captain, goalkeeper against goalkeeper, quarterback against quarterback. The individual is plucked out from the team because he is more manageable and presentable than nine, or eleven, or fifteen happen to be.

Television, too, now controls the tempo and timing of the game. The pace of American sport, for instance, precisely fits the pattern of television advertising in the short breaks that constantly punctuate its football code and baseball. The continuous play of soccer and rugby make both hard to transpose to such an advertising system, but they sit comfortably within the British pattern of fewer and longer commercial breaks. Television had to apply little pressure to existing practice, beyond persuading footballers to take a rather longer half-time interval to allow for two commercial breaks. It has, though, exerted powerful influence on the format of other games, particularly one-day cricket. The Sunday afternoon John Player League was essentially television-shaped

– it was predictable and confined as to time, from 2.00 to 6.30 p.m., it had an assured result, weather apart, and both weather and the state of the wicket were given much less consideration than in the first-class game.

Ironically, with much more Sunday sporting fare to choose from, television has since given up its full coverage of these games, concentrating now only on the last half-hour or so of each innings, when the play is usually at its most hectic. Through its fostering of one-day games, though, television has played a large part in altering the game itself, in all its forms. Fielding has become a much more essential skill. The bowler who could hardly see, the batsman too heavy to run or with too weak an arm to throw – all are liabilities that teams can no longer afford. Bowlers learn that saving runs is at least as important as taking wickets, while batsmen have to learn to score from the start, not just to survive.

Other sports were also given their new television times and shapes. Rugby League found a regular television slot through a floodlit knock-out competition in midweek, again cigarette sponsored, and again subsequently relegated in the broadcast schedules, so that it moved to weekend play. A television audience was weaned for snooker on another weekly competition, the single-frame play of 'Pot Black' for a knock-out cup, until it was ready for the much more extended coverage of long tournaments. Other sports have had their indoor versions encouraged by television. Bowls, in particular, lends itself well to artificial surfaces, and presents a much more predictable package to programmers if played indoors, away from the weather, and unconfined as to its season.[20] Indoor tennis and athletics also bring release from time and calendar, and, at a less ambitious level, six-a-side soccer and indoor hockey have suddenly found themselves with national audiences.

To what extent then, has the control of sport passed from its governing bodies to the television companies? There must be several answers. A sport like rugby union found television an easy and early partner. With no recognized salaries to pay its players, and only dependent on gate money to a limited extent for most of its games up and down the country, it soon realized that television fees for internationals and other major events could make it financially independent of any possible sources of public funding, and free to pursue whatever policies it chose in relation to its own game and to the rest of the world. From the start, television cameras and commentators, quite unlike their reception at Lord's, were given prime viewing positions at Twickenham. Association football, by contrast, saw television as an implacable opponent, the scapegoat for its falling attendances. Edited recordings on Saturday nights were as much as it could stomach, until at last the

157

authorities recognized that they needed the publicity of television rather more than television, with ever-expanding world-wide sporting opportunities at hand, needed football. It was a bitter lesson to accept for a ruling body whose autocracy over the generations almost passed belief, and whose practices in relation to its players had flouted most of the rules of natural justice.[21] It took the threat of leading clubs to break away and form a super league, in alliance with television, to persuade the Football Association and Football League to reach agreements which brought live cup and league football to the screens on Sunday afternoons.

The governing bodies are now in uneasy control of the major sports. In large measure, their control is subject to the co-operation and acquiescence of the television companies, who prefer to have complaisant organizations providing their sport for them, rather than having the responsibility for it themselves. The example of the 1977 cricket 'rebellion' is there to demonstrate that the latter is quite possible. It began in Australia, but soon spread over the whole cricket world, and it sprang immediately from the issue of television rights. The publishing and television magnate, Kerry Packer, was cut out from carrying the Australia v. England test series. His radical response was to recruit players from all over the globe for his own newly created World Series Cricket Organization. The salaries he offered were enough to make players defy the threats of life bans from their national ruling bodies, and the new organization remoulded the game specifically for mass appeal to both live and viewing audiences. It was not only the name that was redolent of transatlantic practice – Melbourne cricket ground came to look much more like Yankee Stadium than Lord's, with teams in coloured track-suits, a white ball, and presentation designed throughout to heighten the sensationalism of the play, already fired up by the high bonuses on offer for victories.

Although Packer handed back the game to the cricket authorities after a couple of years, in return for the television rights he had always sought, the whole episode showed the power of television companies to assume control of the sports themselves if that should prove the only way open to bring them to their screens.

A final look at those screens, with their instantaneous action, their personalized drama, and their hyped-up conflicts, sees them becoming obsessed with a new sporting deity, and one that they are excellently equipped to serve. It is the god of the sporting statistic. The certainty suggested by attaching a number to a performance has, like the picture of the performance itself, been made instantly available. The computer flashes the figure onto the screen and the action is given an apparently hard reality that supercedes the transient picture let alone the feeble message of mere words. The range of the instant statistic becomes

*29 Wisden*: literature and statistics become increasingly central to sports presentation (Author's collection)

almost limitless, and its potency again lies in its new immediacy – it is there the moment the performance is over, or even, in some game settings, is updated second by second as the action plays out. Some sports have a long history of statistical analysis, cricket and baseball in particular. Their followers have been accustomed to detailed break-downs of the achievements of players and teams, with whole volumes devoted to them. The statistics are there in every dimension, whether by the game or by the season, by the individual career or the club history. The existing record, and the breaking of it, have become the bench-marks against which all competitive performance is ultimately judged. What is new is the immediate availability, not only of the customary statistics of the past, but of a whole fresh galaxy of figures in sports both old and new. And it is the watcher of the television screen who usually finds him- or herself better instructed in this new knowledge than the spectator on the ground. He or she it is who is given the fullest guidance into the new sporting wonderland.

Thus the continuing story of sport and time continues to unfold, and to promise ramifications that test the imagination beyond its limits. An exploration that began with the magic of the dawn dance ends with today's magic of the number – with the batting average, the passing yardage, the speed over the ground, the height or distance leapt, the score for the figure skaters. But is it still the same magic, the same sport? Is there any relevance at all to our present sporting lives in the experience of an often distant past which has occupied many of these pages? Many would doubt it. They would see modern sport separated almost irrevocably from the play of the past by such elements as secularization, concepts of equal opportunity for competitors, of specialization of skills and functions in the players, and of the bureaucratization and formalizing of the whole activity. Of the importance of these processes and developments there can be no doubt, but history cautions against seeing over-dramatic divisions between one stage and another in the human story. The fact that we live today through a sporting revolution does not divorce us from our past. It is the pace of change, its timing, which is the novelty, rather than the fact of change itself. Revolutions are often little more than evolution played on the fast-forward button of the time machine.

To see sport as we know it as an entirely modern phenomenon is to take an unduly limited view of its personal and social significance. It is to become over-sophisticated, and to miss sport's simple and eternal essence. Competitive play is scarcely any more 'modern' than, say, hunting, fighting, dancing, singing, and sex. In spite of all the changes that sport has undergone over the centuries, the same central psychosocial urge has remained at its heart. However larded over the zest and pleasures of competitive play may have been from time to time by communal, religious, and commercial considerations, this deep chord of personal striving, the pursuit of achievement and satisfaction – even at the expense of pain – has been of its essence. And it can exist vicariously in the spectator as well as directly in the player. Given this common resilient thread, it becomes unreasonably restricting to deny the relevance of our long sporting past to our contemporary enjoyments from play, to imprison our notions of sport within the confines of what the last century or so has brought in its wake.

We are sternly warned not to expect to find meaningful messages about modern sports in their pre-industrial manifestations, that function and meaning – to use that dangerous word – do not necessarily follow form.[22] It is, of course, a mistake to look for anything, as you will almost surely find it. Nowhere is this truer than in the vast untilled acres of pre-Victorian organized sport, which has made it such an attractive spoiling ground for social theorists. But there is no call for a defence of ignorance, even though so little has yet been revealed of our considerable early sporting lives. The 'feel' of sport has surely altered little down the ages. Some anthropologists are now suggesting that even our hunter-gatherer ancestors hunted for fun as well as for food, and the

160

sweating Yorkshire peasant who charged into his home alehouse with the Haxey Hood must surely have experienced – fertility symbol or not – the same surge of triumph as his descendant who dives over the try-line in the Rugby League cup final at Wembley Stadium. The sensation of the contest, the exhilaration of the play, is sport's life blood. Arthur Shrewsbury, one of England's greatest cricketers, pioneer sports entrepreneur, and manufacturer, always appeared to be the true percentage professional, ranking profit at least on a par with play. Yet it was when his health failed, and he saw the coming end of his cricket days, that he went out and bought a revolver, climbed quietly up to his bedroom in his sister's house, and shot himself through the head. He could not face the close of play.

To see an essential continuity in the history of sport does not mean that we can derive precise lessons from the past. To expect such would be naïve, and that applies as much to the Edwardian age as to the Neolithic. The cycle can never repeat itself exactly enough. As we contemplate today's sporting scene we have to be aware of its unique moment. It is not the sporting world of FitzStephen's medieval London, nor is it the world of Jesse Owens's Berlin Olympics, yet it inherits the legacies of both. We strive to grasp the actuality of today by seizing a still photograph or two from the ever-moving pictures of time. It is a moving film, however blurred and faded many of its images, which reaches back to the earliest human experience of play. Even to contemplate and understand something of its present, let alone to speculate on sport's future, we have a need to be released into its past, to have the whole of that past open and accessible to us. The temptation to see the present as the final revelation should have died with the eighteenth century. Ours is not the ultimate sporting moment and, short of Armageddon, it cannot be. Our own sporting times are at least as transient as those of the past.

So there can be no final reflections on this theme of sport and time. There is no bottom line to be drawn. The pace of the years and the centuries will continue to wreak its changes for as long as humans continue to play. The splitting of the seconds will become finer and finer. Time will continue to conquer distance. Sport will more and more create its own environments. And both time present and time past will bathe in brighter illumination from new generations of sport historians. Some counter-revolution may create a post-sporting world in which the impetus to play is given outlets beyond our present imagination. But it remains safe to venture that even such novel play forms will have their recognized occasions, their allotted time spans, and that these will be of concern to governors and priests, to producers and consumers, and that sport and time will remain in their fascinating and ever-changing interrelationship.

# Notes

### PREFACE

1 Sebastian de Grazia, *Of Time, Work and Leisure*, New York, Twentieth Century Fund, 1962.
2 Malcolm Bradbury, *The History Man*, London, Secker & Warburg, 1975, Arrow Books edn, 1977, pp. 106–7.

### 1  ECHOES FROM A LOST WORLD

1 Henry Bourne, *Antiquitates Vulgares; or, the Antiquities of the Common People*, Newcastle, 1725, p. 241; W. S. Walsh, *Curiosities of Popular Custom*, London, 1898, p. 358; John Goulstone, *The Summer Solstice Games: A Study of Early English Fertility Religion*, privately published, no details, 1985, p. 40.
2 See Goulstone, op. cit., p. 7.
3 *The Times*, 2 January, 20 and 27 April, and 24 December 1987.
4 Robert W. Malcolmson, *Popular Recreations in English Society, 1700–1850*, Cambridge, Cambridge University Press, 1973, pp. 26–7.
5 Robert Scott Fittis, *Sports and Pastimes of Scotland*, Paisley, Alexander Gardner, 1891, p. 154.
6 Geoffrey Cousins, *Golf in Britain: A Social History from the Beginnings to the Present Day*, London, Routledge & Kegan Paul, 1975, p. 55.
7 Percy M. Young, *A History of British Football*, London, Stanley Paul, 1968, pp. 47–9.
8 Malcolmson, op. cit., p. 29.
9 See Simon Inglis, *Soccer in the Dock: A History of British Football Scandals 1900 to 1965*, London, Collins Willow, 1985, pp. 144–55.
10 These tend to be in the industrial north, paradoxically in view of the region's earlier preference for a Good Friday rather than an Easter Monday holiday. The two games in 1987 were at Wigan and Bury. *The Times*, 17 April 1987.
11 In 1987 there were a few Rugby Union games on Good Friday, virtually all evening matches. In the northern code about half the clubs were playing, the matches split between the afternoon and evening. *The Times*, 17 April 1987.
12 In the Act of 1541 (33 Hy VIII, c. 9), primarily aimed to promote archery practice. See Alfred H. Haynes, *The Story of Bowls*, London, Sporting Handbooks, 1972, p. 24; Dennis Brailsford, *Sport and Society: Elizabeth to Anne*, London and Toronto, Routledge & Kegan Paul, 1969, p. 31.

13 See, for example, Malcolmson, op. cit., p. 28.
14 Quoted by D. I. Benning, 'The development of physical recreation in the Staffordshire Potteries 1850–1875', unpublished dissertation, University of Liverpool, 1979, p. 119.
15 Some groups of workers, notably in the industrial north, negotiated their own modifications, preferring New Year's Day and Easter Monday to Christmas Day and Good Friday. See Hugh Cunningham, *Leisure in the Industrial Revolution*, London, Croom Helm, 1980, p. 61.
16 See the 'Pugilistic register' and 'Pedestrian register' published annually in *Bell's Life in London*, usually in the first issue of the new year.
17 F. A. Pottle (ed.), *Boswell's London Journal 1762–1763*, London, Reprint Society, 1950, p. 61.
18 T. F. Thistleton Dyer, *British Popular Customs: Present and Past*, London, Bell & Sons, 1911, pp. 31–2; E. O. James, *Seasonal Feasts and Festivals*, London, Thames & Hudson, 1961, pp. 298–9; Malcolmson, op. cit., p. 28; Brailsford, op. cit., p. 56. The *Independent*, 7 January 1987, has an interesting account of the game as currently played.
19 Goulstone, op. cit., p. 40.
20 ibid., p. 9.
21 'Summa Predicantium', in G. R. Owst, *Literature and the Pulpit in Medieval England*, Oxford, Oxford University Press, 1961, p. 393.
22 H. R. Trevor Roper, *Archbishop Laud*, London, Macmillan, 2nd edn, 1962, p. 159.
23 *Dictionary of National Biography*.
24 *The Times*, 23 March 1925.
25 Brailsford, op. cit., p. 203, describes the locally named 'cock-kibbit' at Hartland, Devon. See also A. R. Wright, *British Calendar Customs: England Vol. I: Movable Festivals*, London, Folk Lore Society, 1936, pp. 76–7.
26 *Public Advertiser*, 17 February 1768. Shrove Tuesday cock-throwing was still giving minor problems at the end of the century – the *Sporting Magazine*, March 1795, p. 331, reports a thwarted attempt in Clerkenwell, and some Spanish villages still indulge in a version where pigeons are hoisted in pots up telegraph poles.
27 Pierce Egan, *Book of Sports*, London, T. T. & J. Tegg, 1832, pp. 321–2.
28 J. A. R. Pimlott, *The Englishman's Holiday: A Social History*, London, Faber & Faber, 1947, pp. 87–93; Benning, op. cit., p. 129.
29 John Wesley, *Journal*, London, Dent, 1906 edn, 4 vols, vol. I, p. 420.
30 Golf and tennis clubs in particular. Warwick Boat Club forbade the use of its property on both Sundays and Good Friday, on pain of expulsion. (Minute Book 2, 1896–1907.) I am indebted to R. J. Davis for this reference.
31 William Whellan, *The History and Topography of the Counties of Cumberland and Westmorland*, Pontefract, 1860, p. 479; Malcolmson, op. cit., p. 83.
32 *Sporting Magazine*, April 1795. ('Kelwick', in the text, is a fairly obvious misprint.)
33 e.g. Owen Swift v. William Murray, at Coombe Warren, on Easter Tuesday 1833. *Bell's Life in London*, 14 April 1833.
34 See Chapter 5, below.
35 *Post Boy*, 28 March 1700.
36 *Sporting Magazine*, April 1795, p. 55.
37 ibid., pp. 37–8.
38 *Sporting Magazine*, April 1811, p. 2.
39 Cunningham, op. cit., p. 143; Pimlott, op. cit., pp. 145–6.
40 Pimlott, op. cit., p. 89.

41 Fittis, op. cit., p. 112.

42 Weatherby's *Racing Calendar*, 1883. Four Oaks was the one new commercial 'Park' course of the 1870s to fail.

43 E.g. that at Malvern. *Malvern Advertiser*, 20 April 1889. I am indebted to R. J. Davis for this reference.

44 See Malcolmson, op. cit., p. 146.

45 Described extensively in A. R. Wright, op. cit., pp. 9–36.

46 House of Lords debate, 16 July 1987. *The Times*, 17 July 1987.

47 24 Geo. II, c. 23, 1751.

48 Goulstone, op. cit., p. 16, quotes some examples from the later 1750s.

49 Brailsford, op. cit., p. 57. See also J. Brand, *Observations on Popular Antiquities*, Newcastle upon Tyne, 1977. Revised edn, London, 1813, 2 vols, I, p. 210; Thistleton Dyer, op. cit., p. 214.

50 *Sporting Magazine*, May 1814, p. 94.

51 Goulstone, op. cit., p. 20.

52 From a cudgel match at a forbidden feast in Somerset during the Interregnum, to athletics meetings at Belsize Park in the eighteenth century, and numerous pedestrian events in the nineteenth. *Quarter Sessions Records for the County of Somerset: Vol. III: Commonwealth 1646–1660*, Somerset Record Society, XXVIII, 1912, p. 285; *Sports History*, no. 7, 1985, p. 10; *Bell's Life in London, passim*.

53 By the Banking and Financial Dealings Act, 1971.

54 Goulstone, op. cit., p. 20.

55 Malcolmson, op. cit., pp. 21, 31, and *passim*; Peter Bailey, *Leisure and Class in Victorian England*, London, Toronto, and Buffalo, Routledge & Kegan Paul, 1978, p. 46 and *passim*.

56 Bailey, op. cit., p. 15.

57 Kingsley Amis, *Lucky Jim*, Harmondsworth, Penguin Books edn, 1961, p. 227.

58 Christopher Whitfield (ed.), *Robert Dover and the Cotswold Games: Annalia Dubrensia*, London, Henry Southeran, 1962, p. 102.

59 Lord John Manners, *A Plea for National Holy Days*, London, Painter, 2nd edn, 1843, pp. 1, 31.

60 *Sports History*, no. 6, 1985, p. 2; Cunningham, op. cit., p. 87; *Sporting Magazine*, August 1808, p. 243; *Bell's Life in London*, 24 April 1836, 10 September 1837; *Sports History*, no. 1, 1982, pp. 25–7, no. 8, 1986, p. 2. For fuller accounts of Dover's Games see Whitfield (ed.), op. cit., pp. 1–60; Brailsford, op. cit., pp. 111–14.

61 An early meeting of the Highland Games, at Inverness, is reported in the *Sporting Magazine*, October 1821, p. 41.

62 Malcolmson, op. cit., pp. 82, 146.

63 Reports from the *Daily Express* in James McMillan, *The Way We Were*, London, Kimber, 1978, pp. 255–6.

64 Haynes, op. cit., pp. 10–19.

65 Owst, op. cit., *passim*.

66 In, for example, Eric Dunning and Kenneth Sheard, *Barbarians, Gentlemen and Players: A Sociological Study of the Development of Rugby Football*, Oxford, Martin Robertson, 1979, Table 1.2, pp. 33–4; Allen Guttman, *From Ritual to Record: The Nature of Modern Sports*, New York, Columbia University Press, 1978, pp. 15–16.

67 Particularly by Joachim K. Rühl, in, for example, 'Behind the scene of popular spectacle and courtly tradition: who is the best jouster?' Paper presented at HISPA Congress, Gubbio, Italy, 1987.

68 The Earl of Worcester's rules, as Constable of England, were reissued by Elizabeth I. Reprinted in *Sporting Magazine*, July 1801, pp. 187–8.

69 ibid., p. 188.

70 Dennis Brailsford, *Bareknuckles: A Social History of Prize-fighting*, Cambridge, Lutterworth Press, 1988, p. 6; 'Morals and maulers: the ethics of early pugilism', *Journal of Sport History*, vol. 12, no. 2, summer 1985, p. 130.

71 There were only 72 races, as against 93 two-horse matches, at Newmarket in 1797. Weatherby's *Racing Calendar*, 1797.

72 Young, op. cit., p. 106.

73 Lance Tingay, *100 Years of Wimbledon*, Enfield, Guinness Superlatives, 1977, p. 48. The challenge round had never operated in the 'new' competitions, the women's doubles and the mixed doubles, introduced in 1913.

## 2 MAKING MUCH OF TIME

1 Members had been more enthusiastic ten years earlier when 231 of them voted in a division on Christmas Day, 1646. *House of Commons Journals*, vol. V, p. 28.

2 Samuel Pepys, *Diary*, 12 February 1660.

3 Dennis Brailsford, *Sport and Society: Elizabeth to Anne*, London and Toronto, Routledge & Kegan Paul, 1969, pp. 6–33.

4 Thomas Lovell, *A Dialogue between Custom and Veritie concerning the use and abuse of Dauncing and Minstrelsie*, London, n.d., quoted in Robert W. Malcolmson, *Popular Recreations in English Society*, 1700–1850, Cambridge, Cambridge University Press, 1973, p. 9; D. Wilkins, *Concilia*, vol. III, 1727, p. 823, the Anglican Injunctions of 1567; also quoted in Christopher Hill, *Society and Puritanism in Pre-revolutionary England*, London, Secker & Warburg, 1964, p. 171.

5 William Hinde, *A Faithful Remonstrance of the Holy Life and Happy Death of John Bruen of Bruen Stapleford, in the County of Cheshire, Esquire*, 1641, in F. R. Raines (ed.), *The Journal of Nicholas Assheton of Downham*, Manchester, Chetham Society, 1848, p. 9, n. Raines quotes extensively from Hinde.

6 F. J. Furnivall (ed.), *Phillip Stubbes' Anatomy of the Abuses in England in Shakespeare's Youth*, London, 1879, p. 136; W. B. Whitaker, *Sunday in Tudor and Stuart Times*, London, Houghton, 1933, p. 34.

7 William Hinde, in Raines (ed.), op. cit., p. 13, n.

8 Richard Baxter, *A Christian Directory: or a Sermon of Practical Theology and Cases of Conscience*, London, 2nd edn, 1678, p. 367.

9 ibid., p. 227.

10 T. F. Merrill (ed.), *William Perkins, 1558–1602: English Puritanist. His Pioneer Works on Casuistry*, Nieuwkoop, 1966, p. 222; Malcolmson, op. cit., p. 9.

11 John Northbrooke, *Spiritus est vicarius Christi in terra. A Treatise wherein Dicing, Dauncing, Vaine plaies or Enterludes with other idle pastimes, etc. commonly used on the Sabboth day, are reprooved*, London, 1579, fols 11v–12r.

12 Sir Paul Harvey (ed.), *The Oxford Companion to English Literature*, 3rd edn, Oxford, Clarendon Press, 1946, Table IV, 'Fixed feasts and saints' days frequently used in dating documents', pp. 930–1.

13 By, for instance, Sebastian de Grazia, who claimed that there were 115 holidays plus 'the inviolable 52 Sundays'. *Of Time, Work, and Leisure*, New York, Twentieth Century Fund, 1962, p. 89.

14 J. Raine (ed.), *The Fabric Rolls of York Minster and Illustrative Documents*, London, Surtees Society, 1859, pp. 181–2.

15 'Articles of the Guild of Wiremongers', 15 October 1481, in A. R. Myers (ed.),

*English Historical Documents Vol. IV 1327–1485*, London, Eyre & Spottiswoode, 1969, p. 1103.

16 G. R. Owst, *Preaching in Medieval England*, Cambridge, Cambridge University Press, 1926, p. 303.

17 Hill, op. cit., p. 171.

18 J. A. Hessey, *Sunday: Its Origin, History and Present Obligation*, London, Brampton Lecture, 1860.

19 Hill, op. cit., pp. 153–62.

20 F. F. Braby, *Churchwardens' presentments from the Vale of Evesham 1660–1717, Pt. II*, Vale of Evesham Historical Society: Research Papers, vol. VI, 1977, p. 111.

21 The Independent Church at Bedford, for instance, admonished 'back-sliders' for playing cards, going to alehouses, gaming, and 'light unbecoming actions about stool ball and the may pole'. H. G. Tibbutt (ed.), *The Minutes of the First Independent Church (now Bunyan Meeting) at Bedford 1656–1766*, Bedfordshire Historical Records Society, vol. 55, 1976, pp. 76–7, 124, 156–8.

22 Orton even disapproved of walking abroad merely for pleasure on Sundays. *The Practical Works of Job Orton*, London, 1842, vol. I, p. 111.

23 Methodists were barred, for instance, from any wake or feast, and bound to 'bear a public testimony against them'. *Digest of the Minutes of the Methodist Conference*, Halifax, 1827, p. 18.

24 See J. T. Ward, *The Factory Movement 1830–1855*, London, Macmillan, 1962, *passim*.

25 A few Yorkshire Mechanics' Institutes had their own cricket grounds but, more typically, Manchester gave up its gymnasium for a new library and never got round to producing the promised replacement. Mabel Tylecote, *The Mechanics' Institutes of Lancashire and Yorkshire before 1851*, Manchester, Manchester University Press, 1957, pp. 160, 275.

26 R. S. S. Baden-Powell, *Scouting for Boys*, London, Cox, 1908. See Brian Dobbs, *Edwardians at Play: Sport 1890–1914*, London, Pelham Books, 1973, p. 31 and *passim*.

27 See, for example, *The Times*, 9 October 1980. With more justification he once described soccer's World Cup trophy as 'one of the most hideous artefacts Western Man has ever produced in his long history of bad taste'. Bernard Levin, *The Pendulum Years: Britain in the Sixties*, London, Jonathan Cape, 1970, p. 234. See also p. 236.

28 Harry Hopkins, *The New Look: A Social History of the Forties and Fifties in Britain*, London, Secker & Warburg, 1969, p. 105.

29 See Dennis Brailsford, 'Sporting days in eighteenth century England', *Journal of Sport History*, vol. 9, no. 3, winter 1982, p. 51.

30 Christopher Brookes, *English Cricket: The Game and its Players Through the Ages*, London, Weidenfeld & Nicolson, 1978, p. 78.

31 They took in £20 million in 1934–5, and had more than doubled this by the outbeak of war. Robert Graves and Alan Hodge, *The Long Week-End: A Social History of Great Britain 1918–1939*, London, Faber & Faber, 1940, p. 384.

32 Arthur Marwick, *Britain in the Century of Total War: War, Peace and Social Change 1900–1967*, London, Bodley Head, 1968, p. 439.

33 For the enlargement of women's recreation see Chapter 8, below.

34 Millwall F.C., for example, did much to retrieve a once bad reputation by communal efforts bringing in the whole family.

35 See David Miller, 'Fair play forfeited in the lust for victory', *The Times*, 4 January 1989.

36 In the interests of promoting 'manliness' it should not shun pain, and there is a lingering suspicion in Britain, where toughness often tends to outweigh skill, that sport has elsewhere degenerated into softness, with space-suit padding on the gridiron and baseball players needing a massive glove to catch the ball with.

37 For example, the invention of the microscope confirmed William Harvey's revolutionary account of the motion of the blood, in circulation.

38 Jeremy Taylor, 'Rules of conducting our sports and recreations', in *The Rule of Conscience*, in *Works*, London, 1822, vol. XIV, p. 334.

39 Though it has been pointed out that baseball is theoretically timeless. Allen Guttman, *From Ritual to Record: The Nature of Modern Sports*, New York, Columbia University Press, 1978, p. 107.

40 In the Sunday League, for instance, forty overs have to be bowled in two hours, with the added constraint of a limited run-up for bowlers.

41 Such as the four minutes claimed for the one-mile run between Charterhouse Wall and Shoreditch Church in 1720. Mervyn Watman, *History of British Athletics*, London, Robert Hale, 1968, p. 17.

42 See, for example, *Sporting Magazine*, October 1819, p. 40; November 1819, p. 87.

43 Named after Captain Allardyce Barclay, all-round athlete and sportsman, who first performed the feat on Newmarket Heath in the 1800s.

44 *Races* over short distances, as against wagers against time, were always popular, for both sexes, but had less status than longer events. For instance, a 100 yards race at Lord's was described as 'a distance much too short for a fair trial of the real powers of agility and wind'. *Sporting Magazine*, June 1805, p. 167.

45 See Chapter 6, below.

### 3  THE GOVERNING OF PLAY

1 *The Times*, 17 June 1988.

2 Crowd disorder was so commonplace in early spectator events that reporters always made a point of stressing the good behaviour of spectators. We are told, for instance, of the 'perfect crowd' of pitmen at one prize-fight in 1846, and an 'excellent' gathering of yeomen and farm labourers at another. Henry Downes Miles, *Pugilistica*, Edinburgh, Grant, 1906, vol. III, pp. 196, 237.

3 Such as destroying mills or pulling down enclosure fences. James Walvin, *The People's Game: A Social History of British Football*, London, Allen Lane, 1975, pp. 24–5.

4 By the 1740 Act, 13 Geo. II, c. 19, which limited matches of less than £50 stakes to Newmarket and Black Hambleton.

5 See Dennis Brailsford, *Bareknuckles: A Social History of Prize-fighting*, Cambridge, Lutterworth Press, 1988, p. 10.

6 By the Sunday Observance Act, 1780, 21 Geo. III, c. 49.

7 There has, for instance, been an understandable reaction to the past Anglo-Saxon domination of international sports organizations in general, and a particular reaction in football's ruling bodies, equally understandable in view of the long disdain of them by the British associations and the latter's continued insistence on fielding three international teams.

8 Lord Killanin, *My Olympic Years*, London, Secker & Warburg, 1983, pp. 2–3.

9 It was removed by the Statute Law Repeals Act.

10 The theme of sport's 'predominance as a focus for collective identification'

is taken up in Norbert Elias and Eric Dunning, *Quest for Excitement: Sport and Leisure in the Civilising Process*, Oxford, Basil Blackwell, 1956, p. 223.

11 For example, the 1388 Act, 12 Rich. II, c. 6, which prohibited named games on Sundays, when archery was to be practised.

12 For example, under Henry VIII an early Act, 3 Hy VIII, c. 3, demanded stricter adherence to earlier statutes, and his 1541 Act, 33 Hy VIII, c. 9, went into detail over who should practise, and how.

13 In 1606, when the Bill failed to pass the House of Lords in time; in 1614, when no Bills at all were passed; in 1621, when it passed both Houses, but was rejected by the king, which happened again in 1624.

14 W. B. Whitaker, *Sunday in Tudor and Stuart Times*, London, Houghton, 1933, pp. 84–6.

15 L. A. Govett, *The King's Book of Sports: A History of the Declarations of King James I and King Charles I as to the use of Lawful Sports on Sundays, with a reprint of the Declarations and a Description of the Sports then popular*, London, 1890, pp. 29–30.

16 ibid.

17 1 Chas I, c. 1.

18 See David Pannick, 'Sports law ill-fitted for demand on its services', *Independent*, 20 May 1988.

19 Simon Inglis, *Soccer in the Dock: A History of British Football Scandals 1900 to 1965*, London, Collins Willow, 1985, p. vii.

20 29 Chas II, c. 27. The second parliamentary attempt at law-making, in 1663, came to a remarkable end – the Bill, passed by both houses, disappeared from the table in the House of Lords when Charles came down to sign the session's successful statutes, and was literally 'lost'! *House of Lords Journals*, vol. XI, pp. 577–8; vol. XIII, p. 91; *House of Commons Journal*, vol. IX, pp. 421–2, 592.

21 The metricated French Revolutionary calendar was one of the rare exceptions.

22 C. H. Firth and R. S. Rait, *Acts and Ordinances of the Interregnum 1642–1660*, London, HMSO, 1911, vol. I, p. 420.

23 ibid., vol. I, p. 791, under the 'Rules for Suspension of Sacraments'.

24 A. R. Bayley, *The Great Civil War in Dorset 1642–1660*, Taunton, 1909, p. 349.

25 *House of Commons Journal*, vol. VII, pp. 566, 577; Firth and Rait, op. cit., vol. II, pp. 1162–70.

26 Firth and Rait, op. cit., vol. I, pp. 285–6.

27 At Timsbury, in rural Somerset, an attempt was made to mount the traditional parish feast some ten years after it had been banned, and three or four hundred 'strangers' turned up for it. *Quarter Sessions Records for the County of Somerset: Vol. III: Commonwealth 1646–1660*, Somerset Record Society, vol. XXVIII, 1912, p. 285.

28 ibid., p. 324.

29 Bayley, op. cit., p. 349.

30 Godfrey Davies, *The Early Stuarts 1603–1660*, Oxford, Oxford University Press, 1959, p. 180.

31 'Ordinance for prohibiting Cock-Matches', Firth and Rait, op. cit., vol. II, p. 861.

32 R. S. Paul, *The Lord Protector: Religion and Politics in the Life of Oliver Cromwell*, London, Lutterworth Press, 1955, p. 314.

33 As noted by, for example, Pepys, Dorothy Osborne, and John Evelyn. Dennis Brailsford, *Sport and Society: Elizabeth to Anne*, London and Toronto, Routledge & Kegan Paul, 1969, p. 138.

34 In spite of their reshaping of the whole leisure calendar, the 'years of

Cromwell's rule' have been described as 'sports history's blank pages'. Allen Guttman, 'English sports spectators: the Restoration to the early nineteenth century', *Journal of Sport History*, vol. 12, no. 2, summer 1985, p. 103.

35 See, for example, the 1541 Act, note 12, above. Local records often reveal the difficulties of implementing the statutes – e.g. J. Harland (ed.), *Court Leet Records of the Manor of Manchester*, Manchester, Chetham Society, 1864, pp. 86, 143–4; Tom Atkinson, *Elizabethan Winchester*, London, Faber & Faber, 1963, p. 226.

36 W. Le Hardy (ed.), *County of Middlesex: Calendar of the Sessions Records Vol. II 1614–1615*, London, Middlesex County Council, 1936, pp. 27, 95.

37 '. . . thus the fun was in some degree legalized.' *Sporting Magazine*, November 1824, p. 116.

38 W. B. Whitaker, *The Eighteenth Century English Sunday*, London, Epworth Press, 1940, p. 194.

39 By the Military Service Act, 1803, 43 Geo. III, c. 96.

40 W. F. Mandle, 'Sport as politics: the Gaelic Athletic Association 1884–1916', in Richard Cashman and Michael McKernan (eds), *Sport in History: The Making of Modern Sporting History*, Queensland, University of Queensland Press, 1979, pp. 99ff.

41 Lord Killanin, op. cit., p. 36, quoting a letter from Brundage.

42 *Sporting Magazine*, April 1813, p. 29.

43 C. H. McIlwain (ed.), *The Political Works of James I*, Cambridge, Mass., Harvard University Press, 1918. Brailsford, op. cit., pp. 71–2.

44 William Hinde, in F. R. Raines (ed.), *The Journal of Nicholas Assheton of Downham*, Manchester, Chetham Society, 1848, p. 99, n. (See note 5, Chapter 2.)

45 Sir Sidney Lee, 'Bearbaiting, bullbaiting, and cockfighting', in *Shakespeare's England*, Oxford, Oxford University Press, 1916, vol. II, p. 433.

46 Pepys has many references to the court's sporting activities, e.g. royal visits to Newmarket, which he much disliked. *Diary*, 7 March 1668. See also, Richard Onslow, *Headquarters: A History of Newmarket and its Racing*, Cambridge, Great Ouse Press, 1983, p. 6; Brailsford, op. cit., pp. 71–2.

47 A better authenticated claim now than it once was. Alfred H. Haynes, *The Story of Bowls*, London, Sporting Handbooks, 1972, pp. 59–61.

48 To be run for annually on the second Tuesday in October – but the first major race to be run on a Sunday, on 11 October 1981.

49 *Sporting Magazine*, September 1852, p. 105.

50 The eldest, the Prince of Wales, made pugilism fashionable by his presence at major fights for a few years; much later, at his coronation as George IV, he had a corps of prize-fighters to keep order in Westminster Abbey. Dennis Brailsford, *Bareknuckles: A Social History of Prize-fighting*, Cambridge, Lutterworth Press, 1988, pp. 23–6, 79.

51 ibid., p. 42.

52 From at least 1583. See John Field, *God's Judgement showed at Paris Garden, 13th January, 1583, being the Sabbath-day, at bear-baiting, at the meeting of about 1000 persons, whereof divers were slain, most maimed and hurt; set out with an Exhortation for the better observation of the Sabbath*, London, 1583.


## 4  MONEY MATTERS

1 William Haller, *The Rise of Puritanism* (1938), New York, Harper Torchbooks, 1957 edn, p. 123.

2 R. H. Tawney, *Religion and the Rise of Capitalism* (1926), London, Penguin Books edn, 1938. Dennis Brailsford, *Sport and Society: Elizabeth to Anne*, London and Toronto, Routledge & Kegan Paul, 1969, pp. 120–1, 200.

3 Richard Baxter, *A Christian Directory: or a Sermon of Practical Theology and Cases of Conscience*, London, 2nd edn, 1678, p. 377.

4 William Hinde, *A Faithful Remonstrance of the Holy Life and Happy Death of John Bruen of Bruen Stapleford, in the County of Cheshire, Esquire*, 1641, in F. R. Raines (ed.), *The Journal of Nicholas Assheton of Downham*, Manchester, Chetham Society, 1848, p. 18, n.

5 8 Geo. II, c. 26.

6 *Sporting Magazine*, January 1808, p. 195.

7 ibid., November 1808, p. 64.

8 *Gentleman's Magazine*, September 1743.

9 13 Geo. II, c. 19.

10 This process is well described by Robert W. Malcolmson, *Popular Recreations in English Society 1700–1850*, Cambridge, Cambridge University Press, 1973, particularly Chapters 6 and 7.

11 Quoted in J. T. Ward, *The Factory Movement 1830–1855*, London, Macmillan, 1962, p. 16.

12 *Leeds Intelligencer*, 20 January 1800.

13 P. Brady (ed.), *Churchwardens' presentments from the Vale of Evesham 1680–1717, Pt. II*, Vale of Evesham Historical Society: Research Papers vol. VI, 1977, p. 106.

14 N. Curnock (ed.), *Journal of John Wesley*, 8 vols, London, 1909, vol. IV, p. 176.

15 See Chapter 2, note 23.

16 Robert F. Wearmouth, *Methodism and the Common People in the Eighteenth Century*, London, 1945, p. 76.

17 See Chapter 2, note 21.

18 Vanessa S. Doe (ed.), *The Diary of James Clegg of Chapel en le Frith 1708–1755*, Derbyshire Record Society, 3 parts, 1978–1981, pt II, p. 368 and *passim*.

19 See Malcolmson, op. cit., pp. 99–101.

20 Robert L. Schuyler (ed.), *Josiah Tucker: A Selection from his Economic and Political Writings*, New York, Columbia University Press, 1931, p. 261.

21 Peter Bailey, *Leisure and Class in Victorian England: Rational Recreation and the Contest for Control 1830–1885*, London, Toronto, and Buffalo, Routledge & Kegan Paul, 1978, p. 13.

22 Ward, op. cit., p. 16.

23 See Chapter 1, above.

24 Bailey, op. cit., pp. 25–6.

25 See, for example, Roy A. Church, *Economic and Social Change in a Midland Town: Victorian Nottingham 1815–1900*, London, Frank Cass, 1966, p. 375; also Chapter 7, below.

26 Malcolmson, op. cit., p. 99.

27 *Sporting Magazine*, September 1852, p. 306.

28 J. G. O'Leary (ed.), *The Autobiography of Joseph Arch*, London, MacGibbon & Kee, 1966 edn, p. 70.

29 Rugby Union, as a more or less genuinely amateur sport, is an exception among the major spectator games.

30 J. H. Turner (ed.), *The Rev. Oliver Heywood, B.A., 1630–1702: His Autobiography, Diaries, Anecdotes and Event Books*, Bradford and Bingley, 1881–5, 4 vols, vol. II, p. 81.

31 Peter Clark, *The English Alehouse: A Social History 1200–1830*, London and New York, Longman, 1983, p. 154 and *passim*.

32 For example, a new bowling green ('very rustic') was opened at The Bell, Brierley Hill, in 1829; there was a fives court at Birmingham's Welsh Harp, and another 'extensive' one at the Shakespeare Inn, Bilston, when it went on the market. *Aris's Birmingham Gazette*, 26 October 1829; *Birmingham Journal*, 13 May 1848.

33 The tavern claimed to have its 'Bowling Green and Gardens . . . tastefully laid out, also Skittle and Quoit grounds'. *Birmingham Journal*, 5 February 1848.

34 The landlord might even pay the players – the winners of a match at Smitham Bottom, near Croydon, were to receive 10s. 6d. each and the losers 5s. 3d., paid by the publican, who advertised the good fare his house provided. *Daily Advertiser*, 12 May 1769.

35 As at Great Horwood, Buckinghamshire, in 1405. Clark, op. cit., p. 23.

36 *Daily Register*, 2 July, 12 July 1787.

37 George Borrow, *Lavengro*, London, John Murray, 1900 edn, pp. 166ff.

38 Great Britain, *Parliamentary Papers* (Commons), *Report of the Select Committee on Drunkenness*, 1834, Evidence, pp. 316–17.

39 John Stockwood, *A Sermon Preached at Paules Crosse on Barthelmew Day, being the 24 of August 1578*, London, n.d. See also Mary McElroy and Kent Cartwright, 'Public fencing contests on the Elizabethan stage', *Journal of Sport History*, vol. 13, no. 3, winter 1986, pp. 193–211.

40 The licence was granted to John Seconton, according to Hessey – there may well have been two of them. J. A. Hessey, *Sunday: Its Origin, History and Present Obligation*, London, Brampton Lecture, 1860.

41 W. B. Whitaker, *Sunday in Tudor and Stuart Times*, London, Houghton, 1933, p. 27.

42 Brailsford, op. cit., pp. 31, 106.

43 Robert Scott Fittis, *Sports and Pastimes of Scotland*, Paisley, Alexander Gardner, 1891, p. 151.

44 Geoffrey Cousins, *Golf in Britain: A Social History from the Beginnings to the Present Day*, London, Routledge & Kegan Paul, 1975, p. 3.

45 Alfred H. Haynes, *The Story of Bowls*, London, Sporting Handbooks, 1972, p. 49.

46 Cecil N. Cullingford, *A History of Dorset*, Letchworth, Phillimore, 1980, p. 77.

47 A. F. J. Brown, *English History from Essex Sources*, Chelmsford, Essex Record Office Publications, no. 18, 1952, p. 158; Mrs Ridout's account book, 'My expence', 19 July and 12 August 1775, unpublished. I am indebted to Pamela McLintock for a sight of these papers.

48 For example, the £100,000 shared by John Gully, the former champion boxer, and John Ridsdale from just two races. Wray Vamplew, *The Turf: A Social and Economic History of Horse Racing*, London, Allen Lane, 1976, pp. 178–9.

49 *Sporting Magazine*, September 1821, p. 283; September 1822, p. 309.

50 ibid., September 1823, p. 303.

51 ibid., October 1827, p. 396.

52 ibid., October 1832, p. 491.

53 See Lord's Day Observance Society, *Quarterly Publication*, no. 10, January 1846, for examples of such suppressions.

54 *Sporting Magazine*, August 1852, p. 247.

55 ibid.

56 For example, at both Bromsgrove, Worcestershire, and Dorchester, Dorset, there were two phases of racing, one in the later eighteenth century and the other in the nineteenth.

57 At 7s. 6d. to one guinea, according to the quality of the paper. *Daily Register*, 22 August 1787.

58 Great Britain, *Parliamentary Papers* (Commons), *Report of the Select Committee into the Laws and Practices relating to the Observance of the Lord's Day*, p. 247. Evidence of the Bishop of London, former Vicar of Chesterford, 26 July 1830.

59 *Daily Register*, 13 October 1787.

60 Stud fees were rising so rapidly that there were complaints that this could 'ultimately prove the ruin of our breed of horses' by excluding owners of moderate means. *Sporting Magazine*, April 1795, p. 6.

61 For example, Inglemere was to go to Van Diemen's Land and Carib to 'the new Swan River Settlement'; ibid., March 1830, p. 348.

62 ibid., May 1842, pp. 68–70.

63 See Dennis Brailsford, 'The geography of eighteenth century English spectator sports', *Sport Place*, vol. I, no. 1, winter 1987, pp. 41–55.

64 Who were not won over by the proprietor's efforts to set up a benevolent fund for them. *Sporting Magazine*, February 1838, p. 302.

65 ibid., 20 June 1852, p. 69. See also below, Chapter 7.

66 Wray Vamplew, 'The sport of kings and commoners: the commercialisation of British horse-racing in the nineteenth century', in Richard Cashman and Michael McKernan, *Sport in History: The Making of Modern Sporting History*, Queensland, University of Queensland Press, 1979, p. 321.

67 *Penny London Morning Advertiser*, 6 July 1744.

68 The *Daily Register*, 22 June 1787, has details of Lord's new ground.

69 Great Britain, *Parliamentary Papers* (Commons), *Select Committee on Public Walks*, 1833, pp. 61, 67.

70 G. B. Buckley, *Fresh Light on Eighteenth Century Cricket*, Birmingham, Cotterell, 1935, p. 110.

71 *Nottingham Journal*, 18 September 1819.

72 *Sussex Weekly Advertiser*, 30 June, 25 August 1823.

73 John Byrom paid 2s. 6d. to see a major fight in 1725 at Figg's, the earliest amphitheatre. Richard Parkinson (ed.), *The Private Journal and Literary Remains of John Byrom*, vol. I, part I, Manchester, Chetham Society, 1854, p. 117. See also Dennis Brailsford, *Bareknuckles: A Social History of Prizefighting*, Cambridge, Lutterworth Press, 1988, *passim*.

74 Brailsford, 1988, op. cit., pp. 86–8, 123–5, and *passim*.

75 *Bell's Life in London*, 11 January 1868.

76 *Daily Advertiser*, 5 and 18 June 1731. See also *Sports History*, no. 1, 1982, pp. 6–7.

77 *Bell's Life in London*, 30 December 1838.

## 5  SPORTS OUT OF TIME

1 Particularly by Robert W. Malcolmson, *Popular Recreations in English Society 1700–1850*, Cambridge, Cambridge University Press, 1972.

2 *Sporting Magazine*, May 1822, p. 98.

3 Wray Vamplew, 'The sport of kings and commoners: the commercialisation of British horse-racing in the nineteenth century', in Richard Cashman and Michael McKernan (eds), *Sport in History: The Making of Modern Sporting History*, Queensland, University of Queensland Press, 1979, p. 307.

4 Thomas Fawconer, *The Sporting Calendar: Containing an Account of the Plates, Matches, and Sweepstakes that have been run for in Great Britain, Ireland and Jamaica. In the Year 1773*, vol. V, n.d.

5 *Sporting Magazine*, July 1798. The change in fortunes could be sudden – Southampton was attracting crowds of 30,000 in 1822, but two years later it

was said that the meeting would be the last unless there was great improvement in both the racing and the upkeep of the course; ibid., August 1822, p. 261; August 1824, p. 277.

6 *Sporting Magazine*, vol. X, 1798, Appendix, Racing Calendar.

7 ibid.

8 W. M. Thackeray, *The History of Pendennis*, London, 1886 edn, p. 140.

9 *Daily Advertiser*, 6 April 1787. The dissection was, in fact, required by law.

10 Such as Young Dutch Sam, the leading lightweight, who fought at Epsom in July 1826. *Sporting Magazine*, July 1826, p. 252.

11 ibid., June 1821, p. 145. See also, for example, June 1823, p. 169; June 1825, p. 188.

12 A favourite venue was the Cockpit Royal, Westminster. Other matches were almost always associated with race meetings.

13 For example, *Sporting Magazine*, September 1797, p. 328; August 1808, p. 244. The 1808 singlestick contest was a county match, Somerset v. Wiltshire.

14 ibid., October 1822, p. 44. Carlisle also regularly offered wrestling as well as cock-fighting.

15 ibid., June 1821, p. 144.

16 ibid., August 1819, p. 247.

17 ibid., August 1814, p. 227, at York; September 1814, p. 275, at Pontefract.

18 For example, over 15,000 at All-England v. Hampshire in 1772. G. B. Buckley, *Fresh Light on Pre-Victorian Cricket*, Birmingham, Cotterell, 1937, p. 192. Again, in 1822, when 'exclusive of a great number of persons who got out into the ground by stealth, more than 17,000 paid for admission'. Rowland Bowen, *Cricket: A History of its Growth and Development Throughout the World*, London, Eyre & Spottiswoode, 1970, p. 265.

19 For example, 2,000 at the Marsh, Southampton, for a match against the Isle of Wight in 1816, and at a Sheffield game two years later. *Salisbury Journal*, 30 September 1816; *Sheffield Mercury*, 8 August 1818. See also *Sporting Magazine*, July 1819, p. 197.

20 '. . . where, hitherto, it has been but little in practice'; ibid., August 1822, p. 265.

21 ibid., June 1828, p. 192.

22 *Ipswich Journal*, 10 September 1743.

23 *Nottingham Journal*, 13 October 1792.

24 *Salisbury Journal*, 30 September 1816.

25 Sir Pelham Warner, *Lords 1787–1945*, London, Harrap, 1946, *passim*.

26 *Kentish Weekly Post*, 13 July 1873; *Kentish Gazette*, 5 August 1780.

27 *Stamford Mercury*, 20 June 1771.

28 *Lichfield Mercury*, 8 July, 8 August 1817.

29 *Bath Chronicle*, 20 August 1772.

30 *Leeds Mercury*, 27 August 1796.

31 *Daily Advertiser*, 12 June 1755.

32 *Chelmsford Chronicle*, 22 June 1787.

33 William Hazlitt, 'The fight', *New Monthly Magazine*, February 1822. There were 30,000 estimated to be at Tom Spring's fight with Neat a few years later and at least that number at Norwich for the Painter v. Oliver fight. J. C. Reid, *Bucks and Bruisers: Pierce Egan and Regency England*, London, Routledge & Kegan Paul, 1971, p. 17; Pierce Egan, *Boxiana; or, Sketches of Modern Pugilism*, London, Sherwood, Neely, & Jones, 1821, 3 vols, vol. III, 140–2.

34 Henry Downes Miles, *Pugilistica: The History of British Boxing*, Edinburgh, John Grant, 1906, 3 vols, vol. II, pp. 470–1.

35 ibid., vol. III, p. 237.

36 See below, Chapter 6.

37 See, for example, Dennis Brailsford, *Bareknuckles: A Social History of Prize-fighting*, Cambridge, Lutterworth Press, 1988, p. 24.

38 *Sporting Magazine*, November 1824, p. 115.

39 ibid., July 1825, p. 309; Miles, op. cit., vol. II, p. 210.

40 Mr J. J. Brayfield, according to his *Sporting Magazine* obituary, was an extreme example of this tendency: 'Almost from infancy attendant upon all the fairs, boxing matches, races, and diversions of every kind round London, from the ring made by the first rate amateurs of the fancy down to the weekly badger baiting in Black Boy-alley. Also constant at Newgate executions . . .'. March 1821, p. 283.

41 ibid., November 1826, p. 55.

42 ibid., May 1827, p. 59; July 1827, p. 243; Hugh Cunningham, *Leisure in the Industrial Revolution*, London, Croom Helm, 1980, p. 27.

43 A Northamptonshire gentleman hopped 120 yards in one minute, for £500, but Will Hopcraft, a Birmingham pedestrian, just failed (at Lord's) to pick up 100 stones, each a yard distant, in 44 minutes. *Sporting Magazine*, May 1796, p. 80; March 1796, p. 337.

44 *Bell's Life in London*, 30 December 1838, in its first 'Chronology of pedestrianism'.

45 *Sporting Magazine*, June 1813, pp. 139–40; *Bell's Life in London*, 30 December 1838.

46 Joseph Strutt, *The Sports and Pastimes of the People of England*, London Methuen, 1801.

47 'A New gallows was set up a few days ago in Newgate Street, the appearances of which are very favourably spoken of . . .'! *Sporting Magazine*, January 1805, p. 224.

48 Roy A. Church, *Economic and Social Change in a Midland Town: Victorian Nottingham 1815–1900*, London, Frank Cass, 1966, p. 18.

49 *Sporting Magazine*, December 1829, p. 121.

50 ibid., April 1799, p. 25.

51 ibid., June 1811, p. 115.

52 ibid., p. 141.

53 ibid., p. 145.

54 ibid., p. 139.

55 J. A. R. Pimlott, *The Englishman's Holiday: A Social History*, London, Faber & Faber, 1947, p. 81.

56 By, for example, R. W. Malcolmson, op. cit. See also, *inter alia*, E. P. Thompson, 'Time, work-discipline and industrial capitalism', *Past and Present*, vol. 38, 1967, pp. 71ff.; Peter Bailey, *Leisure and Class in Victorian England: Rational Recreation and the Contest for Control*, London, Toronto, and Buffalo, Routledge & Kegan Paul, 1978.

57 See also Dennis Brailsford, 'Sporting days in eighteenth century England', *Journal of Sport History*, vol. 9, no. 2, winter 1982, pp. 41–54.

58 As so often in horse-racing history, Newmarket was the exception. Since the horses were stabled there, racing could begin on Mondays and continue through the week to Friday or even Saturday.

59 Brailsford, 1982, op. cit., p. 50.

60 *Hampshire Times*, 13 and 27 September 1802.

61 See, for example, G. B. Buckley, *Fresh Light on Pre-Victorian Cricket*, Birmingham, Cotterell, 1937, pp. 30, 51.

62 It was rare for even very large pugilistic crowds to defy a Justice of the Peace, often accompanied by no more than a couple of constables.

63 Brailsford, 1982, op. cit., p. 47.

64 *Bell's Life in London*, 7 January 1844.

65 *Sporting Magazine*, December 1818, p. 120.

66 Quoted in Thompson, op. cit., p. 72.

67 Ibid.

68 *Sporting Magazine*, January 1820, p. 187, n.

69 Douglas A. Reid, 'The decline of Saint Monday 1776–1876', *Past and Present*, vol. 7, 1976, p. 78.

70 A Staffordshire potter recalled that, in the 1820s, 'there was generally little, if any work done on Mondays and Tuesdays, and yet it was rare for any of the men to get on Saturday less than a full week's wage. From Wednesday to Saturday they worked themselves and worked others, boys and women, like galley slaves. From four and five in the morning until nine or ten at night the fierce race for wages was run'. 'When I was a child', by an old potter, in John Burnett (ed.), *Useful Toil: Autobiographies of Working People from the 1820s to the 1920s*, London, Allen Lane, 1974, pp. 302–3.

71 Bailey, op. cit., p. 13.

72 Cunningham, op. cit., p. 51.

73 See, for example, 'On pugilism', *Sporting Magazine*, April 1795, pp. 137–8; 'Importance of walking matches', ibid., December 1801, pp. 158–9; 'The comforts of sports and games', ibid., October 1807, pp. 22–3.

74 Reported in Egan, op. cit., vol. III, pp. 580ff.

75 As stakeholder in the Brown v. Sampson fight in 1830 he handed the stakes to Sampson in a disputed ending. At the Staffordshire Assizes he was ordered to return the stakes to Brown, and he had other legal tangles over racing stake money. Miles, op. cit., vol. II, p. 453; *Sporting Magazine*, September 1831, p. 404.

76 ibid., August 1831, p. 288.

77 ibid., June 1828, p. 120.

78 See below, Chapter 7.

## 6  THE PACE OF PLAY

1 See above, Chapter 3.

2 Alfred H. Haynes, *The Story of Bowls*, London, Sporting Handbooks, 1972, p. 8.

3 E. O. James, *Seasonal Feasts and Festivals*, London, Thames & Hudson, 1961, p. 299.

4 Nigel Brown, *Ice-skating: A History*, London, Kaye & Ward, 1959, pp. 30–3.

5 *Salix coerulea*, a cross between the native crack willow and the white willow.

6 Haynes, op. cit., *passim*.

7 'The football match', *Sporting Magazine*, December 1807, pp. 153–5.

8 Percy M. Young, *A History of British Football*, London, Stanley Paul, 1968, pp. 49, 61.

9 G. M. Trevelyan, *English Social History*, London, Longmans, Green, 1942, p. 407.

10 Geoffrey Cousins, *Golf in Britain: A Social History from the Beginnings to the Present Day*, London, Routledge & Kegan Paul, 1975, pp. 3, 22.

11 Hugh Cunningham, *Leisure in the Industrial Revolution*, London, Croom Helm, 1980, p. 178.

12 E. V. Lucas (ed.), *The Hambledon Men*, London, Henry Froude, 1907, p. 136.

13 Christopher Brookes, *English Cricket: The Game and its Players through the Ages*, London, Weidenfeld & Nicolson, 1978, p. 107.

14  *Sporting Magazine*, December 1837, p. 98.

15  The Spring v. Oliver fight; ibid., February 1821, p. 200.

16  Josh Hudson v. Chatham Caulker. Henry Downes Miles, *Pugilistica: The History of British Boxing*, Edinburgh, John Grant, 1906, 3 vols, vol. II, pp. 272–3.

17  *Sporting Magazine*, May 1820, p. 67.

18  J. A. R. Pimlott, *The Englishman's Holiday: A Social History*, London, Faber & Faber, 1947, p. 76.

19  ibid., p. 77.

20  *Bell's Life in London*, 3 September 1843.

21  The Ward v. Bailey fight in October 1839 appears to have been the first major contest to make use of the railway, and the first important river encounter was the resumed fight between William Perry, the 'Tipton Slasher', and the American, Freeman, in 1842. Miles, op. cit., vol. III, pp. 215, 179.

22  ibid., vol. III, pp. 179, 251, and *passim*.

23  The Woolwich based *Nymph*, a favourite with the ring fraternity, was the authorized vessel for the Broome v. Rowe fight in 1845. The *Lord Nelson* was a cut-priced rival, but in his anxiety to keep the first boat in his sights the master found himself grounded under London Bridge; ibid., vol. III, p. 315.

24  Keith Dunstan, *Sports*, Melbourne, Sun Books, 1975, p. 152.

25  *The Times*, 7 January 1953.

26  Though they provided one of the earliest special excursions, on the Brighton line, for the Perry v. Parker fight in 1843. Miles, op. cit., vol. III, p. 215.

27  See *The Times*, 7 September 1863. The £1,000 fight between Mace and Goss was prevented in Gloucestershire. With heavy sarcasm the reporter noted that 'whatever may be said against the Great Western Railway, they certainly do manage a prize-fighting excursion capitally'.

28  One fight crowd, using a scheduled train, was alarmed to find a group of local magistrates mounting the first-class carriages, only to be relieved when they alighted a few stops later, apparently on their way to their sessions meeting. Miles, op. cit., vol. III, p. 215.

29  ibid., p. 219.

30  Dennis Brailsford, *Bareknuckles: A Social History of Prize-fighting*, Cambridge, Lutterworth Press, 1988, p. 155.

31  ibid., pp. 129–30; Miles, op. cit., vol. III, pp. 419–37.

32  Under s. 21 of the act.

33  *Sporting Magazine*, May 1830, p. 46.

34  ibid., February 1838, p. 293.

35  The train started from south of the river as the Waterloo terminus was not yet built. It left passengers with a good four-mile walk to Epsom Downs. Alan Delgado, *The Annual Outing and Other Excursions*, London, Allen & Unwin, 1977, p. 28.

36  Wray Vamplew, *The Turf: A Social and Economic History of Horse Racing*, London, Allen Lane, 1976, pp. 24–6.

37  See Chapter 7, below.

38  See Chapter 5, above.

39  G. B. Buckley, *Fresh Light on Pre-Victorian Cricket*, Birmingham, Cotterell, 1937, p. 200.

40  *Sporting Magazine*, September 1819, p. 283.

41  Delgado, op. cit., p. 29

42  ibid., pp. 62–3.

43  ibid., p. 131.

44  *Felix Farley's Bristol Journal*, 21 August 1819.

45 *Sporting Magazine*, August 1852, p. 247.

46 By, for example, Young, op. cit., pp. 89–94.

47 J. A. Mangan, *Athleticism in the Victorian and Edwardian Public School: The Emergence and Consolidation of an Educational Ideology*, Cambridge, Cambridge University Press, 1981, p. 73.

48 See, for example, William J. Baker, *Sports in the Western World*, Totowa, New Jersey, Rowman & Littlefield, 1982, p. 146.

49 Molyneux fought two great fights with Tom Cribb for what was effectively the championship of the world, Richmond became a pillar of the ring for thirty years, and Freeman was a giant of a man who was drawn reluctantly into prize-fighting. William Fuller, whose first fight of note, incidentally, was against Molyneux, became a pioneering teacher of pugilism in the United States. Brailsford op. cit., *passim*.

50 Miles, op. cit., vol. III, p. 77.

51 Ian Tyrrell, 'The emergence of modern American baseball (c. 1850–80)', Richard Cashman and Michael McKernan, *Sport in History: The Making of Modern Sporting History*, Queensland, University of Queensland Press, 1979, p. 206; Paul Gardner, *Nice Guys Finish Last: Sport and American Life*, London, Allen Lane, 1974, p. 5.

52 K. S. Inglis, 'Imperial cricket: test matches between Australia and England 1877–1900', in Cashman and McKernan, op. cit., p. 206.

53 See Chapter 5, above.

54 See Chapter 1, above.

55 M. A. Bienefeld, *Working Hours in British History*, London, Weidenfeld & Nicolson, 1972, p. 37.

56 ibid., p. 38.

57 ibid., pp. 53–5, 61.

58 ibid., p. 79.

59 S. G. Checkland, *The Rise of Industrial Society in England 1815–1885*, London, Longmans, 1964, p. 36.

60 Roy A. Church, *Economic and Social Change in a Midland Town: Victorian Nottingham 1815–1900*, London, Frank Cass, 1966, p. 375.

61 Douglas A. Reid, 'The decline of Saint Monday 1766–1876', *Past and Present*, vol. 71, May 1976, p. 82.

62 Pimlott, op. cit., p. 162.

63 Reid, op. cit., p. 100.

## 7 THE SPORTING WEEKEND

1 In, for instance, the late arrival of league soccer in East Anglia. Farm workers were among the last to be assured of Saturday afternoon freedom and it was only after the Second World War that Norwich was joined in the league by Ipswich, Peterborough, and Colchester. By then, of course, even in rural areas, agriculture had become a minority occupation.

2 Quoted in James Walvin, *The People's Game: A Social History of British Football*, London, Allen Lane, 1975, p. 54.

3 See above, Chapter 6.

4 A practice still strong enough in the early seventeenth century for Puritans to import it into New England. Alice Morse Earle, *The Sabbath in Puritan New England*, London, Hodder & Stoughton, 1892, pp. 246, 257.

5 Hugh Cunningham, *Leisure in the Industrial Revolution*, London, Croom Helm, 1980, p. 143; Lord's Day Observance Society (henceforth LDOS) Minute Book IV, unpublished, p. 262.

6 Cunningham, op. cit., p. 150.
7 S. G. Checkland, *The Rise of Industrial Society in England 1815–1885*, London, Longmans, 1964, p. 229.
8 *Tait's Edinburgh Magazine*, April 1849, p. 239.
9 J. T. Ward, *The Factory Movement 1830–1855*, London, Macmillan, 1962, p. 152.
10 Cunningham, op. cit., p. 61.
11 Ward, op. cit., p. 405.
12 *The Times*, 7 September 1861.
13 Roy Rees, 'The organisation of sport in nineteenth century Liverpool', in Roland Renson, Pierre Paul de Nayer, Michel Ostyn (eds), *The History, the Evolution and Diffusion of Sports and Games in Different Cultures*, Leuven, 1976, p. 242.
14 Walvin, op. cit., p. 62; P. M. Young, *A History of British Football*, London, Stanley Paul, 1968, pp. 123–5. Everton's entry was successful – they were runners-up in their first season in the league.
15 Brian Harrison, *Drink and the Victorians: The Temperance Question in England 1815–1872*, London, Faber & Faber, 1971.
16 *Dorset County Chronicle*, 19 December 1861.
17 Taken from 'Matches to come', *Bell's Life in London*.
18 J. Weatherby, E. Weatherby, and J. P. Weatherby, *The Racing Calendar for the Year 1888*, London, Weatherby, vol. 116, 1888, *passim*.
19 Sir John Clapham, *An Economic History of Modern Britain: Free Trade and Steel 1850–1886*, Cambridge, Cambridge University Press, 1932, p. 448.
20 See above, Chapter 5.
21 In Surrey's case, for instance, from 230 to 1,000 between 1851 and 1861. Christopher Brookes, *English Cricket: The Game and its Players Through the Ages*, London, Weidenfield & Nicolson, 1978, p. 111.
22 When John Jackson's benefit, Nottinghamshire v. MCC, ended in two days, a special game was arranged between the County XI and a 2nd XV, since 'a third day, and that day a Saturday, is an important pecuniary affair to any man having a benefit match in Nottingham'. *Wisden's Cricketers' Almanac 1875*, p. 160.
23 From fixtures in *Bell's Life in London*, July 1854, July 1865, July 1885.
24 ibid., 2 November 1867. (No hard line was yet being drawn between the football codes – some were described as 'Association', some as 'Rugby', and some were not classified at all.)
25 ibid., 25 September 1875.
26 ibid., 27 November 1875.
27 ibid., 28 December 1878.
28 The process has been well described by Robert W. Malcolmson, *Popular Recreations in English Society 1700–1850*, Cambridge, Cambridge University Press, 1973.
29 Cunningham, op. cit., p. 120. The LDOS, though, complained that its annual meeting was in the habit of invading the Sabbath, LDOS, Minute Book IV, unpublished, p. 81.
30 From *Bell's Life in London*, July and August 1854.
31 Notably, for a time, in athletics. Melvyn Watman, *History of British Athletics*, London, Robert Hale, 1968, p. 18.
32 Hylton Cleaver, *A History of Rowing*, London, Herbert Jenkins, 1957, pp. 122, 127.
33 ibid., p. 122.
34 Arthur Shrewsbury's correspondence gives excellent insights into the

financing of tours. See Peter Wynne-Thomas, *'Give Me Arthur': A Biography of Arthur Shrewsbury*, London, Arthur Barker, 1985, pp. 14, 108.

35 Eric Dunning and Kenneth Sheard, *Barbarians, Gentlemen and Players: A Sociological Study of the Development of Rugby Football*, Oxford, Martin Robertson, 1979, pp. 223–8.

36 *Bell's Life in London*, 6 January 1872.

37 Described as 'stark', and the new recreations as 'stringent', by Walvin, op. cit., p. 56.

38 Mr Spencer Perceval (but not the prime minister, assassinated twenty years earlier) proposing a fast day for the relief of the cholera epidemic. *Bell's Life in London*, 25 March 1832.

39 Checkland, op. cit., p. 229.

40 See, for example, Hugh McLeod, *Class and Religion in the Late Victorian City*, London, Croom Helm, 1974, pp. 56–7.

41 Weatherby *et al.*, op. cit., p. 731.

42 Brookes, op. cit., p. 78; Wray Vamplew, *The Turf: A Social and Economic History of Horse Racing*, London, Allen Lane, 1976, p. 87.

43 Interestingly reported in the *Sporting Magazine*. See, for example, November 1827, p. 10; June 1828, pp. 121–3.

44 Brookes, op. cit., p. 109; *Bell's Life in London*, 1 July 1855, over a 12.30 start to Sussex v. Surrey, then a seventy-minute dinner interval, and 18 November 1871, over a 1.00 p.m. start at Maidstone.

45 William Clarke's 'All England XI' was the first and most enduring of the three major touring professional sides, lasting from 1846 to 1870. Brookes, op. cit., pp. 101–18.

46 See Dennis Brailsford, 'Oxford v. Cambridge: a theme in the early growth of modern sport', in Sandra Kereliuk (ed.), *The University's Role in the Development of Modern Sport: Past, Present, and Future*, proceedings of the FISU Conference – Universiade '83 – in association with the Xth HISPA Congress, Edmonton, Canada, 1983, pp. 38–48.

47 ibid., p. 42.

48 *The Times*, 14 March 1857.

49 ibid., 6 April 1857.

50 ibid., 15 April 1867.

51 At Halton, near Leeds, in several Oxfordshire parishes, at Tunstall in the Potteries, and the Sunday Lansdown Revels at Bath. See LDOS, *Quarterly Publication*, no. 9, October 1845; no. 10, January 1846.

52 ibid., no. 22, January 1849; no. 12, January 1846; no. 17, January 1847.

53 Great Britain, *Parliamentary Papers* (Commons), *Report of the Select Committee Appointed to Inquire into the Laws and Practices Relating to the Lord's Day*, 1830; *Hansard*, vol. XVII, 1833, 1334–5; vol. XXII, 1834, 55; vol. XXIII, 1834, 317–18, 327, 1178; vol. XXXVIII, 1837, 1227.

54 The LDOS was the organizing force behind the closing of the Hippodrome enclosed raceground. A Bill to divert a footpath allowing open access to the site was defeated when a clause forbidding Sunday amusements was omitted. LDOS, Minute Book II, unpublished, p. 2.

55 There was hurried government legislation, for instance, to remit penalties and bar private prosecutions under the 1780 Act when the LDOS began to bring private actions against the Sunday opening of diversions such as the Brighton Aquarium. *Sunday Observance Prosecution Act*, 34 and 35 Vict., c. 87 (1871); *Remission of Penalties Act*, 38 and 39 Vict., c. 80 (1875).

56 Alan Delgado, *The Annual Outing and Other Excursions*, London, George Allen & Unwin, 1977, p. 50.

57 Passenger traffic to Calais and Boulogne, for instance, quadrupled between 1840 and 1872; ibid., p. 159.

58 *The Times*, 14 April 1847.

59 LDOS requests to the Jockey Club that its members refrain from racing abroad on Sundays appear to have gone unanswered. Minute Book VI, unpublished, April 1879; January 1880.

60 The secretary of the Malvern Cycling Club made an extensive defence of the weekend tours in a letter to the *Malvern Advertiser*, 20 April 1889. I am indebted to R. J. Davis for this reference.

61 The proprietor responded by saying that no money had been taken – an exoneration only from crime and not from sin in LDOS eyes. Minute Book VI, unpublished, November 1875.

62 Frederick Alderson, *Bicycling: A History*, Newton Abbot, David & Charles, 1972, pp. 32, 42, 67.

63 LDOS Minute Book VII, 1892, p. 452. See also John Wigley, *The Rise and Fall of the Victorian Sunday*, Manchester, Manchester University Press, 1980, p. 158 and *passim*.

64 John Olliffe, *The Romance of Wimbledon*, London, Hutchinson, n.d. p. 16.

65 LDOS Minute Book VII, 1891, p. 432.

66 LDOS Minute Book VIII, 1909, p. 221.

67 LDOS Minute Book VII, pp. 305, 391; IX, pp. 17, 21; VII, p. 273; XI, p. 147.

68 *Edinburgh Review*, vol. XIII, 1809, p. 342.

69 LDOS Minute Book VIII, 1894, p. 22.

70 LDOS Minute Book IX, pp. 231–8.

71 D. I. Benning, 'The development of physical recreation in the Staffordshire Potteries, 1850–1875', unpublished dissertation, University of Liverpool, 1979, p. 108.

72 LDOS Minute Book VI, November 1877; October 1878; October 1879; May 1880.

73 Lance Tingay, *100 Years of Wimbledon*, Enfield, Guinness Superlatives, 1977, p. 27.

74 See, for example, Young, op. cit., p. 111.

75 ibid., p. 105; Wigley, op. cit., pp. 115, 166.

76 Football Association, *The History of the Football Association*, London, 1953, p. 552.

77 LDOS Minute Book IX, pp. 316–38; *The Times*, 25 February 1919.

78 *The Times*, 12 March 1919.

79 E. W. Swanton (ed.), *The World of Cricket*, London, Michael Joseph, 1966, p. 886; Roland Bowen, *Cricket: A History of its Growth and Development Throughout the World*, London, Eyre & Spottiswoode, 1970, p. 177. MCC members, for instance, formed the Romany Club.

80 *The Times*, 25 February 1919.

81 She had not mentioned her Sabbatarian principles earlier for fear of being thought boastful! Olliffe, op. cit., p. 102.

## 8 THE COMING OF THE LEISURE AGE

1 Peter Bailey, *Leisure and Class in Victorian England: Rational Recreation and the Contest for Control 1830–1885*, London, Toronto, and Buffalo, Routledge & Kegan Paul, 1978, p. 81.

2 S. G. Checkland, *The Rise of Industrial Society in England 1815–1885*, London, Longmans, 1964, p. 231.

3 M. A. Bienefeld, *Working Hours in British History*, London, Weidenfeld & Nicolson, 1972, p. 160.

4 G. D. H. Cole and Raymond Postgate, *The Common People 1746–1938*, London, Methuen, 1938, p. 623.

5 Central Office of Information, *Britain 1987: An Official Handbook*, London, HMSO, 1988, p. 30. A 'holiday' is defined as lasting four or more nights.

6 ibid.

7 Percy M. Young, *A History of British Football*, London, Stanley Paul, 1968, p. 79.

8 Brian Harrison, *Drink and the Victorians: The Temperance Question in England 1815–1872*, London, Faber & Faber, 1971, p. 331.

9 Young, op. cit., p. 104. It is interesting to speculate how the British game might have developed, how ball skills might have emerged earlier had football been played from the start with light balls on hard pitches and not with sodden ones in mud.

10 George Parr and Richard Daft, for instance, were among those Nottinghamshire cricketers involved in the founding of Notts County Football Club; ibid., p. 99.

11 ibid., pp. 120–1.

12 'Electric light' matches were played at the Oval and at Bramall Lane, Sheffield, in 1878; ibid., p. 111. Rugby football tried the experiment for practice games, with limited success, in 1911. James McMillan, *The Way We Were*, London, Kimber, 1978, p. 139.

13 See above, Chapter 7.

14 Christopher Brookes, *English Cricket: The Game and its Players Through the Ages*, London, Weidenfeld & Nicolson, 1978, p. 156.

15 By the Statute Law Repeals Act of 1969. The repeal had no practical effect as the Sunday trading restrictions were already embodied, and more specifically, in other legislation such as the Shops Act, 1930.

16 Starting with a match at Bristol in May 1965.

17 *The Times*, 7, 14 January 1974. See also 'The fans say it again', *The Economist*, 2 February 1974.

18 All listed in *The Times*, 6 March 1981.

19 ibid., 10, 12, 16 October 1981.

20 ibid., 21, 30 January 1988.

21 G. R. Owst, *Literature and Pulpit in Medieval England*, Oxford, Oxford University Press, 1961, p. 393 and *passim*.

22 A. R. Wright, *British Calendar Customs: England, Vol. I: Movable Festivals*, London, Folk Lore Society, 1936, p. 36.

23 Joseph Strutt, *The Sports and Pastimes of the People of England*, London, Methuen, 1801. Bath, Firecrest, 1969 edn, illustrations facing pp. 8, 24, 98, 176, 188.

24 T. F. Thistleton Dyer, *British Popular Customs: Present and Past*, London, Bell & Sons, 1911, p. 86.

25 For example, *Richard III*, Act IV; *Love's Labours Lost*, Act IV, scene 1.

26 Samuel Pepys, *Diary*, July 1662; 14 April 1667.

27 *Sporting Magazine*, April 1799, p. 8.

28 ibid., November 1814, p. 94.

29 ibid., April 1813, p. 17.

30 ibid., October 1822, p. 44; September 1823, p. 309; August 1827, p. 296.

31 ibid., November 1792, p. 51.

32 ibid., September 1799, p. 321. See also, for example, October 1807, p. 42.

33 ibid., July 1813, p. 195. See also Anon, *Pancratia, or A History of Pugilism*, 2nd edn, London, 1815, pp. 113, 120.
34 Pierce Egan, *Boxiana, or, Sketches of Modern Pugilism*, London, Sherwood, Neely, & Jones, 3 vols, 1821, vol. III, p. 139.
35 For example, *Bell's Life in London*, 1 August 1858.
36 'A great deal of amusement was occasioned' when 'one of the fair rivals unfortunately fell overboard'; ibid., 4 September 1842.
37 See above, Chapter 7.
38 'Holland' still described fine linen, not the coarser fabric the name was later applied to.
39 But over-excitable spectators were warned that Captain Vinegar would be on hand with his bruisers and bulldogs, 'that no civil spectators may be incomoded by the rabble'. *Penny London Morning Advertiser*, 11 June 1744.
40 *Sporting Magazine*, March 1805, p. 304.
41 ibid., April 1813, p. 20.
42 See, for example, *Reading Mercury*, 2 July 1781.
43 *Sporting Magazine*, May 1797, p. 98.
44 A further discriminatory prohibition appeared in another notice – 'no ladies permitted to enter the prize lists who may appear to have drank too freely of strong waters'; ibid., May 1797, p. 98.
45 ibid., April 1799, p. 25.
46 For example, a wager to run a mile in five and a half minutes for £2 at Wrotham; ibid., August 1795, p. 280.
47 LDOS, Minute Book VI, unpublished, October 1879; May 1880.
48 *Sporting Magazine*, November 1831, pp. 16–19; December 1831, pp. 116–19; January 1832, pp. 182–4.
49 ibid., September 1822, p. 311.
50 Two ladies' teams competed in Norfolk, for instance, the players 'dressed in jackets and trowsers, tastefully decorated with blue ribands'; ibid., June 1823, p. 164. Married v. unmarried ladies' matches were quite common, such as at Alresford a few months earlier; ibid., September 1822, p. 313.
51 Pierce Egan, *Book of Sports*, London, T. T. & J. Tegg, 1832, pp. 242–4.
52 *Sporting Magazine*, November 1819, p. 60; December 1819, p. 110.
53 Checkland, op. cit., p. 216.
54 Hugh Cunningham, *Leisure in the Industrial Revolution*, London, Croom Helm, 1980, p. 132.
55 E. Royston Pike, *Human Documents of the Industrial Revolution in Britain*, London, George Allen & Unwin, 1966, p. 277.
56 Geoffrey Cousins, *Golf in Britain: A Social History from the Beginnings to the Present Day*, London, Routledge & Kegan Paul, 1975, p. 76.
57 ibid., p. 79.
58 Helen King, 'The sexual politics of sport: an Australian perspective', in Richard Cashman and Michael McKernan, *Sport in History: The Making of Modern Sporting History*, Queensland, University of Queensland Press, 1979, p. 76.
59 W. G. Grace, *'W. G.' Cricketing Reminiscences and Personal Recollections*, London, Hambledon Press, 1980 edn, pp. 218–19.
60 Alfred H. Haynes, *The Story of Bowls*, London, Sporting Handbooks, 1972, pp. 95–7.
61 Lance Tingay, *100 Years of Wimbledon*, Enfield, Middx, Guinness Superlatives, 1977, pp. 66–7, 219.
62 William J. Baker, *Sports in the Western World*, Totowa, NJ, Rowman & Littlefield, 1982, pp. 296–7.

63 Brian Dobbs, *Edwardians at Play: Sport 1890–1914*, London, Pelham Books, 1973, p. 177.
64 Melvyn Watman, *History of British Athletics*, London, Robert Hale, 1968, p. 228.
65 For a radical prescription, see Mary A. Boutilier and Lucinda SanGiovanni, *The Sporting Woman*, Champaign, Ill., Human Kinetics, 1983.
66 *The Times*, 4 January 1989.

## 9  INSTANT SPORT AND OPEN SEASON

1 'People are apt to suppose the bodily sufferings of these pugilists to be much greater than they really are. They are led into this belief from the high-coloured descriptions of their combats which are wrought into the newspapers . . .' 'Dedimus', 'A defence of pugilism', *Sporting Magazine*, November 1829, p. 98.
2 Which was to become *The Times* in January 1788.
3 *Universal Daily Register*, 19 April 1787, and *passim*.
4 ibid., 5 July, 15 November, 5 June 1787.
5 ibid., 28 December, 31 December, 5 June 1787.
6 ibid., 19 July 1787 and *passim*.
7 ibid., 22 June, 4 August, 31 December 1787.
8 ibid., 8 June, 13 August 1787.
9 *Sporting Magazine*, October 1792, p. iv. In fact, Captain Topham's *World* had briefly filled that role until he retired to his Yorkshire estates earlier that year.
10 Great Britain, *Parliamentary Papers* (Commons), *Lords Select Committee on Laws Respecting Gaming*, 1844, p. 89.
11 Over a hundred such telegrams were sent to the Oval on the last afternoon of a key Nottinghamshire v. Surrey match in 1887! Peter Wynne-Thomas, *'Give Me Arthur': A Biography of Arthur Shrewsbury*, London, Arthur Barker, 1985, p. 71.
12 See Simon Inglis, *Soccer in the Dock: A History of British Football Scandals 1900 to 1965*, London, Collins Willow, 1985, *passim*.
13 E. W. Swanton, *Sort of a Cricket Person*, London, Collins, 1972; Fontana, 1974 edn, Ch. 13, 'On the air', pp. 259ff. The cover of the *Radio Times*, 22 April 1938, has a picture of the two cup final captains superimposed on a pitch set out in numbered squares.
14 Swanton, op. cit., p. 261.
15 *Radio Times*, 15 April, 22 April 1938.
16 £120,000, for instance, went to the MCC for cricket.
17 James Walvin, *The People's Game: A Social History of British Football*, London, Allen Lane, 1975, p. 169.
18 For example, Benjamin G. Rader, *In its Own Image: How Television has Transformed Sports*, New York, Free Press, 1984.
19 Christopher Brookes, *English Cricket: The Game and its Players Through the Ages*, London, Weidenfeld & Nicolson, 1978, pp. 120ff.; K. S. Inglis, 'Imperial cricket: test matches between Australia and England 1877–1900', in Richard Cashman and Michael McKernan, *Sport in History: The Making of Modern Sporting History*, Queensland, University of Queensland Press, 1979, pp. 173–6, '"Test matches": a note on usage'.
20 W. G. Grace, international bowler as well as cricketer, had introduced indoor bowling to the Crystal Palace in 1906. Alfred H. Haynes, *The Story of Bowls*, London, Sporting Handbooks, 1972, p. 131.

21 Until the Eastman case in 1963, the game's disciplinary methods ignored accepted rules of procedure, assumption of innocence, and taking of evidence. See Inglis, op. cit., p. vii and *passim*.
22 See, for example, Richard D. Mandell, *Sport: A Cultural History*, New York, Columbia University Press, 1984.

# Index

Note: places in England and Wales are generally indexed under their traditional counties.

185

UBS.
L5796/12.
R40:00.